THE CULTURE OF EDUCATION

▼

THE CULTURE OF EDUCATION

▼

Jerome Bruner

HARVARD UNIVERSITY PRESS
Cambridge, Massachusetts
London, England
1996

Library of Congress Cataloging-in-Publication Data

Bruner, Jerome S. (Jerome Seymour)
    The culture of education / Jerome Bruner.
      p. cm.
    Includes bibliographical references and index.
    ISBN 0-674-17952-8
    1. Educational psychology. 2. Social psychology. 3. Educational
anthropology. 4. Education—Philosophy. 5. Discourse analysis,
Narrative. I. Title.
LB1051.B736   1996
370.15—dc20   95-46844

For David Olson

CONTENTS

▼

PREFACE

▼

This is a book of essays about education. But it is by no means limited to education in the usual sense of classrooms and schools. For it is surely the case that schooling is only one small part of how a culture inducts the young into its canonical ways. Indeed, schooling may even be at odds with a culture's other ways of inducting the young into the requirements of communal living. Our changing times are marked by deep conjectures about what schools should be expected to "do" for those who choose to or are compelled to attend them—or for that matter, what schools *can* do, given the force of other circumstances. Should schools aim simply to reproduce the culture, to "assimilate" (to use a word now considered odious) the young into the ways of being little Americans or little Japanese? Yet assimilation was the unexamined faith even as recently as the beginning of this century. Or would schools, given the revolutionary changes through which we are living, do better to dedicate themselves to the equally risky, perhaps equally quixotic ideal of preparing students to cope with the changing world in which they will be living? And how shall we decide what that changing world will be and what it will demand of them? These are no longer abstract issues: we live with them daily, and they form the substance of the educational debates that reverberate everywhere in the world.

What has become increasingly clear in these debates is that education is not *just* about conventional school matters like curriculum or standards or testing. What we resolve to do in school only makes sense when considered in the broader context of what the society intends to accomplish through its educational investment in the young. How one conceives of education, we have finally come to recognize, is a function of how one conceives of the culture and its aims, professed and otherwise. This has been plain in the cascade of reports on the "state" of education that began with *A Nation at Risk* and seems to go on unceasingly.

The essays that constitute this book not surprisingly range over a wider terrain than usually encountered in a book about "education," though they all have their origin there. Some of them, indeed, reflect my own stances in the educational debates of the last years. But they are not "debate essays." The very first one, Chapter 1, is the antithesis of debating. Written after all the others, it is my attempt to reflect on the underlying implications of the decade's debates, to search out the foundational presuppositions inherent in them.

It is altogether appropriate that this book bears the title *The Culture of Education*. For its central thesis is that culture shapes mind, that it provides us with the toolkit by which we construct not only our worlds but our very conceptions of our selves and our powers. Ideally, perhaps, the book might have included a much broader examination of education in different cultures. But to take a cultural view of education does not really require constant cultural comparison. Rather, it requires that one consider education and school learning in their situated, cultural context, and that is what I have tried to do.

When Angela von der Lippe, my friend and my editor at Harvard University Press, proposed that I do this book, I was at first somewhat resistant. My ideas were in metamorphosis, for I was among those who were preoccupied with formulating a new "cultural psychology." What finally convinced me was recognizing how closely linked were the problems of education and the questions that loomed large in creating such a cultural psychology—questions about the making and negotiating of meanings, about the constructing of self and a sense of agency, about the acquisition of symbolic skills, and especially about the cultural "situatedness" of all mental activity. For you cannot understand mental activity unless you take into account the cultural setting and its resources, the very things that give mind its shape and scope. Learning, remembering, talking, imagining: all of them are made possible by participating in a culture.

Once I got started, it became increasingly clear to me that education was indeed the right "test frame" for budding ideas in a cultural psychology. Let me explain. The test frames we choose for clarifying our ideas tell volumes about our presuppositions. La Mettrie of the notorious *L'Homme Machine,* for example, used as his test frame the water-driven mobile statuary that Louis XIV had installed at Versailles: how do you get from such robots to intelligent creatures—by equipping them with senses? B. F. Skinner's test frame was a pecking pigeon in the isolated world of a Skinner box. Sir Frederic Bartlett seemed to be trying out his ideas about thinking against how a clever cricketer might behave on a cricket pitch, while Max Wertheimer tested his on a thinly disguised version of the young Einstein going about his work. The test frame of educational praxis is strikingly different from all of these and fits a cultural psychology uniquely well.

It presupposes that human mental activity is neither solo nor conducted unassisted, even when it goes on "inside the head." We are the only species that *teaches* in any significant way. Mental life is lived with others, is shaped to be communicated, and unfolds with the aid of cultural codes, traditions, and the like. But this extends beyond school. Education does not only occur in classrooms, but around the dinner table when family members try to make joint sense of what happened that day, or when kids try to help each other make sense of the adult world, or when a master and apprentice interact on the job. So there is nothing more appropriate than educational practice for testing a cultural psychology.

Some years after I first became actively engaged with education, I set down what seemed to me some reasonable conclusions in *The Process of Education.* It now seems to me in retrospect, some three decades later, that I was then much too preoccupied with solo, intrapsychic processes of knowing and how these might be assisted by appropriate pedagogies. I'll summarize the main points of that initial effort. Educational encounters, to begin with, should result in understanding, not mere performance. Understanding consists in grasping the place of an idea or fact in some more general structure of knowledge. When we understand something, we understand it as an exemplar of a broader conceptual principle or theory. Knowledge itself, moreover, is organized in such a way that the grasp of its conceptual structure renders its particulars more self-evident, even as redundant. Acquired knowledge is most useful to a learner, moreover, when it is "discovered" through the learner's own cognitive efforts, for it is then related to and used in reference to what one has known before. Such acts of discovery are enormously facilitated by the structure of knowledge itself, for however complicated any domain of knowledge may be, it can be represented in ways that make it accessible through less complex elaborated processes. It was this conclusion that led me to propose that any subject could be taught to any child at any age in some form that was honest—although "honest" was left undefined and has haunted me ever since!

This line of reasoning in turn implied that the object of instruction was not *coverage* but *depth:* to teach or instantiate general principles that rendered self-evident as many particulars as possible. It was a short step from there to the idea that the shape of a curriculum be conceived as a spiral, beginning with an intuitive depiction of a domain of knowledge, circling back to represent the domain more powerfully or formally as needed. The teacher, in this version of pedagogy, is a guide to understanding, someone who helps you discover on your own.

It was, of course, the ongoing cognitive revolution in psychology that inspired my initial approach to the process of education—a Revolution that began in the relatively affluent, rather complacent late 1950s and early 1960s. At least the times seemed so to many of us then. Besides, there was one "outside" disturbance that took precedence over any internal concerns. It was the Cold War. Not only was it ideological and military; it was a "technical" war as well. There were "knowledge gaps," and our schools were under accusation for creating them. Could our schools keep America technologically ahead of the Soviet Union in the endless Cold War? It is not surprising that the principal focus of the educational reform movement of the day was on science and mathematics. And those were the subjects that lent themselves best to the principles of the new cognitive psychology. Guided by these new principles, science and mathematics curricula flourished. Almost everything else was taken for granted. The reformers assumed, for example, that kids in school were just as interested in mastering the improved curriculum as they had been in constructing it. And it was also taken for granted that students lived in some sort of educational vacuum, untroubled by the ills and problems of the culture at large.

It was the "discovery of poverty" and the civil rights movement in America that woke most of us from our unthinking complacency about reforming education—specifically, the discovery of the impact of poverty, racism, and alienation on the mental life and growth of the child victims of these blights. A theory of education that was to serve all could no longer take for granted the supporting assistance of a benign, even a neutral culture. Something more was needed to compensate for what many of us then thought of as the "deficit" created by "cultural deprivation." And the remedies proposed for overcoming such deprivation were eventually converted into Head Start and similar programs.

In the years following, I found myself increasingly preoccupied with how *culture* affected the way in which children went about their school learning. My own research drove me deeper and deeper into the problem—laboratory research on infancy as well as field work on mental development and schooling in Africa. I was not alone in this. My students and post-docs, my colleagues, were equally involved; even my travels conspired to involve me. I recall particularly visits with Alexander Luria, that enthusiastic exponent of Lev Vygotsky's "cultural historical" theories of development. His ebullient espousal of the role of language and culture in the functioning of mind soon undermined my confidence in the more self-contained, formalistic theories of the towering Jean Piaget, theories that had very little room for the enabling role of culture in mental development. While I am hardly a Vygotskian in any strict sense of the term, I found this new work enormously helpful in thinking about education. But a concern with "culture in mind" does not rest on adherence to any "school" of psychology. Indeed, it goes beyond psychology altogether and relies today on the work of primatologists, anthropologists, linguists, sociologists in the great lineage of Emile Durkheim, even on the work of historians of the *Annales* school preoccupied with how peoples form their distinctive *mentalités*. Indeed, in the last decade there has been a veritable renaissance of interest in the culture of education—not only in theory but in the guidance of classroom practice. Since I will discuss some of this work in later chapters, I need say no more about it here.

This book was written in the midst of a collaborative research project with my wife and colleague, Carol Fleisher Feldman, a project principally concerned with *narrative* as both a mode of thought and an expression of a culture's world view. It is through our own narratives that we principally construct a version of ourselves in the world, and it is through its narrative that a culture provides models of identity and agency to its members. Appreciation of the centrality of narrative comes not from any single discipline, but from a confluence of many: literary, socio-anthropological, linguistic, historical, psychological, even computational. And I have come to take this confluence as a fact of life, not only in our own narrative studies but in educational studies generally.

Given all this new work, given the surge of effort since the cognitive revolution, are we any better able to improve the education of children suffering the blight of poverty, discrimination, alienation? Have we developed any promising leads about how to organize the culture of school in ways to help children toward a fresh start? What does it take to create a nurturing school culture that empowers the young effectively to use the resources and opportunities of the broader culture?

Obviously there are no sure-fire answers. But there are certainly enough promising hints to encourage serious efforts. One of the most promising involves experiments in schools that have established "mutual learning cultures." Such classroom cultures are organized to model how the broader culture should work if it were operating at its best and liveliest and if it were concentrating on the task of education. There is mutual sharing of knowledge and ideas, mutual aid in mastering material, division of labor and exchange of roles, opportunity to reflect on the group's activities. That, in any case, is one possible version of "culture at its best." School, in such a dispensation, is conceived of both as an exercise in consciousness raising about the possibilities of communal mental activity, and as a means for acquiring knowledge and skill. The teacher is the enabler, *primus inter pares*. This is only one of the successful experiments being tried, and there are others.

But is all this "realistic"? Given the pressures under which schools operate, can ideals such as mutual communities really be achieved? Is this more educational utopia? Utopia is hardly the issue. Nobody doubts that there are powerful constraints on what schools can do. They are never free even to try out all the things they think would help, but neither are they knee-jerk agents of the status quo. We systematically underestimate the impact of educational innovations. Even the relatively feeble and much-criticized efforts of Head Start produced some stunning results, as we shall see presently. Besides, we already know more than we have put to use—including the fact that kids in classrooms organized as mutual communities do well on intellectual performance and get their sights raised. And there are many other lessons to be learned from bringing cultural psychology to bear on education. I hope I can be convincing when I say that we are not at the end of the road where education is concerned. Indeed, there is good reason to believe that we may just be starting out on a new one.

Let me say a few words about the plan of the book. While each chapter can be read on its own, together they form parts of a broader point of view. That point of view is set forth and elaborated in the opening chapter in the form of "tenets" about the nature of individual human minds operating in an enabling culture. The chapters following elaborate further on those tenets. The "educational" topics covered are many and varied—ranging from the influence of folk conceptions of pedagogy on education to the inherent anomalies of educational policy, from the uses of narrative to primate pedagogy, from "reading" other people's minds to the question of how we represent the world to each other. Coverage, to pick up an old theme, is not the issue. Nor are there many confrontations with the hot issues of educational politics. I am convinced that such issues cannot be resolved without our first achieving some deeper understanding of the culture of education. And that is what this book is about.

I must express a special debt of gratitude to those who have made this work possible: to the Spencer Foundation, which has generously supported my research; to the Department of Psychology at New York University, which has provided a place to work and facilities for doing so; and particularly to the Law School of New York University, in whose intellectual life I have participated with profit and where I have had the continuing privilege of teaching a seminar on the theory of interpretation in law, literature, and the human sciences with my friends and colleagues Tony Amsterdam, Peggy Davis, and David Richards—a seminar whose echoes are audible in every chapter of this book.

I have dedicated *The Culture of Education* to David Olson—former post-doc, longtime friend, buoyant co-conspirator, always available interlocutor whether in collaboration or in debate. There are too many others to whom I owe a debt of gratitude to list in a preface. I shall have occasion to mention them in context later.

Reenogreena
Glandore, County Cork
Republic of Ireland
September 1995

1

▼

CULTURE, MIND, AND EDUCATION

The essays in this volume are all products of the 1990s, expressions of the fundamental changes that have been altering conceptions about the nature of the human mind in the decades since the cognitive revolution. These changes, it now seems clear in retrospect, grew out of two strikingly divergent conceptions about how mind works. The first of these was the hypothesis that mind could be conceived as a computational device. This was not a new idea, but it had been powerfully reconceived in the newly advanced computational sciences. The other was the proposal that mind is both constituted by and realized in the use of human culture. The two views led to very different conceptions of the nature of mind itself, and of how mind should be cultivated. Each led its adherents to follow distinctively different strategies of inquiry about how mind functions and about how it might be improved through "education."

The first or *computational* view is concerned with *information processing:* how finite, coded, unambiguous information about the world is inscribed, sorted, stored, collated, retrieved, and generally managed by a computational device. It takes information as its given, as something already settled in relation to some preexisting, rule-bound code that maps onto states of the world.[1] This so-called "well-formedness" is both its strength and its shortcoming, as we shall see. For the process of knowing is often messier, more fraught with ambiguity than such a view allows.

Computational science makes interesting general claims about the conduct of education,[2] though it is still unclear what specific lessons it has to teach the educator. There is a widespread and not unreasonable belief that we *should* be able to discover something about how to teach human beings more effectively from knowing how to program computers effectively. One can scarcely doubt, for example, that computers provide a learner with powerful aids in mastering bodies of knowledge, particularly if the knowledge in question is well defined. A well-programmed computer is especially useful for taking over tasks that, at last, can be declared "unfit for human production." For computers are faster, more orderly, less fitful in remembering, and do not get bored. And of course, it is revealing of our own minds and our human situation to ask what things we do better or worse than our servant computer.

It is considerably more uncertain whether, in any deep sense, the tasks of a teacher can be "handed over" to a computer, even the most "responsive" one that can be theoretically envisioned. Which is not to say that a suitably programmed computer cannot lighten a teacher's load by taking over some of the routines that clutter the process of instruction. But that is not the issue. After all, books came to serve such a function after Gutenberg's discovery made them widely available.[3]

The issue, rather, is whether the computational view of mind itself offers an adequate enough view about how mind works to guide our efforts in trying to "educate" it. It is a subtle question. For in certain respects, "how the mind works" is itself dependent on the tools at its disposal. "How the *hand* works," for example, cannot be fully appreciated unless one also takes into account whether it is equipped with a screwdriver, a pair of scissors, or a laser-beam gun. And by the same token, the systematic historian's "mind" works differently from the mind of the classic "teller of tales" with his stock of combinable myth-like modules. So, in a sense, the mere existence of computational devices (and a theory of computation about their mode of operating) can (and doubtless will) change our minds about how "mind" works, just as the book did.[4]

This brings us directly to the second approach to the nature of mind—call it *culturalism*. It takes its inspiration from the evolutionary fact that mind could not exist save for culture. For the evolution of the hominid mind is linked to the development of a way of life where "reality" is represented by a symbolism shared by members of a cultural community in which a technical-social way of life is both organized and construed in terms of that symbolism. This symbolic mode is not only shared by a community, but conserved, elaborated, and passed on to succeeding generations who, by virtue of this transmission, continue to maintain the culture's identity and way of life.

Culture in this sense is *superorganic*.[5] But it shapes the minds of individuals as well. Its individual expression inheres in *meaning making,* assigning meanings to things in different settings on particular occasions. Meaning making involves situating encounters with the world in their appropriate cultural contexts in order to know "what they are about." Although meanings are "in the mind," they have their origins and their significance in the culture in which they are created. It is this cultural situatedness of meanings that assures their negotiability and, ultimately, their communicability. Whether "private meanings" exist is not the point; what is important is that meanings provide a basis for cultural exchange. On this view, knowing and communicating are in their nature highly interdependent, indeed virtually inseparable. For however much the individual may seem to operate on his or her own in carrying out the quest for meanings, nobody can do it unaided by the culture's symbolic systems. It is culture that provides the tools for organizing and understanding our worlds in communicable ways. The distinctive feature of human evolution is that mind evolved in a fashion that enables human beings to utilize the tools of culture. Without those tools, whether symbolic or material, man is not a "naked ape" but an empty abstraction.

Culture, then, though itself man-made, both forms and makes possible the workings of a distinctively human mind. On this view, learning and thinking are always *situated* in a cultural setting and always dependent upon the utilization of cultural resources.[6] Even individual variation in the nature and use of mind can be attributed to the varied opportunities that different cultural settings provide, though these are not the only source of variation in mental functioning.

Like its computational cousin, culturalism seeks to bring together insights from psychology, anthropology, linguistics, and the human sciences generally, in order to reformulate a model of mind. But the two do so for radically different purposes. Computationalism, to its great credit, is interested in any and all ways in which information is organized and used—information in the well-formed and finite sense mentioned earlier, regardless of the guise in which information processing is realized. In this broad sense, it recognizes no disciplinary boundaries, not even the boundary between human and non-human functioning. Culturalism, on the other hand, concentrates exclusively on how human beings in cultural communities create and transform meanings.

I want to set forth in this opening chapter some principal motifs of the cultural approach and explore how these relate to education. But before turning to that formidable task, I need first to dispel the shibboleth of a necessary contradiction between culturalism and computationalism. For I think the apparent contradiction is based on a misunderstanding, one that leads to gross and needless over-dramatization. Obviously the approaches are very different, and their ideological overspill may indeed overwhelm us if we do not take care to distinguish them clearly. For it surely matters ideologically what kind of "model" of the human mind one embraces.[7] Indeed, the model of mind to which one adheres even shapes the "folk pedagogy" of schoolroom practice, as we shall see in the following chapter. Mind as equated to the power of association and habit formation privileges "drill" as the true pedagogy, while mind taken as the capacity for reflection and discourse on the nature of necessary truths favors the

Socratic dialogue. And each of these is linked to our conception of the ideal society and the ideal citizen.

Yet in fact, neither computationalism nor culturalism is so linked to particular models of mind as to be shackled in particular pedagogies. Their difference is of quite a different kind. Let me try to sketch it.

The objective of computationalism is to devise a formal redescription of *any* and *all* functioning systems that manage the flow of well-formed information. It seeks to do so in a way that produces foreseeable, systematic outcomes. One such system is the human mind. But thoughtful computationalism does *not* propose that mind is like some particular "computer" that needs to be "programmed" in a particular way in order to operate systematically or "efficiently." What it argues, rather, is that any and all systems that process information must be governed by specifiable "rules" or procedures that govern what to do with inputs. It matters not whether it is a nervous system or the genetic apparatus that takes instruction from DNA and then reproduces later generations, or whatever. This is the ideal of Artificial Intelligence, so-called. "Real minds" are describable in terms of the same AI generalization—systems governed by specifiable rules for managing the flow of coded information.

But, as already noted, the rules common to all information systems do not cover the messy, ambiguous, and context-sensitive processes of meaning making, a form of activity in which the construction of highly "fuzzy" and metaphoric category systems is just as notable as the use of specifiable categories for sorting inputs in a way to yield comprehensible outputs. Some computationalists, convinced a priori that even meaning making can be reduced to AI specifications, are perpetually at work trying to prove that the messiness of meaning making is not beyond their reach.[8] The complex "universal models" they propose are sometimes half-jokingly referred to by them as "TOEs," an acronym for "theories of everything."[9] But though they have not even come near to succeeding and, as many believe, will probably never in principle succeed, their efforts nonetheless are interesting for the light they shed on the divide between meaning making and information processing.

The difficulty these computationalists encounter inheres in the kinds of "rules" or operations that are possible in computation. All of them, as we know, must be specifiable in advance, must be free of ambiguity, and so on. They must, in their ensemble, also be computationally consistent, which means that while operations may alter with feedback from prior results, the alterations must also adhere to a consistent, prearranged systematicity. Computational rules may be contingent, but they cannot encompass unforeseeable contingencies. Thus Hamlet cannot (in AI) tease Polonius with ambiguous banter about "yonder cloud shaped like a camel, nay 'tis backed like a weasel," in the hope that his banter might evoke guilt and some telltale knowledge about the death of Hamlet's father.

It is precisely this clarity, this prefixedness of categories that imposes the most severe limit on computationalism as a medium in which to frame a model of mind. But once this limitation is recognized, the alleged death struggle between culturalism and computationalism evaporates. For the meaning making of the culturalist, unlike the information processing of the computationalist, is in principle interpretive, fraught with ambiguity, sensitive to the occasion, and often after the fact. Its "ill-formed procedures" are like "maxims" rather than like fully specifiable rules.[10] But they are hardly unprincipled. Rather, they are the stuff of *hermeneutics,* an intellectual pursuit no less disciplined for its failure to produce the click-clear outputs of a computational exercise. Its model case is text interpretation. In interpreting a text, the meaning of a part depends upon a hypothesis about the meanings of the whole, whose meaning in turn is based upon one's judgment of meanings of the parts that compose it. But, as we shall have many occasions to see in the following chapters, a wide swath of the human cultural enterprise depends upon it. Nor is it clear that the infamous "hermeneutic circle" deserves the knocks it gets from those in search of clarity and certainty. After all, it lies at the heart of meaning making.

Hermeneutic meaning making and well-formed information processing are incommensurate. Their incommensurability can be made evident even in a simple example. Any input to a computational system must, of course, be encoded in a specifiable way that leaves no room for ambiguity. What happens, then, if (as in human meaning making) an input needs to be encoded according to the context in which it is encountered? Let me give a homely example involving language, since so much of meaning making involves language. Say the input into the system is the word *cloud*. Shall it be taken in its "meteorological" sense, its "mental condition" sense, or in some other way? Now, it is easy (indeed necessary) to provide a computational device with a "look-up" lexicon that provides alternative senses of *cloud*. Any dictionary can do it. But to determine *which* sense is appropriate for a particular context, the computational device would also need a way of encoding and interpreting all contexts in which the word *cloud* might appear. That would then require the computer to have a look-up list for all possible contexts, a "contexticon." But while there are a finite number of words, there are an infinite number of contexts in which particular words might appear. Encoding the context of Hamlet's little riddle about "yonder cloud" would almost certainly escape the powers of the best "contexticon" one could imagine!

There is no decision procedure known that could resolve the question whether the incommensurability between culturalism's meaning making and computationalism's information processing could ever be overcome. Yet, for all that, the two have a kinship that is difficult to ignore. For once meanings are established, it is their formalization into a well-formed category system that *can* be managed by computational rules. Obviously one loses the subtlety of context dependency and metaphor in doing so: *clouds* would have to pass tests of truth functionality to get into the play. But then again, "formalization" in science consists of just such maneuvers: treating an array of formalized and operationalized meanings "as if" they were fit for computation. Eventually we come to believe that scientific terms actually were born and grew that way: decontextualized, disambiguated, totally "lookuppable."

There is equally puzzling commerce in the other direction. For we are often forced to interpret the output of a computation in order to "make some sense" of it—that is, to figure out what it "means." This "search for the meaning" of final outputs has always been customary in statistical procedures such as factor analysis where the association between different "variables," discovered by statistical manipulation, needed to be interpreted hermeneutically in order to "make sense." The same problem is encountered when investigators use the computational option of parallel processing to discover the association between a set of coded inputs. The final output of such parallel processing similarly needs interpretation to be rendered meaningful. So there is plainly some complementary relationship between what the computationalist is trying to explain and what the culturalist is trying to interpret, a relationship that has long puzzled students of epistemology.[11]

I shall return to this puzzling problem in Chapter 5. For now it suffices to say that in an undertaking as inherently reflexive and complicated as characterizing "how our minds work" or how they might be made to work better, there is surely room for two perspectives on the nature of knowing.[12] Nor is there any demonstrable reason to suppose that without a single and legitimately "true" way of knowing the world, we could only slide helplessly down the slippery slope that leads to relativism. It is surely as "true" to say that Euclid's theorems are computable as to say, with the poet, that "Euclid alone has looked on beauty bare."

II

To begin with, if a theory of mind is to be interesting educationally, it should contain some specifications for (or at least implications bearing on) how its functioning can be improved or altered in some significant way. All-or-none and once-for-all theories of mind are not educationally interesting. More specifically, educationally interesting theories of mind contain specifications of some kind about the "resources" required for a mind to operate effectively. These include not only instrumental resources (like mental "tools"), but also settings or conditions required for effective operations—anything from feedback within certain time limits to, say, freedom from stress or from excessive uniformity. Without specification of resources and settings required, a theory of mind is all "inside-out" and of limited applicability to education. It becomes interesting only when it becomes more "outside-in," indicating the kind of world needed to make it possible to use mind (or heart!) effectively—what kinds of symbol systems, what kinds of accounts of the past, what arts and sciences, and so on. The approach of computationalism to education tends to be inside-out—though it smuggles the world into the mind by inscribing bits of it in memory, as with our earlier dictionary example, and then relies on "look-up" routines. Culturalism is much more outside-in, and although it may contain specifications about mental operations *eo ipso,* as it were, they are not as binding as, say, the formal requirement of computability. For the approach of the computationalist to education is indeed bound by the constraint of computability—that is, whatever aids are offered to mind must be operable by a computational device.

When one actually examines how computationalism has approached educational issues, there seem to be three different styles. The first of these consists in "restating" classical theories of teaching or learning in a computable form. But while some clarity is gained in so doing (for example, in locating ambiguities), not much is gained by way of power. Old wine does not improve much for being poured into differently shaped bottles, even if the glass is clearer. The classic reply, of course, is that a computable reformulation yields "surplus insight." Yet "association theory," for example, has gone through successive translations from Aristotle to Locke to Pavlov to Clark Hull without much surplus yield. So one is justifiably impatient with new claims for veiled versions of the same—as with many so-called PDP "learning models."[13]

But in fact, computationalism can and does do better than that. Its second approach begins with a rich description or protocol of what actually transpires when somebody sets out to solve a particular problem or master a particular body of knowledge. It then seeks to redescribe what has been observed in strict computational terms. In what order, for example, does a subject ask for information, what confuses him, what kinds of hypotheses does he entertain? This approach then asks what might be going on computationally in devices that operate that way, for instance, like the subject's "mind." From this it seeks to reformulate a plan about how a learner of this kind might be helped—again within limits of computability. John Bruer's interesting book is a nice example of what can be gained from this fresh approach.[14]

But there is an even more interesting third route that computationalists sometimes follow. The work of Annette Karmiloff-Smith[15] provides an example if taken in conjunction with some abstract computational ideas. All complex "adaptive" computational programs involve redescribing the output of prior operations in order both to reduce their complexity and to improve their "fit" to an adaptation criterion. That is what "adaptive" means: reducing prior complexities to achieve greater "fitness" to a criterion.[16] An example will help. Karmiloff-Smith notes that when we go about solving particular problems, say language acquisition, we characteristically "turn around" on the results of a procedure that has worked locally and try to redescribe it in more general, simplified terms. We say, for example, "I've put an *s* at the end of that noun to pluralize it; how about doing the same for *all* nouns?" When the new rule fails to pluralize *woman,* the learner may generate some additional ones. Eventually, he ends up with a more or less adequate rule for pluralizing, with only a few odd "exceptions" left over to be handled by rote. Note that in each step of this process that Karmiloff-Smith calls "redescription," the learner "goes meta," considering how he is thinking as well as what he is thinking about. This is the hallmark of "metacognition," a topic of passionate interest among psychologists—but also among computational scientists.

That is to say, the rule of redescription is a feature of *all* complex "adaptive" computation, but in the present instance, it is also a genuinely interesting *psychological* phenomenon. This is the rare music of an overlap between different fields of inquiry—if the overlap turns out to be fertile. So, REDESCRIBE, a TOE-like rule for adaptive computational systems that also happens to be a good rule in human problem solving, may turn out to be a "new frontier." And the new frontier may turn out to be next door to educational practice.[17]

So the computationalist's approach to education seems to take three forms as noted. The first reformulates old theories of learning (or teaching, or whatever) in computable form in the hope that the reformulation will yield surplus power. The second analyzes rich protocols and applies the apparatus of computational theory to them to discern better what might be going on computationally. Then it tries to figure out how the process can be helped. This, in effect, is what Newell, Shaw, and Simon did in their work on the General Problem Solver,[18] and what is currently being done in studies of how "novices" become "experts."[19] Finally there is the happy fortuity where a central computational idea, like "redescription," seems to map directly onto a central idea in cognitive theory, like "metacognition."

The culturalist approaches education in a very different way. Culturalism takes as its first premise that education is not an island, but part of the continent of culture. It asks first what function "education" serves in the culture and what role it plays in the lives of those who operate within it. Its next question might be why education is situated in the culture as it is, and how this placement reflects the distribution of power, status, and other benefits. Inevitably, and virtually from the start, culturalism also asks about the enabling resources made available to people to cope, and what portion of those resources is made available through "education," institutionally conceived. And it will constantly be concerned with constraints imposed on the process of education—external ones like the organization of schools and class-rooms or the recruitment of teachers, and internal ones like the natural or imposed distribution of native endowment, for native endowment may be as much affected by the accessibility of symbolic systems as by the distribution of genes.

Culturalism's task is a double one. On the "macro" side, it looks at the culture as a system of values, rights, exchanges, obligations, opportunities, power. On the "micro" side, it examines how the demands of a cultural system affect those who must operate within it. In that latter spirit, it concentrates on how individual human beings construct "realities" and meanings that adapt them to the system, at what personal cost, with what expected outcomes. While culturalism implies no particular view concerning inherent psycho-biological constraints that affect human functioning, particularly meaning making, it usually takes such constraints for granted and considers how they are managed by the culture and its instituted educational system.

Although culturalism is far from computationalism and its constraints, it has no difficulty incorporating its insights—with one exception. It obviously cannot rule out processes relating to human meaning making, however much they do not meet the test of computability. As a corollary, it cannot and does not rule out subjectivity and its role in culture. Indeed, as we shall see, it is much concerned with *inter*subjectivity—how humans come to know "each other's minds." In both these senses, culturalism is to be counted among the "sciences of the subjective." And, in consequence, I shall often refer to it as the "cultural psychological" approach, or simply as "cultural psychology." For all that it embraces the subjective in its purview and refers often to the "construction of reality," cultural psychology surely does not rule out "reality" in any ontological sense. It argues (on epistemological grounds) that "external" or "objective" reality can only be known by the properties of mind and the symbol systems on which mind relies.[20]

A final point relates to the place of emotion and feeling. It is often said that all "cognitive psychology," even its cultural version, neglects or even ignores the place of these in the life of mind. But it is neither necessary that this be so nor, at least in my view, is it so. Why should an interest in cognition preclude feeling and emotion?[21] Surely emotions and feelings are represented in the processes of meaning making and in our constructions of reality. Whether one adopts the Zajonc view that emotion is a direct and unmediated response to the world with subsequent cognitive consequences, or the Lazarus view that emotion requires prior cognitive inference, it is still "there," still to be reckoned with.[22] And as we shall see, particularly in dealing with the role of schools in "self" construction, it is very much a part of education.

III

Let me now set out some tenets that guide a psycho-cultural approach to education. In doing so I shall commute back and forth between questions about the nature of mind and about the nature of culture, for a theory of education necessarily lies at the intersect between them. We shall, in consequence, constantly be inquiring about the interaction between the powers of individual minds and the means by which the culture aids or thwarts their realization. And this will inevitably involve us in a never-ending assessment of the fit between what any particular culture deems essential for a good, or useful, or worthwhile way of life, and how individuals adapt to these demands as they impinge on their lives. We shall be particularly mindful of the resources that a culture provides in making this fit possible. These are all matters that relate directly to how a culture or society manages its system of education, for education is a major embodiment of a culture's way of life, not just a preparation for it.[23]

Here, then, are the tenets and some of their consequences for education.

1. The perspectival tenet. First, about meaning making. The meaning of any fact, proposition, or encounter is relative to the perspective or frame of reference in terms of which it is construed. A treaty that legitimizes the building of the Panama Canal, for example, is an episode in the history of North American imperialism. It is also a monumental step in the history of inter-ocean transportation, as well as a landmark in man's effort to shape nature to his own convenience at whatever cost. To understand well what something "means" requires some awareness of the alternative meanings that can be attached to the matter under scrutiny, whether one agrees with them or not.

Understanding something in one way does not preclude understanding it in other ways. Understanding in any one particular way is only "right" or "wrong" from the particular perspective in terms of which it is pursued.[24] But the "rightness" of particular interpretations, while dependent on perspective, also reflects rules of evidence, consistency, and coherence. Not everything goes. There are inherent criteria of rightness, and the possibility of alternative interpretations does not license all of them equally. A perspectival view of meaning making does *not* preclude common sense or "logic." Something that happens a century after an event cannot be taken as a "cause" or "condition" of that event. I shall return to this issue of common sense, logic, and reason in a later tenet.

Interpretations of meaning reflect not only the idiosyncratic histories of individuals, but also the culture's canonical ways of constructing reality. Nothing is "culture free," but neither are individuals simply mirrors of their culture. It is the interaction between them that both gives a communal cast to individual thought and imposes a certain unpredictable richness on any culture's way of life, thought, or feeling. There are, as it were, "official" versions of all of these—"Frenchmen are realistic," for example—and some of them are even inscribed in the law or in widely accepted kinship practices. And of course, they are also portrayed (often ambiguously and even problematically) in a culture's literature and its folk theories.

Life in culture is, then, an interplay between the versions of the world that people form under its institutional sway and the versions of it that are products of their individual histories. It rarely conforms to anything resembling a cookbook of recipes or formulas, for it is a universal of all cultures that they contain factional or institutional interests. Nonetheless, any particular individual's idiosyncratic interpretations of the world are constantly subject to judgment against what are taken to be the canonical beliefs of the culture at large. Such communal judgments, though often governed by "rational" and evidentiary criteria, are just as often dominated by commitments, tastes, interests, and expressions of adherence to the culture's values relating to the good life, decency, legitimacy, or power. In consequence of all of the foregoing, a culture's judgments about the idiosyncratic construals of its members are rarely univocal. And to cope with this ever-present cultural multivocality, every society requires some "principle of tolerance," a phrase that David Richards has used to characterize the way in which constitutional systems cope with contending interests and their interpretive claims.[25]

An "official" educational enterprise presumably cultivates beliefs, skills, and feelings in order to transmit and explicate its sponsoring culture's ways of interpreting the natural and social worlds. And as we shall see later, it also plays a key role in helping the young construct and maintain a concept of Self. In carrying out that function, it inevitably courts risk by "sponsoring," however implicitly, a certain version of the world. Or it runs the risk of offending some interests by openly examining views that might be taken as like the culture's canonically tabooed ones. That is the price of educating the young in societies whose canonical interpretations of the world are multivocal or ambiguous. But an educational enterprise that fails to take the risks involved becomes stagnant and eventually alienating.

It follows from this, then, that effective education is always in jeopardy either in the culture at large or with constituencies more dedicated to maintaining a status quo than to fostering flexibility. The corollary of this is that when education narrows its scope of interpretive inquiry, it reduces a culture's power to adapt to change. And in the contemporary world, change is the norm.

In a word, the perspectival tenet highlights the interpretive, meaning-making side of human thought while, at the same time, recognizing the inherent risks of discord that may result from cultivating this deeply human side of mental life. It is this double-facing, Janus-like aspect of education that makes it either a somewhat dangerous pursuit or a rather drearily routine one.

2. The constraints tenet. The forms of meaning making accessible to human beings in any culture are constrained in two crucial ways. The first inheres in the nature of human mental functioning itself. Our evolution as a species has specialized us into certain characteristic ways of knowing, thinking, feeling, and perceiving. We cannot, even given our most imaginative efforts, construct a concept of Self that does not impute some causal influence of prior mental states on later ones. We cannot seem to accept a version of our own mental lives that denies that what we thought before affects what we think now. We are obliged to experience ourselves as invariant across circumstances and continuous across time. Moreover, to pick up a theme that will concern us later, we need to conceive of ourselves as "agents" impelled by self-generated intentions. And we see others in the same way. In answer to those who deny this version of selfhood on philosophical or "scientific" grounds, we reply simply, "But that's how it is: can't you *see?*" All this despite the fact that there have always been rhetorically compelling philosophers (or in more recent centuries, psychologists) who have denied this "folk psychological" view and even called it mischievous.

Indeed, we even institutionalize these so-called folk beliefs. Our legal system takes it as a given and constructs a *corpus juris* based upon notions like "voluntary consent," "responsibility," and the rest. It does not matter whether "selfhood" can be proved scientifically or whether it is merely a "fiction" of folk psychology. We simply take it as in the "nature of human nature." Never mind what critics say.[26] "Common sense" asserts it to be so. To be sure, we bend slightly for the critics. The law, typically, meets its critics by enunciating "principled exceptions"—as in the extension and clarification of the *mens rea* doctrine.[27]

Such intrinsic constraints on our capacities to interpret are by no means limited only to subjective concepts like "selfhood." They even limit our ways of conceiving of such presumably impersonal, "objective" matters as time, space, and causality. We see "time" as having a homogeneous continuity—as flowing evenly whether measured by clocks, phases of the moon, climatic changes, or any other form of recurrence. Discontinuous or quantal conceptions of time offend common sense to such an extent that we come to believe that continuous time is the state of nature that we experience directly. And this despite the fact that Immanuel Kant, one of the most highly honored philosophers in the Western tradition, made so strong a case for time and space as categories of mind rather than facts of nature. Faced with the fact, adduced by anthropologists, that there are local cultural variations in conceptions of time and space, and that these have practical implications in a culture's ways of life and thought,[28] we tend to "naturalize" them by labeling them exotic. It seems to be a human universal that we nominate certain forms of interpreted experience as hard-edged, objective realities rather than "things of the mind." And it is widely believed, both among lay people and scientists, that the "nominees" for such objective status reflect certain natural or native predispositions to think and interpret the world in a particular way.

These universals are generally considered to constitute the "psychic unity of mankind." They can be considered as limits on human capacity for meaning making. And they require our attention because they presumably reduce the range of the perspectival tenet discussed in the preceding section. I think of them as constraints on human meaning making, and it is for that reason that I have labeled this section "the constraints tenet." These constraints are generally taken to be an inheritance of our evolution as a species, part of our "native endowment."

But while they may reflect the evolution of the human mind, these constraints should not be taken as man's *fixed* native endowment. They may be common to the species, but they also reflect how we represent the world through language and folk theories. And they are not immutable. Euclid, after all, finally altered our way of conceiving of, even looking at space. And in time, doubtless, Einstein will have done the same. Indeed, the very predispositions that we take to be "innate" most often require shaping by exposure to some communally shared notational system, like language. Despite our presumably native endowment, we seem to have what Vygotsky called a Zone of Proximal Development,[29] a capacity to recognize ways beyond that endowment. The famous slave-boy in Plato's *Meno* was indeed capable of certain "mathematical" insights (at least in response to the questions posed by the masterful Socrates). Would his insights have been possible without the queries of Socrates?

The educational implications that follow from the foregoing are both massive and subtle. If pedagogy is to empower human beings to go beyond their "native" predispositions, it must transmit the "toolkit" the culture has developed for doing so. It is a commonplace that any math major in a halfway decent modern university can do more mathematics than, say, Leibniz, who "invented" the calculus—that we stand on the shoulders of the giants who preceded us. Obviously, not everybody benefits equally from instruction in the culture's toolkit. But it hardly follows that we should instruct only those with the most conspicuous talent to benefit from such instruction. That is a political or economic decision that should never be allowed to take on the status of an evolutionary principle. Decisions to cultivate "trained incompetencies" will concern us presently.

I mentioned *two* constraints on human mental activity at the start of this discussion. The second comprises those constraints imposed by the symbolic systems accessible to human minds generally—limits imposed, say, by the very nature of language—but more particularly, constraints imposed by the different languages and notational systems accessible to different cultures. The latter is usually called the Whorf-Sapir hypothesis[30]—that thought is shaped by the language in which it is formulated and/or expressed.

As for the "limits of language," not much can be said with any certainty—or with much clarity. It has never been clear whether our ability to entertain certain notions inheres in the nature of our minds or in the symbolic systems upon which mind relies in carrying out its mental operations. Is it in mind or in language that it is "necessary" that something cannot be both A and not-A? Or is it "in the world"—except for the part of the world covered by quantum theory? Is it in the structure of natural language that the world divides into subjects and predicates, or is this a reflection of how human attention works naturally?

Some have gone to the fanciful length of likening language to an instinct.[31] But that dubious claim relates only to the formal syntax of language and is belied, in the main, by the profusion of expressive forms that mark its *use*—the pragmatics of language. The crafts of the storyteller, the orator, the gossip, or the poet/novelist, while caught in the web of syntax, hardly seem constrained by that fact. And as literary linguists continue to remind us, novelists keep surprising us by inventing new genres, still using the "old" language.[32]

As for the Whorf–Sapir hypothesis, its power and reach are also still not clearly understood.[33] But as with the "limits of language" question, it poses an interesting question for the cultural psychology of education. All that is known for sure is that consciousness or "linguistic awareness" seems to reduce the constraints imposed by any symbolic system.[34] The real victims of the limits of language or of the Whorfian hypothesis are those least aware of the language they speak.

But as the greatest linguist of our century, Roman Jakobson, long ago noted,[35] the *metalinguistic* gift, the capacity to "turn around" on our language to examine and transcend its limits, is within everybody's reach. There is little reason to believe that anybody, even the speech-disabled, cannot be helped to explore more deeply the nature and uses of his language. Indeed, the spread of literacy may itself have increased linguistic awareness just by virtue of externalizing, decontextualizing, and making more permanent "what was said," as David Olson has recently argued.[36]

The pedagogical implications of the foregoing are strikingly obvious. Since the limits of our inherent mental predispositions can be transcended by having recourse to more powerful symbolic systems, one function of education is to equip human beings with the needed symbolic systems for doing so. And if the limits imposed by the languages we use are expanded by increasing our "linguistic awareness," then another function of pedagogy is to cultivate such awareness. We may not succeed in transcending all the limits imposed in either case, but we can surely accept the more modest goal of improving thereby the human capacity for construing meanings and constructing realities. In sum, then, "thinking about thinking" has to be a principal ingredient of any empowering practice of education.

3. The constructivism tenet. This tenet has already been implied in all that has gone before. But it is worth making explicit. The "reality" that we impute to the "worlds" we inhabit is a constructed one. To paraphrase Nelson Goodman,[37] "reality is made, not found." Reality construction is the product of meaning making shaped by traditions and by a culture's toolkit of ways of thought. In this sense, education must be conceived as aiding young humans in learning to use the tools of meaning making and reality construction, to better adapt to the world in which they find themselves and to help in the process of changing it as required. In this sense, it can even be conceived as akin to helping people become better architects and better builders.

4. *The interactional tenet.* Passing on knowledge and skill, like any human exchange, involves a subcommunity in interaction. At the minimum, it involves a "teacher" and a "learner"—or if not a teacher in flesh and blood, then a vicarious one like a book, or film, or display, or a "responsive" computer.

It is principally through interacting with others that children find out what the culture is about and how it conceives of the world. Unlike any other species, human beings deliberately teach each other in settings outside the ones in which the knowledge being taught will be used. Nowhere else in the animal kingdom is such deliberate "teaching" found—save scrappily among higher primates.[38] To be sure, many indigenous cultures do not practice as deliberate or decontextualized a form of teaching as we do. But "telling" and "showing" are as humanly universal as speaking.

It is customary to say that this specialization rests upon the gift of language. But perhaps more to the point, it also rests upon our astonishingly well developed talent for "intersubjectivity"—the human ability to understand the minds of others, whether through language, gesture, or other means.[39] It is not just words that make this possible, but our capacity to grasp the role of the settings in which words, acts, and gestures occur. We are the intersubjective species par excellence. It is this that permits us to "negotiate" meanings when words go astray.

Our Western pedagogical tradition hardly does justice to the importance of intersubjectivity in transmitting culture. Indeed, it often clings to a preference for a degree of explicitness that seems to ignore it. So teaching is fitted into a mold in which a single, presumably omniscient teacher explicitly tells or shows presumably unknowing learners something they presumably know nothing about. Even when we tamper with this model, as with "question periods" and the like, we still remain loyal to its unspoken precepts. I believe that one of the most important gifts that a cultural psychology can give to education is a reformulation of this impoverished conception. For only a very small part of educating takes place on such a one-way street—and it is probably one of the least successful parts.

So back to the innocent but fundamental question: how best to conceive of a subcommunity that specializes in learning among its members? One obvious answer would be that it is a place where, among other things, learners help each other learn, each according to her abilities. And this, of course, need not exclude the presence of somebody serving in the role of teacher. It simply implies that the teacher does not play that role as a monopoly, that learners "scaffold" for each other as well. The antithesis is the "transmission" model first described, often further exaggerated by an emphasis on transmitting "subject matter." But in most matters of achieving mastery, we also want learners to gain good judgment, to become self-reliant, to work well with each other. And such competencies do not flourish under a one-way "transmission" regimen. Indeed, the very institutionalization of schooling may get in the way of creating a subcommunity of learners who bootstrap each other.

Consider the more "mutual" community for a moment. Typically, it models ways of doing or knowing, provides opportunity for emulation, offers running commentary, provides "scaffolding" for novices, and even provides a good context for teaching deliberately. It even makes possible that form of job-related division of labor one finds in effective work groups: some serving pro tem as "memories" for the others, or as record keepers of "where things have got up to now," or as encouragers or cautioners. The point is for those in the group to help each other get the lay of the land and the hang of the job.

One of the most radical proposals to have emerged from the cultural-psychological approach to education is that the classroom be reconceived as just such a subcommunity of mutual learners, with the teacher orchestrating the proceedings. Note that, contrary to traditional critics, such subcommunities do not reduce the teacher's role nor his or her "authority." Rather, the teacher takes on the additional function of encouraging others to share it. Just as the omniscient narrator has disappeared from modern fiction, so will the omniscient teacher disappear from the classroom of the future.

There is obviously no single formula that follows from the cultural-psychological approach to interactive, intersubjective pedagogy. For one thing, the practices adopted will vary with subject: poetry and mathematics doubtless require different approaches. Its sole precept is that where human beings are concerned, learning (whatever else it may be) is an interactive process in which people learn from each other, and not just by showing and telling. It is surely in the nature of human cultures to form such communities of mutual learners. Even if we are the only species that "teaches deliberately" and "out of the context of use," this does not mean that we should convert this evolutionary step into a fetish.

5. *The externalization tenet.* A French cultural psychologist, Ignace Meyerson,[40] first enunciated an idea that today, a quarter-century after his death, now seems both obvious and brimming with educational implications. Briefly, his view was that the main function of all collective cultural activity is to produce "works"—*oeuvres,* as he called them, works that, as it were, achieve an existence of their own. In the grand sense, these include the arts and sciences of a culture, institutional structures such as its laws and its markets, even its "history" conceived as a canonical version of the past. But there are minor oeuvres as well: those "works" of smaller groupings that give pride, identity, and a sense of continuity to those who participate, however obliquely, in their making. These may be "inspirational"—for example, our school soccer team won the county championship six years ago, or our famous Bronx High School of Science has "produced" three Nobel Laureates. Oeuvres are often touchingly local, modest, yet equally identity-bestowing, such as this remark by a 10-year-old student: "Look at *this* thing we're working on if you want to see how *we* handle oil spills."[41]

The benefits of "externalizing" such joint products into oeuvres have too long been overlooked. First on the list, obviously, is that collective oeuvres produce and sustain group solidarity. They help *make* a community, and communities of mutual learners are no exception. But just as important, they promote a sense of the division of labor that goes into producing a product: Todd is our real computer wonk, Jeff's terrific at making graphics, Alice and David are our "word geniuses," Maddalena is fantastic at explaining things that puzzle some of the rest of us. One group we will examine in later discussions even devised a way to highlight these "group works" by instituting a weekly session to hear and discuss a report on the class's performance for the week. The report, presented by a "class ethnographer" (usually one of the teaching assistants), highlights *overall* rather than individual progress; it produces "metacognition" on the class's oeuvre and usually leads to lively discussion.

Works and works-in-progress create *shared* and *negotiable* ways of thinking in a group. The French historians of the so-called *Annales* school, who were strongly influenced by Meyerson's ideas, refer to these shared and negotiable forms of thought as *mentalités,*[42] styles of thinking that characterize different groups in different periods living under various circumstances. The class's approach to its "weekly ethnography" produces just such a *mentalité.*

I can see one other benefit from externalizing mental work into a more palpable oeuvre, one that we psychologists have tended to ignore. Externalization produces a *record* of our mental efforts, one that is "outside us" rather than vaguely "in memory." It is somewhat like producing a draft, a rough sketch, a "mock-up." "It" takes over our attention as something that, in its own right, needs a transitional paragraph, or a less frontal perspective there, or a better "introduction." "It" relieves us in some measure from the always difficult task of "thinking about our own thoughts" while often accomplishing the same end. "It" embodies our thoughts and intentions in a form more accessible to reflective efforts. The process of thought and its product become interwoven, like Picasso's countless sketches and drawings in reconceiving Velásquez's *Las Meninas.*[43] There is a Latin motto, "scientia dependit in mores," knowledge works its way into habits. It might easily be retranslated as "thinking works its way into its products."

All viable cultures, Ignace Meyerson noted, make provisions for conserving and passing on their "works." Laws get written down, codified, and embodied in the procedure of courts. Law schools train people in the ways of a "profession" so that the *corpus juris* can be assured for the future. These "hard copy" externalizations are typically supported as well by myth-like ones: the indomitable Lord Mansfield bringing the skepticism of Montaigne and Montesquieu into English law, the equally indomitable Mr. Chief Justice Holmes injecting a new, Darwinian "realism" into American jurisprudence, and even John Mortimer's fictional Rumpole struggling commonsensically against the legal pedants. What finally emerges is a subtle mix of starchy procedures and their informal human explication.

Obviously, a school's classroom is no match for the law in tradition-making. Yet it can have long-lasting influence. We carry with us habits of thought and taste fostered in some nearly forgotten classroom by a certain teacher. I can remember one who made us relish as a class "less obvious" interpretations of historical happenings. We lost our embarrassment about offering our "wilder" ideas. She helped us invent a tradition.[44] I still relish it. Can schools and classrooms be designed to foster such tradition-inventing? Denmark is experimenting with keeping the same group of children and teachers together through all the primary grades—an idea that goes back to Steiner. Does that turn "work" into "works" with a life of their own? Modern mobility is, of course, the enemy of all such aspirations. Yet the creation and conservation of culture in shared works is a matter worth reflecting upon. Nor are we without good examples in our own time. Sarah Lightfoot has documented how certain public high schools create a sense of their enduring meaning,[45] and Michael Cole's "computer networking" seems to yield the interesting by-product of widely separated groups of children finding a wider, more enduring, and palpable world through contact with each other by e-mail.[46]

Externalizing, in a word, rescues cognitive activity from implicitness, making it more public, negotiable, and "solidary." At the same time, it makes it more accessible to subsequent reflection and metacognition. Probably the greatest milestone in the history of externalization was literacy, putting thought and memory "out there" on clay tablets or paper. Computers and e-mail may represent another step forward. But there are doubtless myriad ways in which jointly negotiated thought can be communally externalized as oeuvres—and many ways in which they can be put to use in schools.

6. *The instrumentalism tenet.* Education, however conducted in whatever culture, always has consequences in the later lives of those who undergo it. Everybody knows this; nobody doubts it. We also know that these consequences are instrumental in the lives of individuals, and even know that, in a less immediately personal sense, they are instrumental to the culture and its various institutions (the latter are discussed in the following tenet). Education, however gratuitous or decorative it may seem or profess to be, provides skills, ways of thinking, feeling, and speaking, that later may be traded for "distinctions" in the institutionalized "markets" of a society. In this deeper sense, then, education is never neutral, never without social and economic consequences. However much it may be claimed to the contrary, education is always political in this broader sense.

There are two pervasive considerations that need to be taken into account in pursuing the implications of these hard-edged facts. One has to do with *talent;* the other with *opportunity.* And while the two are by no means unrelated, they need to be discussed separately first. For, as in the recent book by Herrnstein and Murray,[47] the two are often confounded—as if opportunity followed talent like its shadow.

About talent, it is by now obvious that it is more multifaceted than any single score, like an IQ test, could possibly reveal. Not only are there many ways of using mind, many ways of knowing and constructing meanings, but they serve many functions in different situations. These ways of using mind are enabled, indeed often brought into being, by learning to master what I earlier described as a culture's "toolkit" of symbolic systems and speech registers. There is thinking and meaning making for intimate situations different in kind from what one uses in the impersonal setting of a shop or office.

Some people seem to have great aptitude in using certain powers of mind and their supporting registers, others less. Howard Gardner has made a good case for certain of these aptitudes (he calls them "frames of mind") having an innate and universal basis—like the ability to deal with quantitative relations, or with linguistic subtleties, or with skilled movement of the body in dance, or with sensing the feelings of others.[48] And he is engaged in constructing curricula for fostering these differing aptitudes.

Beyond the issue of differing native aptitudes, however, it is also the case that different cultures place different emphasis upon the skilled use of different modes of thought and different registers. Not everybody is supposed to be numerate, but if you occupy the role of engineer, you're something of a queer duck if you're not. But everybody is supposed to be passingly competent in managing interpersonal relations. Different cultures distribute these skills differently. The French even have an expression that refers to the "shape" of one's trained capabilities, "professional deformation" in literal translation. And these very rapidly get "typed" and consolidated through training and schooling: girls used to be considered more "sensitive" to poetry, were given more experience in it, and more often than not *became* more sensitive. But this is a harmless example of the kinds of considerations that affect the *opportunity* young people have for developing the skills and ways of thinking that they will later trade for distinctions and rewards in the larger society.

There are many uglier features of opportunity that blight lives far more profoundly. Racism, social-class entitlements, and prejudice, all of them amplified by the forms of poverty they create, have powerful effects on how much and how we educate the young. Indeed, even the so-called innate talents of children from "socially tainted" backgrounds are altered before they ever get to school—in ghettos, barrios, and those other settings of poverty, despair, and defiance that seem to suppress and divert the mental powers of the young who "grow up" in them. Indeed, it was principally to counteract these early blighting effects of poverty (and, of course, racism) that Head Start was founded (see Chapter 3). But schools themselves, given that they are locally situated, also tend to continue and perpetuate the subcultures of poverty or defiance that initially nipped or diverted children's "natural" talents of mind in the first place.

Schools have always been highly selective with respect to the uses of mind they cultivate—which uses are to be considered "basic," which "frills," which the school's responsibility and which the responsibility of others, which for girls and which for boys, which for working-class children and which for "swells." Some of this selectivity was doubtless based on considered notions about what the society required or what the individual needed to get along. Much of it was a spillover of folk or social class tradition. Even the more recent and seemingly obvious objective of equipping all with "basic literacy" is premised on moral-political grounds, however pragmatically those grounds may be justified. School curricula and classroom "climates" always reflect inarticulate cultural values as well as explicit plans; and these values are never far removed from considerations of social class, gender, and the prerogatives of social power. Should girls, to take a case pending before the U.S. Supreme Court, be admitted into state-supported military academies formerly reserved for young men?[49] Is affirmative action a covert form of discrimination against the middle class?[50]

Nothing could be more expressive of a culture than the conflicts and compromises that swirl around quasi-educational questions of this order. What is striking in most democratic states is that the compromises that emerge initially get buried in the rhetoric of official blandness, after which (and partly as a result of which) they become candidates for bitter and rather poorly considered attack. All children should have the same curricula? Of course. And then there is an exposé of what "the same" means in the schools, say, of a South Bronx ghetto and those in suburban Forest Hills. With increased community awareness, formerly innocent issues like curriculum soon become political ones—and quite appropriately so. The trouble, of course, is that purely political debate specializes in oversimplification. And these are not simple issues.

So the "underground curriculum" continues to loom larger—a school's way of adapting a curriculum to express its attitudes toward its pupils, its racial attitudes, and the rest. And in the community's politicized reaction, political slogans become at least as determinative of educational policy as do theories about the cultivation of the multiple powers of mind.

Surely one of the major educational tenets of a cultural psychology is that the school can never be considered as culturally "free standing." *What* it teaches, what modes of thought and what "speech registers" it actually cultivates in its pupils, cannot be isolated from how the school is situated in the lives and culture of its students. For a school's curriculum is not only *about* "subjects." The chief subject matter of school, viewed culturally, is school itself. That is how most students experience it, and it determines what meaning they make of it.

This, of course, is what I mean by the "situatedness" of school and school learning. Yet, for all its pervasiveness, there is little question that, with thought and will, it can be changed. Change can occur even by little symbolic innovations—like creating a chess club in a ghetto school, and providing real coaching. Joining the chess club (indeed, *having* a chess club) in a mainly black Harlem middle school creates a quite different communal self-image than joining one (or having one) in Cincinnati's well-to-do Walnut Hills. And winning the National Junior High School Chess Team Championship for Mott High Middle School in Harlem is no ho-hum matter. In some cryptic way it can mean "beating the oppressor at his own brainy games."[51] But bits of symbolism scarcely touch the problem at large.

None of this is new. What does the cultural psychologist have to say about such matters? Certainly one general thing: education does not stand alone, and it cannot be designed as if it did. It exists in a culture. And culture, whatever else it is, is also about power, distinctions, and rewards. We have, in the laudable interest of protecting freedom of thought and instruction, officially buffered schools against political pressures. School is "above" politics. In some important sense, this is surely true—but it is a threadbare truth. Increasingly, we see something quite different. For, as it were, the secret is out. Even the so-called man in the street knows that how one equips minds matters mightily later in our postindustrial, technological era. The public, to be sure, has a rather unformed sense of this—and certainly the press does. But they are aware. The *New York Times* carried as front-page news in the spring of 1995 that achievement levels had gone up in the city's schools; and Dublin's *Irish Times* in the summer of that same year carried on its front page the news that Irish students had scored "above the average" in a comparative study of reading ability in European schools.

Why not, then, treat education for what it is? It has always been "political," though cryptically so in more settled, less aware times. There has now been a revolution in public awareness. But it has not been accompanied by a comparable revolution in our ways of taking this awareness into account in the forging of educational policies and practices. All of which is not to propose that we "politicize" education, but simply that we recognize that it is already politicized and that its political side needs finally to be taken into account more explicitly, not simply as though it were "public protest." I will return to this issue in more detail later in this chapter.

7. *The institutional tenet.* My seventh tenet is that as education in the developed world becomes institutionalized, it behaves as institutions do and often must, and suffers certain problems common to all institutions. What distinguishes it from others is its special role in preparing the young to take a more active part in other institutions of the culture. Let us explore now what this implies.

Cultures are not simply collections of people sharing a common language and historical tradition. They are composed of institutions that specify more concretely what roles people play and what status and respect these are accorded—though the culture at large expresses its way of life through institutions as well. Cultures can also be conceived as elaborate exchange systems,[52] with media of exchange as varied as respect, goods, loyalty, and services. Exchange systems become focalized and legitimized in institutions which provide buildings, stipends, titles, and the rest. They are further legitimized by a complex symbolic apparatus of myths, statutes, precedents, ways of talking and thinking, and even uniforms. Institutions impose their "will" through coercion, sometimes implicit as in incentives and disincentives, sometimes explicit as in restriction backed by the power of the state, such as the disbarring of a lawyer or the refusal of credit to a defaulting merchant.

Institutions do the culture's serious business. But for all that, they do so through an unpredictable mix of coercion and voluntarism. I say "unpredictable" because it remains perpetually unclear both to participants in a culture and to those who observe it from "outside" when and how the power of enforcement will be brought to bear by those delegated or otherwise thought privileged to use it. So if it can be said that a culture's institutions do "serious business," it can equally be said that it is often ambiguous and uncertain business.

It is also characteristic of human cultures that individuals rarely owe allegiance to any single institution: one "belongs" to a family of origin and one by marriage, an occupational group, a neighborhood, as well as to more general groups like a nation or a social class. Each institutional grouping struggles to achieve its distinctive pattern of rights and responsibilities. This adds further to the inherent ambiguity of life in culture. As Walter Lippmann and John Dewey long ago pointed out,[53] how any given individual forms his interpretation on issues of public concern will usually involve him in a conflict of interests and identities. For while institutions may complement each other functionally, they also compete for privilege and power. Indeed, the power of a culture inheres in its capacity to integrate its component institutions through a dialectic of conflict resolution.

Institutions, as Pierre Bourdieu has suggested,[54] provide the "markets" where people "trade" their acquired skills, knowledge, and ways of constructing meanings for "distinctions" or privileges. Institutions often compete in getting their "distinctions" prized above those of others, but the competition must never be "winner take all," for institutions are mutually dependent upon each other. Lawyers and businessmen need each other as much as patients and doctors do. So, as in Diderot's delightful *Jacques le fataliste et son maître,* bargaining for distinction becomes a subtle game, often a source of sly humor. The struggle for distinction seems to be a feature of all cultures.[55]

While all this may at first seem remote from schools and the process of education, the remoteness is an illusion. Education is up to its elbows in the struggle for distinctions. The very expressions *primary, secondary,* and *tertiary* are metaphors for it. It has even been argued recently that the "new" bourgeoisie in France after the Revolution used the schools as one of their principal tools for "turning around" the system of prestige and distinction previously dominated by the aristocracy and gentry of the *ancien régime*.[56] Indeed, the very concept of a meritocracy is precisely an expression of the new power that schools are expected to exercise in fixing the distribution of distinctions in contemporary bureaucratic society.

It was the "tug" of institutional competition that mainly concerned us in the preceding section, often converted into a more conventionalized political form. I commented there that there had been an "evolution in awareness" about education. Let me pursue that now. Few democracies today are short of cultural critics who bring educational issues before the public, sometimes vividly: a Paulo Freire in Latin America, a Pierre Bourdieu in France, a Neil Postman in America, or an A. H. Halsey in Britain. There is lively public discussion of education in virtually every developed country of the world. Despite that, most countries still lack public forums for informed consideration of educational issues. I believe such forums are crucial for responding to and, indeed, informing the kinds of politicized debates discussed earlier. But they are emerging. And though they may not turn out to be as stately or noncontroversial as Her Majesty's Inspectorate of Education in Queen Victoria's class-dominated days, they at least are bringing education out from behind its screen of "neutrality." We already have some foretaste of what is to come, as when the President of the United States discusses educational issues on television with a selected forum of experts and participants, or when Shirley Williams, formerly Britain's Minister of Education, instituted widely covered broadcasts of regional discussions. Many regional Italian teachers' unions now hold annual discussion meetings on the state and progress of education, with provincial ministers and leading researchers actively in attendance.[57] In the United States, where sectarian acrimony often increases faster than responsible and informed discussion, many state governors have established quasi-official groups at whose meetings pending state policy decisions on education get discussed. The goals of education seem again to have become a topic worthy of study as well as debate.

But there is more to the matter than public opinion and the need to inform it. For, as I remarked at the outset, educational systems are themselves highly institutionalized, in the grip of their *own* values. Educators have their own usually well informed views about how to cultivate and how to "grade" the human mind. And like other institutions, education perpetuates itself and its practices: by establishing graduate schools of education, *grandes écoles* like the École Normale Supérieure in France, even elite academies like the chartered National Academy of Education in America and the informal All Souls Group in Britain. And as often happens, it invents durable ways of distributing skills, attitudes, and ways of thinking in the same old unjust demographic patterns. A reliable example of this can be found in procedures for examining students that, somehow, long outlive exposés of their unfairness to less privileged groups in the population. In consequence, the goodness of fit between school practices and society's demands comes increasingly under scrutiny.

Yet, in a sense, the public discussions that occur in consequence of this scrutiny are by no means strictly about "education." It is not simply that we are trying to reevaluate the balance between schools as a fixed Educational Establishment, on the one side, and a set of well-established needs of the culture, on the other. The issues are much broader than that. They have to do with the emerging role of women in society, with the vexing problem of the ethnic loyalties of the children of guest workers, with minority rights, with sexual mores, with unmarried mothers, with violence, with poverty. The Educational Establishment, for all its fingertip expertise in dealing with educational routines, has little by way of established doctrine for dealing with such problems. Nor do other institutions within the culture, though they nonetheless seem always tempted to "blame education" for its particular set of troubles—whether it be the falling competitiveness of the auto industry, the increase in births out of wedlock, or violence on the streets.

It is astonishing how little systematic study is devoted to the institutional "anthropology" of schooling, given the complexity of its situatedness and its exposure to the changing social and economic climate. Its relation to the family, to the economy, to religious institutions, even to the labor market, is only vaguely understood.[58] But suggestive work is beginning. I find it encouraging that one distinguished contributor to this current debate on the role of education in the economy is no less a figure than the serving Secretary of Labor in the Clinton administration. His discussion of the place of symbolic "meta-skills" in *The Work of Nations* could serve as a policy document in our times. And one wonders, indeed, whether the institutional challenges of our changing society might call not only for the proverbial New Man, but also for some New Institutions (as Daniel Bell suggests).[59]

Let me offer two such institutions, though entirely in the spirit of illustration. Each is intended to address the range of institutional questions just discussed—both very much in the spirit of the cultural-ist approach. Each takes for granted that there is a reciprocal relation between education and the other major institutional activities of a culture: communication, economics, politics, family life, and so on. The first is designed to recognize the shortage of useful information on such crucial matters, the second that we lack a deliberative apparatus that can convert useful knowledge into wise policy alternatives.

In connection with the first of these, gathering useful information, what I envision is something that might be called an "anthropology" of education, a term that for me goes far beyond the collection of "classroom ethnographies," however helpful such exercises have been. This kind of "anthropology" should be dedicated to work on the situatedness of education in the society at large—to its institutions, as just noted, but also to "crisis" problems like poverty and racism. Or, in a word, what role does schooling play in coping with or exacerbating the "predicament of culture" that James Clifford has described so vividly?[60]

Well, there is no such "field" as this one, really: only a lot of scattered investigators working in different academic departments. So, one invents a field and even legitimizes it by granting a broad charter to, say, a National Institute of Education, to be financed (in the interest of maintaining the "compromise control" mentioned earlier) by federal, state, and private foundation support and sponsorship. And since these are all thoughts that come even before a "drawing board" gets involved, I will also suggest that such an institute not be exclusively for research, but also for consultation. But let me turn to the other institutional invention, this one concerned principally with forging possible policy alternatives in a setting of competing institutions.

We still have reason to celebrate Clemenceau's remark that war is too important to leave to the generals. Not generals alone—too many other interests and constituencies are affected. In this same sense, as I've tried to make clear in this opening chapter, education is too consequential to too many constituencies to leave to professional educators. And I'm sure most thoughtful professionals would agree. Thus, to bring judgment, balance, and a broader social commitment to the educational scene in America, we would need to engage "the best and the brightest" as well as the most publicly committed to the task of formulating alternative policies and practices. I know this is not easy, but imagine a task force or a board whose members were recruited from many "walks of life," as we like to put it. It might take many different forms: its only requirement is that it be made up of those who have achieved a reputation for their acumen, their fair-mindedness, and their public commitment. Imagine such a body as a White House Board, say, in the spirit of the Board of Economic Advisers or the National Security Council, with the function of advising the President of the United States on educational issues in the broad sense, including the impact of federal policy generally on the conduct of education, and vice versa. Or a more vigorous model might be the Federal Reserve Board, though obviously such a model would violate the American constitutional mandate of leaving education to the "several states." In any case, I offer these suggestions in the spirit of recognizing that education is not a free-standing institution, not an island, but part of the continent.

Having offered these rather grandiose examples, I must conclude this discussion of "institutionalization" on a more homely note. Improving education requires teachers who understand and are committed to the improvements envisioned. So banal a point would scarcely be worth mentioning were it not so easily overlooked by many efforts at educational reform. We need to equip teachers with the necessary background training to take an effective part in reform.[61] The people who run them make institutions. However thoughtful our educational plans may become, they must include a crucial place for teachers. For ultimately, that is where the action is.

8. *The tenet of identity and self-esteem.* I have put this tenet late in the list. For it is so pervasive as to implicate virtually all that has gone before. Perhaps the single most universal thing about human experience is the phenomenon of "Self," and we know that education is crucial to its formation. Education should be conducted with that fact in mind.

We know "Self" from our own inner experience, and we recognize others as selves. Indeed, more than one distinguished scholar has argued that self-awareness requires as its necessary condition the recognition of the Other as a self.[62] Though there are universals of selfhood—and we will consider two of them in a moment—different cultures both shape it differently and set its limits in varying ways. Some emphasize autonomy and individuality, some affiliation;[63] some link it closely to a person's position in a divine or secular social order,[64] some link it to individual effort or even to luck. Since schooling is one of life's earliest institutional involvements outside the family, it is not surprising that it plays a critical role in the shaping of Self. But I think this will be clearer if we first examine two aspects of selfhood that are regarded as universal.

The first is *agency.* Selfhood, most students of the subject believe, derives from the sense that one can initiate and carry out activities on one's own.[65] Whether this is "really" so or simply a folk belief, as radical behaviorists would have us believe, is beyond the scope of this inquiry. I shall simply take it as so. People experience themselves as agents. But then too, any vertebrate distinguishes between a branch *it* has shaken and one that has shaken *it*.[66] So there must be something more to selfhood than the recognition of simple sensorimotor agentivity. What characterizes human selfhood is the construction of a conceptual system that organizes, as it were, a "record" of agentive encounters with the world, a record that is related to the past (that is, "autobiographical memory," so-called)[67] but that is also extrapolated into the future—self with history and with possibility. It is a "possible self" that regulates aspiration, confidence, optimism, and their opposites.[68] While this "constructed" self-system is inner, private, and suffused with affect, it also extends outward to the things and activities and places with which we become "ego-involved"[69]—William James's "extended self." Schools and school learning are among the earliest of those places and activities.

But just as important as the inner psychodynamics of selfhood are the ways in which a culture institutionalizes it. All natural languages, for example, make obligatory grammatical distinctions between agentive and patientive forms: *I hit him; he hit me*. And even the simplest narratives are built around, indeed depend upon, an agent-Self as a protagonist with his or her own goals operating in a recognizable cultural setting.[70] There is a moral aspect to selfhood as well, expressed simply by such ubiquitous phenomena as "blaming yourself" or "blaming another" for acts committed or outcomes that result from our acts. At a more evolved level, all legal systems specify (and legitimize) some notion of *responsibility* by which Self is endowed with obligation in regard to some broader cultural authority—confirming "officially" that we, our Selves, are presumed to be agents in control of our own actions.

Since agency implies not only the capacity for initiating, but also for completing our acts, it also implies *skill* or *know-how*. Success and failure are principal nutrients in the development of selfhood. Yet we may not be the final arbiters of success and failure, which are often defined from "outside" according to culturally specified criteria. And school is where the child first encounters such criteria—often as if applied arbitrarily. School judges the child's performance, and the child responds by evaluating himself or herself in turn.

Which brings us to a second ubiquitous feature of selfhood: *evaluation*. Not only do we experience self as agentive, we evaluate our efficacy in bringing off what we hoped for or were asked to do. Self increasingly takes on the flavor of these valuations. I call this mix of agentive efficacy and self-evaluation "self-esteem." It combines our sense of what we believe ourselves to be (or even hope to be) capable of and what we fear is beyond us.[71]

How self-esteem is experienced (or how it is expressed) varies, of course, with the ways of one's culture. Low esteem sometimes manifests itself in guilt about intentions, sometimes simply in shame for having been "found out"; sometimes it is accompanied by depression, even to the point of suicide, sometimes by defiant anger.[72] In some cultures, particularly those that emphasize achievement, high self-esteem increases level of aspiration;[73] in others it leads to status display and standing pat. There may even be an individual temperamental component in how people deal with threatened self-esteem—whether one blames oneself, others, or circumstances.[74]

Only two things can be said for certain and in general: the management of self-esteem is never simple and never settled, and its state is affected powerfully by the availability of supports provided from outside. These supports are hardly mysterious or exotic. They include such homely resorts as a second chance, honor for a good if unsuccessful try, but above all the chance for discourse that permits one to find out why or how things didn't work out as planned. It is no secret that school is often rough on children's self-esteem, and we are beginning to know something about their vulnerability in this area.[75] Ideally, of course, school is supposed to provide a setting where our performance has fewer esteem-threatening consequences than in the "real world," presumably in the interest of encouraging the learner to "try things out." Yet radical critics, like Paulo Freire,[76] have argued that school often metes out failures to those children the society would later "exploit." And even moderate critics, like Roland Barthes and Pierre Bourdieu, make the provocative case that school is principally an agent for producing, say, "little Frenchmen and French-women" who will conform to the niche where they will end up.[77]

Obviously there are other "markets" where even school children can "trade" their skills for distinctions, to use Bourdieu's interesting terms again. And these "markets" often compensate for sensed failure in school—as when "street smarts" are traded on the market of petty crime, or when defiance of the majority community earns black teenagers respect among their peers. School, more than we have realized, competes with myriad forms of "anti-school" as a provider of agency, identity, and self-esteem—no less at a middle-class suburban mall than on the ghetto streets.

Any system of education, any theory of pedagogy, any "grand national policy" that diminishes the school's role in nurturing its pupils' self-esteem fails at one of its primary functions. The deeper problem—from a cultural-psychological point of view, but in worka-day common sense as well—is how to cope with the erosion of this function under modern urban conditions. Though I shall touch on some specific efforts to cope with these problems in later chapters, one point can certainly be made clear in this opening chapter. Schools do not simply equip kids with skills and self-esteem or not. They are in competition with other parts of society that can do this, but with deplorable consequences for the society. America manages to alienate enough black ghetto boys to land nearly a third of them in jail before they reach the age of thirty.

More positively, if agency and esteem are central to the construc-tion of a concept of Self, then the ordinary practices of school need to be examined with a view to what contribution they make to these two crucial ingredients of personhood. Surely the "community of learners" approach mentioned earlier contributes to both. But equally, the granting of more responsibility in setting and achieving goals in all aspects of a school's activities could also contrib-ute—everything from maintenance of a school's physical plant to a share in decisions about academic and extracurricular projects to be undertaken. Such a conception, earlier so dear to the progressive tradition in education, is also in the image of the constitutional principle that (in a democracy) rights and responsibilities are two sides of the same coin. If, as I noted at the outset, school is an entry into the culture and not just a preparation for it, then we must constantly reassess what school does to the young student's conception of his own powers (his sense of agency) and his sensed chances of being able to cope with the world both in school and after (his self-esteem). In many democratic cultures, I think, we have become so preoccupied with the more formal criteria of "performance" and with the bureaucratic demands of education as an institution that we have neglected this personal side of education.

9. *The narrative tenet.* I want finally to leapfrog over the issue of school "subjects" and curricula in order to deal with a more general matter: the mode of thinking and feeling that helps children (indeed, people generally) create a version of the world in which, psychologically, they can envisage a place for themselves—a personal world. I believe that story making, narrative, is what is needed for that, and I want to discuss it briefly in this final tenet.

I still hold firmly to the views expressed in my earlier work about subject-matter teaching: the importance of giving the learner a sense of the generative structure of a subject discipline, the value of a "spiral curriculum," the crucial role of self-generated discovery in learning a subject matter, and so forth.[78] The issue I want to address now has to do more directly with the issue of how growing children create meanings from school experience that they can relate to their lives in a culture. So let me turn to narrative as a mode of thought and as a vehicle of meaning making.

I shall begin with some basics. There appear to be two broad ways in which human beings organize and manage their knowledge of the world, indeed structure even their immediate experience: one seems more specialized for treating of physical "things," the other for treating of people and their plights. These are conventionally known as *logical-scientific* thinking and *narrative* thinking. Their universality suggests that they have their roots in the human genome or that they are (to revert to an earlier tenet) givens in the nature of language. They have varied modes of expression in different cultures, which also cultivate them differently. No culture is without both of them, though different cultures privilege them differently.[79]

It has been the convention of most schools to treat the arts of narrative—song, drama, fiction, theater, whatever—as more "decoration" than necessity, something with which to grace leisure, sometimes even as something morally exemplary. Despite that, we frame the accounts of our cultural origins and our most cherished beliefs in story form, and it is not just the "content" of these stories that grip us, but their narrative artifice. Our immediate experience, what happened yesterday or the day before, is framed in the same storied way. Even more striking, we represent our lives (to ourselves as well as to others) in the form of narrative.[80] It is not surprising that psychoanalysts now recognize that personhood implicates narrative,[81] "neurosis" being a reflection of either an insufficient, incomplete, or inappropriate story about oneself. Recall that when Peter Pan asks Wendy to return to Never Never Land with him, he gives as his reason that she could teach the Lost Boys there how to tell stories. If they knew how to tell them, the Lost Boys might be able to grow up.

The importance of narrative for the cohesion of a culture is as great, very likely, as it is in structuring an individual life. Take law as an illustration. Without a sense of the common trouble narratives that the law translates into its common law writs, it becomes arid.[82] And those "trouble narratives" appear again in mythic literature and contemporary novels, better contained in that form than in reasoned and logically coherent propositions. It seems evident, then, that skill in narrative construction and narrative understanding is crucial to constructing our lives and a "place" for ourselves in the possible world we will encounter.

It has always been tacitly assumed that narrative skill comes "naturally," that it does not have to be taught. But a closer look shows this not to be true at all. We know now, for example, that it goes through definite stages,[83] is severely impaired in brain damage of certain kinds,[84] fares poorly under stress,[85] and ends up in literalism in one social community while becoming fanciful in a neighboring one with a different tradition.[86] Observe law students or young lawyers preparing their final arguments for litigation or mock court and it will quickly be plain that some people have the knack more than others—they have simply learned how to make a story believable and worth thinking about.

Feeling at home in the world, knowing how to place oneself into self-descriptive stories, is surely not made easier by the enormous increase in migration in the modern world. It is not easy, however multicultural your intentions, to help a ten-year-old create a story that includes him in the world beyond his family and neighborhood, having been transplanted from Vietnam to the San Fernando Valley, from Algeria to Lyons, from Anatolia to Dresden. If school, his *pied-à-terre* outside the family, can't help him, there are alienated countercultures that can.

None of us know as much as we should about how to create narrative sensibility. Two commonplaces seem to have stood the test of time. The first is that a child should "know," have a "feel" for, the myths, histories, folktales, conventional stories of his or her culture (or cultures). They frame and nourish an identity. The second commonplace urges imagination through fiction. Finding a place in the world, for all that it implicates the immediacy of home, mate, job, and friends, is ultimately an act of imagination. So, for the culturally transplanted, there is the imaginative challenge of the fiction and "quasi-fiction" that takes him or her into the world of possibilities—as in the novels of a Maxine Hong Kingston or the poems of a Maya Angelou. And for any schoolboy pondering how it all came about, there is a Simon Schama narratively restoring the human plights to the "dead certainties" of the past, to use his telling phrase.[87]

Obviously, if narrative is to be made an instrument of mind on behalf of meaning making, it requires work on our part—reading it, making it, analyzing it, understanding its craft, sensing its uses, discussing it. These are matters much better understood today than a generation ago.[88]

All of which is not intended to undervalue the importance of logical-scientific thinking. Its value is so implicit in our highly technological culture that its inclusion in school curricula is taken for granted. While its teaching may still be in need of improvement, it has become strikingly better since the curriculum reform movements of the 1950s and 1960s. But it is no secret that for many of the young now in school, "science" has come to seem "inhuman" and "uncaring" and "off-putting"—despite the first-class efforts of science and mathematics teachers and their associations.[89] Indeed, the image of science as a human and cultural undertaking might itself be improved if it were also conceived as a history of human beings overcoming received ideas—whether Lavoisier overcoming the dogma of phlogiston, Darwin rethinking respectable creationism, or Freud daring to look under the smug surface of our self-satisfaction.[90] We may have erred in divorcing science from the narrative of culture.

A summary is hardly necessary. A system of education must help those growing up in a culture find an identity within that culture. Without it, they stumble in their effort after meaning. It is only in the narrative mode that one can construct an identity and find a place in one's culture. Schools must cultivate it, nurture it, cease taking it for granted. There are many projects now in the making, not only in literature but also in history and social studies, that are following up interesting leads in this field. We will have an opportunity in later chapters to consider them in more detail.

IV

More as a postscript than as a general conclusion, I offer one last reflection on the set of tenets I've put forth in the spirit of a cultural-psychological perspective on education. I realize, reading back over them, to what degree they emphasize the powers of consciousness, reflection, breadth of dialogue, and negotiation. In all systems that depend on authority, even duly constituted and representative authority, all of these factors seem to pose risks by opening discussion of currently institutionalized authority. And they are risky. Education *is* risky, for it fuels the sense of possibility. But a failure to equip minds with the skills for understanding and feeling and acting in the cultural world is not simply scoring a pedagogical zero. It risks creating alienation, defiance, and practical incompetence. And all of these undermine the viability of a culture.

Let me revert finally to the theme with which this chapter opened. I tried to show at the start that education is not simply a technical business of well-managed information processing, nor even simply a matter of applying "learning theories" to the classroom or using the results of subject-centered "achievement testing." It is a complex pursuit of fitting a culture to the needs of its members and of fitting its members and their ways of knowing to the needs of the culture.

In the chapters that follow, we will encounter "in the particular" many of the issues discussed in more general terms in this one. My aim in the foregoing has been to set education in the broader context it requires to be properly understood. Now we can proceed with the particulars.

2

▼

FOLK PEDAGOGY

Thoughtful people have been forever troubled by the enigma of applying theoretical knowledge to practical problems. Applying psychological theory to educational practice is no exception to the rule, not much less puzzling than applying science to medicine. Aristotle comments (rather touchingly) in the *Nichomachean Ethics* (Book V, 1137a): "It is an easy matter to know the effects of honey, wine, hellebore, cautery, and cutting. But to know how, for whom, and when we should apply these as remedies is no less an undertaking than being a physician." Even with scientific advances, the physician's problem is not much easier today than it was in the times of hellebore and cautery: "how, for whom, and when" still loom as problems. The challenge is always to *situate* our knowledge in the living context that poses the "presenting problem," to borrow a bit of medical jargon. And that living context, where education is concerned, is the schoolroom—the schoolroom situated in a broader culture.

That is where, at least in advanced cultures, teachers and pupils come together to effect that crucial but mysterious interchange that we so glibly call "education." Obvious though it may seem, we would do better to concentrate in what follows on "learning and teaching in the setting of school" rather than, as psychologists sometimes do, generalizing from learning in a rat maze, from the nonsense-syllable learning of sophomores incarcerated in a laboratory cubicle, or from the performance of an AI computer simulation at Carnegie-Mellon. Keep before you a busy classroom of nine-year-olds, say, with a hard-working teacher, and ask what kind of theoretical knowledge would help them. A genetic theory that assures them that people differ? Well, perhaps, but not much. Do you work harder with the not-so-bright or ignore them? What about an associationist theory that tells you that nonsense syllables are associated with each other through frequency, recency, contiguity, and similarity effects? Would you want to design a curriculum on knowledge about how nonsense syllables are learned? Well, perhaps a little—where things are a little nonsense-like anyway, such as the names of elements in the periodic table: cerium, lithium, gold, lead . . .

There is one "presenting problem" that is always with us in dealing with teaching and learning, one that is so pervasive, so constant, so much part of the fabric of living, that we often fail to notice it, fail even to discover it—much as in the proverb "the fish will be the last to discover water." It is the issue of how human beings achieve a meeting of minds, expressed by teachers usually as "how do I reach the children?" or by children as "what's she trying to get at?" This is the classic problem of Other Minds, as it was originally called in philosophy, and its relevance to education has mostly been overlooked until very recently. In the last decade it has become a topic of passionate interest and intense research among psychologists, particularly those interested in development. It is what this chapter is about—the application of this new work to the process of education.

To a degree almost entirely overlooked by anti-subjective behaviorists in the past, our interactions with others are deeply affected by our everyday intuitive theories about how other minds work. These theories, rarely made explicit, are omnipresent but have only recently been subjected to intense study. Such lay theories are now referred to professionally by the rather condescending name of "folk psychology." Folk psychologies reflect certain "wired-in" human tendencies (like seeing people normally as operating under their own control), but they also reflect some deeply ingrained cultural beliefs about "the mind." Not only is folk psychology preoccupied with how the mind works here and now, it is also equipped with notions about how the child's mind learns and even what makes it grow. Just as we are steered in ordinary interaction by our folk psychology, so we are steered in the activity of helping children learn about the world by notions of *folk pedagogy*. Watch any mother, any teacher, even any babysitter with a child and you'll be struck by how much of what they do is steered by notions of "what children's minds are like and how to help them learn," even though they may not be able to verbalize their pedagogical principles.

From this work on folk psychology and folk pedagogy has grown a new, perhaps even a revolutionary insight. It is this: in theorizing about the practice of education in the classroom (or any other setting, for that matter), you had better take into account the folk theories that those engaged in teaching and learning already have. For any innovations that you, as a "proper" pedagogical theorist, may wish to introduce will have to compete with, replace, or otherwise modify the folk theories that already guide both teachers and pupils. For example, if you as a pedagogical theorist are convinced that the best learning occurs when the teacher helps lead the pupil to discover generalizations on her own, you are likely to run into an established cultural belief that a teacher is an authority who is supposed to *tell* the child what the general case is, while the child should be occupying herself with memorizing the particulars. And if you study how most classrooms are conducted, you will often find that most of the teacher's questions to pupils are about particulars that can be answered in a few words or even by "yes" or "no." So your introduction of an innovation in teaching will necessarily involve changing the folk psychological and folk pedagogical theories of teachers—and, to a surprising extent, of pupils as well.

Teaching, in a word, is inevitably based on notions about the nature of the learner's mind. Beliefs and assumptions about teaching, whether in a school or in any other context, are a direct reflection of the beliefs and assumptions the teacher holds about the learner. (Later, we will consider the other side of this coin: how learning is affected by the child's notion of the teacher's mind-set, as when girls come to believe that teachers expect them not to come up with unconventional answers.) Of course, like most deep truths, this one is already well known. Teachers have always tried to adjust their teaching to the backgrounds, abilities, styles and interests of the children they teach. This is important, but it is not quite what we are after. Our purpose, rather, is to explore more general ways in which learners' minds are conventionally thought about, and the pedagogic practices that follow from these ways of thinking about mind. Nor will we stop there, for we also want to offer some reflections on "consciousness raising" in this setting: what can be accomplished by getting teachers (and students) to think *explicitly* about their folk psychological assumptions, in order to bring them out of the shadows of tacit knowledge.

One way of presenting the general matter of folk psychology and folk pedagogy most starkly is by contrasting our own human species with non-human primates. In our species, children show an astonishingly strong "predisposition to culture"; they are sensitive to and eager to adopt the folkways they see around them. They show a striking interest in the activity of their parents and peers and with no prompting at all try to imitate what they observe. As for adults, as Kruger and Tomasello insist,[1] there is a uniquely human "pedagogic disposition" to exploit this tendency, for adults to demonstrate correct performance for the benefit of the learner. One finds these matching tendencies in different forms in all human societies. But note that these imitative and demonstrational dispositions seem scarcely to exist at all in our nearest primate kin, the chimpanzees. Not only do adult chimpanzees not "teach" their young by demonstrating correct performance, the young for their part seem not to imitate the actions of adults either, at least if we use a sufficiently stringent definition of imitation. If by imitation one means the ability to observe not just the goal achieved but also the means to that achievement, there is little evidence of imitation in chimpanzees raised in the wild[2] and, even more conspicuously, little attempt at teaching. It is very revealing, however, that when a young chimpanzee is raised "as if" he were a human child, and exposed to the ways of humans, he begins to show more imitative dispositions.[3] The evidence on "demonstrational" dispositions in adult chimpanzees is much less clear, but such dispositions may also be there in a rudimentary form.[4]

Tomasello, Ratner, and Kruger have suggested that because non-human primates do not naturally attribute beliefs and knowledge to others, they probably do not recognize their presence in themselves.[5] We humans show, tell, or teach someone something only because we first recognize that they don't know, or that what they believe is false. The failure of non-human primates to ascribe ignorance or false beliefs to their young may, therefore, explain the absence of peda-gogic efforts, for it is only when these states are recognized that we try to correct the deficiency by demonstration, explanation, or discussion. Even the most humanly "enculturated" chimpanzees show little, if any, of the attribution that leads to instructional activity.

Research on lesser primates shows the same picture. On the basis of their observations of the behavior of vervet monkeys in the wild,[6] Cheney and Seyfarth were led to conclude: "While monkeys may use abstract concepts and have motives, beliefs, and desires, they . . . seem unable to attribute mental states to others: they lack a 'theory of mind.'" Work on other species of monkeys reveals similar findings.[7] The general point is clear: assumptions about the mind of the learner underlie attempts at teaching. No ascription of ignorance, no effort to teach.

But to say only that human beings understand other minds and try to teach the incompetent is to overlook the varied ways in which teaching occurs in different cultures. The variety is stunning.[8] We need to know much more about this diversity if we are to appreciate the relation between folk psychology and folk pedagogy in different cultural settings.

Understanding this relationship becomes particularly urgent in addressing issues of educational reform. For once we recognize that a teacher's conception of a learner shapes the instruction he or she employs, then equipping teachers (or parents) with the best available theory of the child's mind becomes crucial. And in the process of doing that, we also need to provide teachers with some insight about their own folk theories that guide their teaching.

Folk pedagogies, for example, reflect a variety of assumptions about children: they may be seen as willful and needing correction; as innocent and to be protected from a vulgar society; as needing skills to be developed only through practice; as empty vessels to be filled with knowledge that only adults can provide; as egocentric and in need of socialization. Folk beliefs of this kind, whether expressed by laypeople or by "experts," badly want some "deconstructing" if their implications are to be appreciated. For whether these views are "right" or not, their impact on teaching activities can be enormous.

A culturally oriented cognitive psychology does not dismiss folk psychology as mere superstition, something only for the anthropological connoisseur of quaint folkways. I have long argued that explaining what children *do* is not enough;[9] the new agenda is to determine what they *think* they are doing and what their reasons are for doing it. Like new work on children's theories of mind,[10] a cultural approach emphasizes that the child only gradually comes to appreciate that she is acting not directly *on* "the world" but on beliefs she holds *about* that world. This crucial shift from naive realism to an understanding of the role of beliefs, occurring in the early school years, is probably never complete. But once it starts, there is often a corresponding shift in what teachers can do to help children. With the shift, for example, children can take on more responsibilities for their own learning and thinking.[11] They can begin to "think about their thinking" as well as about "the world." It is not surprising, then, that achievement testers have become increasingly concerned not just with what children *know* but with how they think they came by their knowledge.[12] It is as Howard Gardner puts it in *The Unschooled Mind:* "We must place ourselves inside the heads of our students and try to understand as far as possible the sources and strengths of their conceptions."[13]

Stated boldly, the emerging thesis is that educational practices in classrooms are premised on a set of folk beliefs about learners' minds, some of which may have worked advertently toward or inadvertently against the child's own welfare. They need to be made explicit and to be reexamined. Different approaches to learning and different forms of instruction—from imitation, to instruction, to discovery, to collaboration—reflect differing beliefs and assumptions about the learner—from actor, to knower, to private experiencer, to collaborative thinker.[14] What higher primates lack and humans continue to evolve is a set of beliefs about the mind. These beliefs, in turn, alter beliefs about the sources and communicability of thought and action. Advances in how we go about understanding children's minds are, then, a prerequisite to any improvement in pedagogy.

Obviously, all this involves much more than learners' minds. Young learners are people in families and communities, struggling to reconcile their desires, beliefs, and goals with the world around them. Our concern may be principally cognitive, relating to the acquisition and uses of knowledge, but we do not mean to restrict our focus to the so-called "rational" mind. Egan reminds us that "Apollo without Dionysus may indeed be a well-informed, good citizen, but he's a dull fellow. He may even be 'cultured,' in the sense one often gets from traditionalist writings in education. . . . But without Dionysus he will never make and remake a culture."[15] Although our discussion of folk psychology and folk pedagogy has emphasized "teaching and learning" in the conventional sense, we could as easily have emphasized other aspects of the human spirit, ones equally important for educational practice, like folk conceptions of desire, intention, meaning, or even "mastery." But even the notion of "knowledge" is not as peacefully Apollonian as all that.

Consider for example the issue of what knowledge is, where it comes from, how we come by it. These are also matters that have deep cultural roots. To begin with, take the distinction between knowing something concretely and in particular and knowing it as an exemplar of some general rule. Arithmetic addition and multiplication provide a stunning example. Somebody, say, has just learned a concrete arithmetic fact. What does it mean to grasp a "fact" of multiplication, and how does that differ from the idea that multiplication is simply repeated addition, something you already "know"? Well, for one thing, it means that you can *derive* the unknown from the known. That is a pretty heady notion about knowledge, one that might even delight the action-minded Dionysus.

In some much deeper sense, grasping something abstractly is a start toward appreciating that seemingly complicated knowledge can often be derivationally reduced to simpler forms of knowledge that you already possess. The Ellery Queen mystery stories used to include a note inserted on a crucial page in the text telling the reader that he or she now had all the knowledge necessary to solve the crime. Suppose one announced in class after the children had learned multiplication that they now had enough knowledge to understand something called "logarithms," special kinds of numbers that simply bore the names "1," "2," "3," "4," and "5," and that they ought to be able to figure out what these logarithm names "mean" from three examples, each example being a series that bore those names. The first series is 2, 4, 8, 16, 32; the second series 3, 9, 27, 81, 243, and the third series 1, 10, 100, 1,000, 10,000, 100,000. The numbers in each series correspond to the logarithmic names 1, 2, 3, 4, and 5. But how can 8 be called "3," and so too 27 and 1,000? Not only do children "discover" (or invent) the idea of an *exponent* or *power,* but they also discover/invent the idea of exponents to some *base:* that 2 to the third power is 8, that 3 to the third power is 27, and that 10 to the third power is 1,000. Once children (say around age ten) have gone through that experience, their conception of mathematical knowledge as "derivational" will be forever altered: they will grasp that once you know addition and know that addition can be repeated different numbers of times to make multiplication, you already know what logarithms are. All you need to determine is the "base."

Or if that is too "mathematical," you can try getting children to act out Little Red Riding Hood, first as a class drama with everybody having a part, then by actors chosen to represent the main characters to an audience, and finally as a story to be told or read by a storyteller to a group. How do they differ? The moment some child informs you that in the first instance there are only actors and no audience, but in the second there are both, the class will be off and running into a discussion of "drama" to match Victor Turner for excitement.[16] As with the previous example, you will have led children to recognize that they know far more than they thought they ever knew, but that they have to "think about it" to know what they know. And that, after all, was what the Renaissance and the Age of Reason were all about! But to teach and learn that way means that you have adopted a new theory of mind.

Or take the issue of where you get knowledge, an equally profound matter. Children usually begin by assuming that the teacher has the knowledge and passes it on to the class. Under appropriate conditions, they soon learn that others in the class might have knowledge too, and that it can be shared. (Of course they know this from the start, but only about such matters as where things are to be found.) In this second phase, knowledge exists in the group—but inertly in the group. What about group discussion as a way of *creating* knowledge rather than merely finding who has what knowledge?[17] And there is even one step beyond that, one of the most profound aspects of human knowledge. If nobody in the group "knows" the answer, where do you go to "find things out"? This is the leap into culture as a warehouse, a toolhouse, or whatever. There are things known by each individual (more than each realizes); more still is known by the group or is discoverable by discussion within the group; and much more still is stored somewhere else—in the "culture," say, in the heads of more knowledgeable people, in directories, books, maps, and so forth. Virtually by definition, nobody in a culture knows all there is to know about it. So what do we do when we get stuck? And what are the problems we run into in getting the knowledge we need? Start answering that question and you are on the high road toward under-standing what a culture is. In no time at all, some kid will begin to recognize that knowledge is power, or that it is a form of wealth, or that it is a safety net.

So let us consider more closely, then, some alternative conceptions about the minds of learners commonly held by educational theorists, teachers, and ultimately by children themselves. For these are what may determine the educational practices that take place in classrooms in different cultural contexts.

Models of Mind and Models of Pedagogy

There are four dominant models of learners' minds that have held sway in our times. Each emphasizes different educational goals. These models are not only conceptions of mind that determine how we teach and "educate," but are also conceptions about the relations between minds and cultures. Rethinking educational psychology requires that we examine each of these alternative conceptions of human development and reevaluate their implications for learning and teaching.

1. Seeing children as imitative learners: The acquisition of "know-how." When an adult demonstrates or models a successful or skilled action to a child, that demonstration is implicitly based on the adult's belief that (a) the child does not know how to do x, and (b) the child can learn how to do x by being *shown.* The act of modeling also presupposes that (c) the child wants to do x, and (d) that she may, in fact, be trying to do x. To learn by imitation the child must recognize the goals pursued by the adult, the means used to achieve those goals, and the fact that the demonstrated action will successfully get her to the goal. By the time children are two years of age, they are capable, unlike chimpanzees raised in the wild, of imitating the act in question. Adults, recognizing children's proclivity for imitation, usually turn their own demonstrative actions into *performances,* acting in a way to demonstrate more vividly just what is involved in "doing it right." In effect, they provide "noiseless exemplars,"[18] of the act, preternaturally clear examples of the desired action.[19]

Such modeling is the basis of apprenticeship, leading the novice into the skilled ways of the expert. The expert seeks to transmit a skill he has acquired through repeated practice to a novice who, in his turn, must then practice the modeled act in order to succeed. There is little distinction in such an exchange between procedural knowledge (knowing how) and propositional knowledge (knowing that). An underlying assumption is that the less skilled can be taught by showing, and that they have the ability to learn through imitation. Another assumption in this process is that modeling and imitating make possible the accumulation of culturally relevant knowledge, even the transmission of culture[20] from one generation to the next.

But using imitation as the vehicle for teaching entails an additional assumption about human competence as well: that it consists of talents, skills, and abilities, rather than knowledge and understanding. Competence on the imitative view comes only through practice. It is a view that precludes teaching about logarithms or drama in the way described earlier. Knowledge "just grows as habits" and is linked neither to theory nor to negotiation or argument. Indeed, we even label cultures that rely heavily upon an imitative folk psychology and folk pedagogy as "traditional." But more technically advanced cultures also rely heavily upon such implicit imitative theories—for example, on apprenticeships for transmitting sophisticated skills. Becoming a scientist or a poet requires more than "knowing the theory"[21] or knowing the rules of iambic pentameter. It is Aristotle and the physician all over again.

So what do we know about demonstration and apprenticeship? Not much, but more than one might suspect. For example, simply demonstrating "how to" and providing practice at doing so is known not to be enough. Studies of expertise demonstrate that just learning how to perform skillfully does not get one to the same level of flexible skill as when one learns by a combination of practice and conceptual explanation—much as a really skillful pianist needs more than clever hands, but needs as well to know something about the theory of harmony, about solfège, about melodic structure. So if a simple theory of imitative learning suits a "traditional" society (and it usually turns out on close inspection that there is more to it than that),[22] it certainly does not suit a more advanced one. Which leads us to the next set of assumptions about human minds.

2. *Seeing children as learning from didactic exposure: The acquisition of propositional knowledge.* Didactic teaching usually is based on the no-

tion that pupils should be presented with facts, principles, and rules of action which are to be learned, remembered, and then applied. To teach this way is to assume that the learner "does not know that p," that he or she is ignorant or innocent of certain facts, rules, or principles that can be conveyed by telling. What is to be learned by the pupil is conceived as "in" the minds of teachers as well as in books, maps, art, computer databases, or wherever. Knowledge is simply to be "looked up" or "listened to." It is an explicit canon or corpus—a representation of the what-is-known. Procedural knowledge, knowing how to, is assumed to follow automatically from knowing certain propositions about facts, theories, and the like: "the square of the hypotenuse of a right triangle is equal to the squares of the other two sides."

In this teaching scenario, abilities are no longer conceived as knowing how to *do* something skillfully, but rather as the ability to acquire new knowledge by the aid of certain "mental abilities": verbal, spatial, numerical, interpersonal, or whatever. This is probably the most widely adhered to line of folk pedagogy in practice today—whether in history, social studies, literature, geography, or even science and mathematics. Its principal appeal is that it purports to offer a clear specification of just what it is that is to be learned and, equally questionable, that it suggests standards for assessing its achievement. More than any other theory of folk pedagogy, it has spawned objective testing in all its myriad guises. To determine whether a student has "learned" the capital of Albania, all one need do is offer him a multiple choice of Tirana, Milano, Smyrna, and Samarkand.

But damning the didactic assumption is too much like beating a dead horse. For plainly there are contexts where knowledge can usefully be treated as "objective" and given—like knowing the different writs under which a case can be brought under English common law, or knowing that the Fugitive Slave Law became an American statute in 1793, or that the Lisbon earthquake destroyed that city in 1755. The world is indeed full of facts. But facts are not of much use when offered by the hatful—either by teacher to student in class, or in the reverse direction as name dropping in an "objective" exam. We shall return to this point later in considering our fourth perspective.

What we must concentrate upon here is the conception of the child's mind that the didactic view imposes on teaching—its folk pedagogy. In effect, this view presumes that the learner's mind is a tabula rasa, a blank slate. Knowledge put into the mind is taken as cumulative, with later knowledge building upon priorly existing knowledge. More important is this view's assumption that the child's mind is passive, a receptacle waiting to be filled. Active interpretation or construal does not enter the picture. The didactic bias views the child from the outside, from a third-person perspective, rather than trying to "enter her thoughts." It is blankly one-way: teaching is not a mutual dialogue, but a telling by one to the other. In such a regimen, if the child fails to perform adequately, her shortcomings can be explained by her lack of "mental abilities" or her low IQ and the educational establishment goes scot-free.

It is precisely the effort to achieve a first-person perspective, to reconstruct the child's point of view, that marks the third folk pedagogy, to which we turn now.

3. *Seeing children as thinkers: The development of intersubjective interchange.* The new wave of research on "other minds" described earlier is the latest manifestation of a more general modern effort to recognize the child's perspective in the process of learning. The teacher, on this view, is concerned with understanding what the child thinks and how she arrives at what she believes. Children, like adults, are seen as constructing a *model* of the world to aid them in construing their experience. Pedagogy is to help the child understand better, more powerfully, less one-sidedly. Understanding is fostered through discussion and collaboration, with the child encouraged to express her own views better to achieve some meeting of minds with others who may have other views.

Such a pedagogy of mutuality presumes that all human minds are capable of holding beliefs and ideas which, through discussion and interaction, can be moved toward some shared frame of reference. Both child and adult have points of view, and each is encouraged to recognize the other's, though they may not agree. They must come to recognize that differing views may be based on recognizable reasons and that these reasons provide the basis for adjudicating rival beliefs. Sometimes you are "wrong," sometimes others are—that depends on how well reasoned the views are. Sometimes opposing views are both right—or both wrong. The child is *not* merely ignorant or an empty vessel, but somebody able to reason, to make sense, both on her own and through discourse with others. The child no less than the adult is seen as capable of thinking about her own thinking, and of correcting her ideas and notions through reflection—by "going meta," as it is sometimes called. The child, in a word, is seen as an epistemologist as well as a learner.

No less than the adult, the child is thought of as holding more or less coherent "theories" not only about the world but about her own mind and how it works. These naive theories are brought into congruence with those of parents and teachers not through imitation, not through didactic instruction, but by discourse, collaboration, and negotiation. Knowledge is what is shared within discourse,[23] within a "textual" community.[24] Truths are the product of evidence, argument, and construction rather than of authority, textual or pedagogic. This model of education is mutualist and dialectical, more concerned with interpretation and understanding than with the achievement of factual knowledge or skilled performance.

It is not simply that this mutualist view is "child-centered" (a not very meaningful term at best), but it is much less patronizing toward the child's mind. It attempts to build an exchange of understanding between the teacher and the child: to find in the intuitions of the child the roots of systematic knowledge, as Dewey urged.

Four lines of recent research have enriched this perspective on teaching and learning. While they are all closely related, they are worth distinguishing. The first has to do with how children develop their ability to "read other minds," to get to know what others are thinking or feeling. It usually gets labeled as research on *intersubjectivity*. Intersubjectivity begins with infant's and mother's pleasure in eye-to-eye contact in the opening weeks of life, moves quickly into the two of them sharing joint attention on common objects, and culminates a first preschool phase with the child and a caretaker achieving a meeting of minds by an early exchange of words—an achievement that is never finished.[25]

The second line of research involves the child's grasp of another's "intentional states"—his beliefs, promises, intentions, desires, in a word his *theories of mind,* as this research is often referred to. It is a program of inquiry into how children acquire their notions about how others come to hold or relinquish various mental states. It is particularly concerned, as well, with the child's sorting of people's beliefs and opinions as being true or right versus being false and wrong, and in the process, this research has found out many intriguing things about the young child's ideas about "false beliefs."[26]

The third line is the study of *metacognition*—what children think about learning and remembering and thinking (especially their own), and how "thinking about" one's own cognitive operations affects one's own mental procedures. The first important contribution to this work, a study by Ann Brown, illustrated how remembering strategies were profoundly changed by the child turning her inner eye on how she herself proceeded in attempting to commit something to memory.[27]

Studies in *collaborative learning* and problem solving constitute the fourth line of new research, which focuses on how children explicate and revise their beliefs in discourse.[28] It has flourished not only in America but also in Sweden, where much recent pedagogical research has been given over to studying how children understand and how they manage their own learning.[29]

What all this research has in common is an effort to understand how children themselves organize their own learning, remembering, guessing, and thinking. Unlike older psychological theories, bent on imposing "scientific" models on children's cognitive activities, this work explores the child's own framework to understand better how he comes to the views that finally prove most useful to him. The child's *own* folk psychology (and its growth) becomes the object of study. And, of course, such research provides the teacher with a far deeper and less condescending sense of what she will encounter in the teaching-learning situation.

Some say that the weakness of this approach is that it tolerates an unacceptable degree of relativity in what is taken as "knowledge." Surely more is required to justify beliefs than merely sharing them with others. That "more" is the machinery of justification for one's beliefs, the canons of scientific and philosophical reasoning. Knowledge, after all, is *justified* belief. One must be pragmatist enough in one's views about the nature of knowledge to recognize the importance of such criticism. It is a foolish "postmodernism" that accepts that all knowledge can be justified simply by finding or forming an "interpretive community" that agrees. Nor need we be so old guard as to insist that knowledge is only knowledge when it is "true" in a way that precludes all competing claims. "True history," without regard to the perspective from which it was written, is at best a mischievous joke and at worst a bid for political hegemony. Claims about "truth" must always be justified.

They must be justified by appeal to reasons that, in the logician's stricter sense, resist disproof and disbelief. Reasons of this kind obviously include appeals to evidence that defy falsifiability. But falsifiability is rarely a "yes-no" matter, for there are often variant interpretations that are compatible with available evidence—if not all of the evidence, then enough of it to be convincing.

There is no reason a priori why the third approach to teaching and learning should not be compatible with this more pragmatic epistemology. It is a very different conception of knowledge from the second perspective, where knowledge was taken to be fixed and independent of the knower's perspective. For the very nature of the knowledge enterprise has changed in our times. Hacking points out, for example, that prior to the seventeenth century an unbridgeable gap was thought to exist between knowledge and opinion, the former objective, the latter subjective.[30] What modernism sponsors is a healthy skepticism about the absoluteness of that gap. We are considering here not "analytic" knowledge—as in logic and mathematics—where the rule of contradiction has a privileged position (that something cannot be both A and not-A). But even at the analytic level the view we are discussing casts a skeptical eye at the premature imposition of formal, logical forms on bodies of empirical knowledge outside the "hard" natural sciences.

In the light of all this, it is surely possible to take one step further in conceiving folk pedagogy—a step that, like the others we have considered, rests on epistemological considerations. At issue is how subjectively held beliefs are turned into viable theories about the world and its facts. How are beliefs turned into hypotheses that hold not because of the faith we place in them but because they stand up in the public marketplace of evidence, interpretation, and agreement with extant knowledge? Hypotheses cannot simply be "sponsored." They must be openly tested. "Today is Tuesday" turns into a conventional fact not by virtue of its being "true" but through conformity with conventions for naming the days of the week. It achieves intersubjectivity by virtue of convention and thereby becomes a "fact" independent of individual beliefs. This is the basis of Popper's well-known defense of "objective knowledge"[31] and of Nagel's view of what he calls "the view from nowhere."[32]

Issues of this order are precisely the ones that this third perspective most admirably and directly deals with. We now turn to the fourth and last of the perspectives on folk pedagogy.

4. *Children as knowledgeable: The management of "objective" knowledge.* Too exclusive a focus on beliefs and "intentional states" and on their negotiation in discourse risks overestimating the importance of social exchange in constructing knowledge. That emphasis can lead us to underestimate the importance of knowledge accumulated in the past. For cultures preserve past reliable knowledge much as the common law preserves a record of how past communal conflicts were adjudicated. In both instances there is an effort to achieve a workable consistency, to shun arbitrariness, to find "general principles." Neither culture nor law is open to abrupt reconstrual. Reconstrual is typically undertaken (to use the legal expression) with "restraint." Past knowledge and reliable practice are not taken lightly. Science is no

different: it too resists being stampeded into "scientific revolutions," profligately throwing out old paradigms.[33]

Now to pedagogy. Early on, children encounter the hoary distinction between what is known by "us" (friends, parents, teachers, and so on) and what in some larger sense is simply "known." In these post-positivist, perhaps "post-modern" times, we recognize all too well that the "known" is neither God-given truth nor, as it were, written irrevocably in the Book of Nature. Knowledge in this dispensation is always putatively revisable. But revisability is not to be confused with free-for-all relativism, the view that since *no* theory is the ultimate truth, *all* theories, like all people, are equal. We surely recognize the distinction between Popper's "World Two" of personally held beliefs, hunches, and opinions and his "World Three" of justified knowledge. But what makes the latter "objective" is not that it constitutes some positivist's free-standing, aboriginal reality, but rather that it has stood up to sustained scrutiny and been tested by the best available evidence. All knowledge has a history.

The fourth perspective holds that teaching should help children grasp the distinction between personal knowledge, on the one side, and "what is taken to be known" by the culture, on the other. But they must not only grasp this distinction, but also understand its basis, as it were, in the history of knowledge. How can we incorporate such a perspective in our pedagogy? Stated another way, what have children gained when they begin to distinguish what is known canonically from what they know personally and idiosyncratically?

Janet Astington offers an interesting twist on this classic problem.[34] She finds that when children begin to understand how evidence is used to check beliefs, they often see the process as akin to forming a belief about a belief: "I now have reason to believe that this belief is true (or false, as the case may be)." "Reasons for believing" a hypothesis are not the same order of thing as the belief embodied in the hypothesis itself, and if the former work out well, then the latter graduates from being a belief (or hypothesis) to becoming something more robust—a proved theory or even a body of fact.

And by the same intuition, one can as easily come to see one's personal ideas or beliefs as relating (or not relating) to "what is known" or what is generally believed to have stood the test of time. In this way, we come to view personal conjecture against the background of what has come to be shared with the historical past. Those presently engaged in the pursuit of knowledge become sharers of conjectures with those long dead. But one can go a step further and ask how past conjecture settled into something more solid over the years. You can share Archimedes with seesaw partners on the playground, and know how he came to hold his view. But what about your interpretation of Kate in *Taming of the Shrew* as being like the class tomboy? That couldn't be what Shakespeare had in mind: he didn't "know about" her in that sense. So was there something else like that in his day? There is something appealing and, indeed, enspiriting about facing off one's own version of "knowledge" with the foibles of the archivally famous in our past. Imagine an inner-city high school class—it was a real one, mostly San Antonio Latinos—staging *Oedipus Rex*. They "knew" things about incest that Sophocles may never have dreamt of. It was plain to their gifted teacher/director that they were not in the least intimidated by the DWEM (Dead White European Male) who had written the play some two millennia ago. Yet they were true to the play's spirit.

So the fourth perspective holds that there is something special about "talking" to authors, now dead but still alive in their ancient texts—so long as the objective of the encounter is not worship but discourse and interpretation, "going meta" on thoughts about the past. Try several trios of teenagers, each staging a play about the astonishingly brief account in Genesis where Abraham at God's instruction takes Isaac, his only son, to sacrifice him to God on Mount Moriah. There is a famous set of "versions" of the Abraham story in Kierkegaard's *Fear and Trembling;* try that on them too. Or try out some teenagers on a dozen different reproductions of Annunciation paintings in which the Angel announces to the Virgin that she is to be Queen of Heaven. Ask them what they judge, from the various pictures, might be going through Mary's mind—in a painting where

Mary looks like a haughty Renaissance princess, in another where she resembles a humble Martha, in yet another where she looks quite a brazen young lady. It is striking how quickly teenagers leap across the gulf that separates Popper's subjective World Two from his "objective" World Three. The teacher, with class exercises like these, helps the child reach beyond his own impressions to join a past world that would otherwise be remote and beyond him as a knower.[35]

Real Schooling

Real schooling, of course, is never confined to one model of the learner or one model of teaching. Most day-to-day education in schools is designed to cultivate skills and abilities, to impart a knowledge of facts and theories, and to cultivate understanding of the beliefs and intentions of those nearby and far away. Any choice of pedagogical practice implies a conception of the learner and may, in time, be adopted by him or her as the appropriate way of thinking about the learning process. For a choice of pedagogy inevitably communicates a conception of the learning process and the learner. Pedagogy is never innocent. It is a medium that carries its own message.

Summary: Rethinking Minds, Cultures, and Education

We can conceive of the four views of teaching-and-learning just set forth as being ordered on two dimensions. The first is an "inside-outside" dimension: call it the *internalist-externalist* dimension. Externalist theories emphasize what adults can do for children from outside to foster learning—the bulk of traditional educational psychology. Internalist theories focus on what the child can do, what the child thinks he or she is doing, and how learning can be premised on those intentional states.

The second dimension describes the degree of intersubjectivity or "common understanding" assumed to be required between the pedagogical theorist and the subjects to whom his theories relate. Let us call this the *intersubjective-objectivist* dimension. Objectivist theories regard children as an entomologist might regard a colony of ants or an elephant-trainer an elephant; there is no presumption that the subjects should see themselves in the same terms that the theorist does. Intersubjective theorists, on the other hand, apply the same theories to themselves as they do to their clients. Hence, they seek to create psychological theories that are as useful for the children in organizing their learning and managing their lives as they are for the adults that work with them.

Internalist theories tend to be intersubjective in emphasis. That is to say, if one is concerned with what the child is up to mentally, one is likely to be concerned with formulating a theory of teaching-and-learning that one can share with him or her in order to facilitate the child's efforts. But this is not necessarily so. Much Western cultural anthropology, for example, is internalist and very concerned with "how natives think." But anthropologists' theories are, as it were, not for the "natives" but for their colleagues back home.[36] It is usually assumed, however tacitly, that the natives are "different" or that they simply would not understand. And, indeed, some psychoanalytically oriented theories of early childhood pedagogy are of this same order—not to be shared with the child. Such theories are much occupied with the child's internal states, but like the native, the child is "different." The adult—theorist or teacher—becomes like an omniscient narrator in nineteenth-century novels: he knows perfectly what is going on in the minds of the novel's protagonist, even though the protagonist herself may not know.

Modern pedagogy is moving increasingly to the view that the child should be aware of her own thought processes, and that it is crucial for the pedagogical theorist and teacher alike to help her to become more metacognitive—to be as aware of how she goes about her learning and thinking as she is about the subject matter she is studying. Achieving skill and accumulating knowledge are not enough. The learner can be helped to achieve full mastery by reflecting as well upon how she is going about her job and how her approach can be improved. Equipping her with a good theory of mind—or a theory of mental functioning—is one part of helping her to do so.

In the end, then, the four perspectives on pedagogy are best thought of as parts of a broader continent, their significance to be understood in the light of their partialness. Nobody can sensibly propose that skills and cultivated abilities are unimportant. Nor can they argue that the accumulation of factual knowledge is trivial. No sensible critic would ever claim that children should not become aware that knowledge is dependent upon perspective and that we share and negotiate our perspectives in the knowledge-seeking process. And it would take a bigot to deny that we become the richer for recognizing the link between reliable knowledge from the past and what we learn in the present. What is needed is that the four perspectives be fused into some congruent unity, recognized as parts of a common continent. Older views of mind and how mind can be cultivated need to be shorn of their narrow exclusionism, and newer views need to be modulated to recognize that while skills and facts never exist *out* of context, they are no less important *in* context.

Modern advances in the study of human development have begun providing us with a new and steadier base upon which a more integrated theory of teaching-and-learning can be erected. And it was with these advances that this chapter was principally concerned—with the child as an active, intentional being; with knowledge as "man-made" rather than simply there; with how our knowledge about the world and about each other gets constructed and negotiated with others, both contemporaries and those long departed. In the chapters following, we will explore these advances and their implications still further.

3

▼

THE COMPLEXITY OF
EDUCATIONAL AIMS

As in most revolutionary times, our times too are caught up in contradictions. Indeed, on closer scrutiny, contradictions in such times often turn out to be antinomies—pairs of large truths, which, though both may be true, nonetheless contradict each other. Antinomies provide fruitful grounds not only for strife, but also for reflection. For they remind us that truths do not exist independently of the perspectives of those who hold them to be so.

Educational truths in revolutionary times are also afflicted by antinomies. And it is not surprising, then, that there are antinomic contradictions even in our objectives for early education—genuine antinomies. It is these that I want to explore in this chapter. I am particularly interested in how our emerging ideas about early education led us into such antinomies, and how, through greater awareness, we can turn them into lessons for the changing times ahead.

Let me begin this exploration by briefly setting out three of the most baffling of these antinomies. They will provide us with themes upon which to play out variations later. Recall that antinomies do not permit of logical but only of pragmatic resolution. As Niels

Bohr liked to remark, the opposites of little truths are false; the opposites of big ones may also be true. So our concern will be principally pragmatic.

The first antinomy is this: on the one hand, it is unquestionably the function of education to enable people, individual human beings, to operate at their fullest potential, to equip them with the tools and the sense of opportunity to use their wits, skills, and passions to the fullest. The antinomic counterpart to this is that the function of education is to reproduce the culture that supports it—not only reproduce it, but further its economic, political, and cultural ends. For example, the educational system of an industrial society should produce a willing and compliant labor force to keep it going: unskilled and semi-skilled workers, clerical workers, middle managers, risk-sensitive entrepreneurs, all of whom are convinced that such an industrial society constitutes the right, valid, and only way of living.

But can schooling be construed both as the instrument of individual realization and at the same time as a reproductive technique for maintaining or furthering a culture? Well, the answer is an inevitably flawed "not quite yes." For the unfettered ideal of individual realization through education inevitably risks cultural and social unpredictability and, even further, the disruption of legitimate order. The second horn, education as cultural reproduction, risks stagnation, hegemony, and conventionalism, even if it holds out the promise of reducing uncertainty. Finding a way within this antinomic pair does not come easily, particularly not in times of rapid change. Indeed, it could never have come easily at any time. But if one does not face it, one risks failing both ideals.

The second antinomy reflects two contradictory views about the nature and uses of mind, again both meritorious when taken singly. One side proclaims that learning is, as it were, principally inside the head, intrapsychic. Learners must, in the end, rely on their own intelligence and their own motivation to benefit from what school has to offer. Education provides the means for strengthening and enabling our native mental powers. While on this view education raises everybody's level of functioning, it should be particularly concerned to cultivate the minds of those with the most superior "native endowment." For the best endowed can benefit most from schooling.

The contrastive view to this one is that all mental activity is situated in and supported by a more or a less enabling cultural setting. We are not simply isolated minds of varying capacity to which skills are then to be added. How well the student does in mastering and using skills, knowledge, and ways of thinking will depend upon how favoring or enabling a cultural "toolkit" the teacher provides for the learner. Indeed, the culture's symbolic toolkit actualizes the learner's very capacities, even determines whether or not they come into being in any practical sense. The cultural contexts that favor mental development are principally and inevitably interpersonal, for they involve symbolic exchanges and include a variety of joint enterprises with peers, parents, and teachers. Through such collaboration, the developing child gains access to the resources, the symbol systems, and even the technology of the culture. And it is the right of every child to have equal access to these resources. If there is a difference in native endowment, the better endowed child will get more from his interaction with the culture.

The risks (and the benefits) inherent in pushing either side of this antinomy to the exclusion of the other are so critical that their discussion is better postponed until we can look at them in context, which we will do in a moment. Otherwise we might get stuck in the nature-nurture controversy, for this antinomy is too easily converted into Herrnstein-Murray rhetoric.[1]

The third and final antinomy is one that is too rarely made explicit in educational debate. It is about how ways of thinking, ways of constructing meaning, and ways of experiencing the world are to be judged, by what standards, and by whom—for example, as embodied in the question, "Who owns the right version of history?" Let me spell out the two sides of this antinomy bluntly and with some needed exaggeration. One side holds that human experience, "local knowledge," as it were, is legitimate in its own right—that it cannot be reduced to some "higher," more authoritative universalistic construal.[2] All efforts to impose more authoritative meanings upon local experience are suspect as hegemonic, serving the ends of power and domination, whether so intended or not. This, of course, is a caricature of the kind of anti-foundationalism sometimes referred to as "postmodernism."[3] It is not only an epistemological stance but a political one. The claim of non-reductiveness and untranslatability often appears in radical feminism, in radical ethnic and anti-imperialist movements, and even in critical legal studies. In education, it doubtless fueled the "deschooling" movement. But even in its extreme versions, it cannot be dismissed out of hand. It expresses something deep about the dilemmas of living in contemporary bureaucratized society.

The contrastive side of this third antinomy—the search for an authoritatively universal voice—is also likely to get puffed up by self-righteousness. But ignore for a moment the pomposity of the self-appointed spokesmen for undisputable universal truths. For there is a compelling claim on this side too. It inheres in the deep integrity, for good or evil, with which any larger culture's way of life expresses its historically rooted aspirations for grace, order, well-being, and justice. Human plights, though they may always express themselves locally in time, place, and circumstance, are nonetheless an expression of some more universal history. To ignore that more universal history is to deny the legitimacy of the broader culture. Working-class history without reference to the larger setting in which it transpired is arbitrary and usually self-aggrandizing. To insist on our own group's self-definition—whether ethnic, gender, race, or class—is to court parochialism and divisiveness. For all that experience and knowledge may be local and particular, they are still part of a larger continent.

We have three antinomies, then: the individual-realization versus the culture-preserving antinomy; the talent-centered versus the tool-centered antinomy; and the particularism versus universalism antinomy. Without keeping them in mind, we risk losing our way in evaluating what we have learned about early schooling and where we are moving. For they help keep the issues in balance. There is no way to get the full measure from both sides of an antinomy, these three included. We need to realize human potential, but we need to maintain a culture's integrity and stability. We need to recognize differing native talent, but we need to equip all with the tools of the culture. We need to respect the uniqueness of local identities and experience, but we cannot stay together as a people if the cost of local identity is a cultural Tower of Babel.

These are all matters that are rarely settled by large-scale general precepts. They demand case-by-case judgment. But to concentrate on individual schools engaged in particular practices, to see what we can learn from them in general, is too large a task. So I shall focus on one particular kind of schooling and how its practices grew from research and practical work. And then I'll move on to more general matters.

II

Let me begin with Head Start, a revealing microcosm. Though it had many incipient precursors, all rather ideological and utopian, it is unique for having been fueled by a series of scientific discoveries about the nature of early development. And like most important facts about the human condition, these were quickly converted from facts to metaphors and then into precepts about practice.

First some history, to get a better sense of what motivated this particular set of happenings. Animals reared in impoverished environments, it was discovered, were found to be deficient when tested later on standard learning and problem-solving tasks.[4] Moreover, their brains seemed to be underdeveloped as well, if I may condense a great many very complicated particulars into an overly simple summary.[5] Some of these findings were literally inadvertent, by-products of other concerns, as when white rats were reared in germ-free environments to see whether they would develop normal antibodies. They did not, but more interesting still, the germ-free environments, being very pallid places, made the rats raised in them exceptionally backward in their learning abilities in comparison with their more friskily and unhygienically raised littermates.[6]

From these meager beginnings, the so-called deprivation hypothesis was born. To grow, you needed an environment of opportunities. Education was not the issue at first; it was newborns raised in respirators, very impoverished places, who were the focus of the new concern.[7] But before long, new research began demonstrating that kids from backgrounds of poverty fell progressively further behind once they started school.[8] And this work alerted a much wider community to the possibility that lack of a "good start" in general (not just starting out in a respirator) might lock a child into later failure. The deprivation hypothesis had found a much broader human locus. Though it was an exceedingly crude formulation, it now had a much broader moral force behind it. The children of poverty might also be the victims of deprivation, a man-made state of affairs rather than an ecological inadvertence. A social condition might be depriving them of something as vital to their growth as were certain vitamins or immunization shots.

Soon after, roughly around the mid-1960s, the direct and carefully designed study of "real" infants began in earnest: their perception, memory, attention, imitation, action. Such work had been rare before then. Why it began at just that time and with that much vigor I will leave for historians to decide.[9] Had there been an implicit taboo on studying little babies in laboratories—a collision between the ethics of tenderness and the cool detachment of research? Or was it just that transistor recording with its miniaturizing possibilities made it possible to do such odd things as letting babies suck blurred pictures into focus or control what came into view by a slight head turn or a flick of the leg?[10] Imagine the excitement of finding that the older the infant, the more complicated was the checkerboard he or she chose to look at,[11] or that an infant's eye movements were not that different from an adult's when scanning a familiar human face.[12]

Not surprisingly, these findings quickly caught the public imagination. Even the august *Times* of London carried a series of articles in praise of the "revolutionary" new work. And the equally august British historian and former Vice Chancellor of Oxford, Lord Bullock, was soon quoted to the effect that we were entering a new era in our conception of man. Infants, it turned out, were much smarter, more cognitively proactive rather than reactive, more attentive to the immediate social world around them, than had been previously suspected. They emphatically did *not* inhabit a world of "buzzing blooming confusion": they seemed to be in search of predictive stability from the very start. And that insight cast a completely different light on what "deprivation" might be all about. Indeed, it shifted attention to the issue of how we *enable* young human beings to grow into effective adults by helping them use and develop their own powers.

These studies suggested that something more active was going on during growth, far more active than implied by "sensory deprivation." For one side of "deprivation" was social or interactive: so-called deprived infants were thwarted of the opportunity to interact with others, for under normal conditions they went out of their way to establish joint attention with them eye to eye[13] but also by following their line of regard to discover what they were looking at. Indeed, infants sought and were even reinforced by eye-to-eye contact with their caregivers. Withholding these opportunities, it was shown by the few studies that undertook to do so (for infancy researchers hate tormenting their subjects), distressed and upset the infants. So the first thing these studies revealed about early life was the importance of two-way human interaction.

The second thing infants seemed to need was self-initiated activity. In a nutshell, what infants *did* to their mundane environments seemed to provide a necessary prelude to their learning what the environment did back to *them*. And what in fact they did in their visual search and awkward groping was far more systematic and means-ends oriented than had been suspected.[14]

Somehow, and despite all these new findings on the role of interaction and self-initiation in early development, the idea of "deprivation" hung on—but now it was changed into "cultural deprivation." The concept of deprivation must have had a powerful grip on the American imagination; it was in that same period of the early 1960s that, as Harrington has remarked,[15] Americans were just "discovering" poverty in their midst. In any case, the old, more passive notion of deprivation was transformed into the more interactive notion of "cultural deprivation."

But whether wittingly or unwittingly, the new deprivation was being judged against a standard of "culture" that was implicitly derived from notions about idealized middle-class American culture. In this version of family life, child rearing consisted of a fully domestic mother and her well-fed child interacting with each other harmoniously, with the child given ample opportunity to initiate things on her own. Falling short of this idealized standard was "cultural deprivation." Soon there were new projects to teach mothers in poverty how to talk more and play more with their infants, how to hand over more self-initiated activity to them, and so on—in short, how to be more like idealized middle-class mothers with their children. And, indeed, these projects produced some real results.[16] For in fact, and not surprisingly, middle-class child rearing *does* produce middle-class kids.

So when Head Start came into being, it was not surprising that its central concepts were patterned on this ideal of overcoming "cultural deprivation" by becoming more middle class in one's child-rearing practices. But note something disquieting. "Cultural deprivation" blames the victim, even if only indirectly. It blames the victim's mother, or at least her "culture." And since in America the mothers in question were predominantly black or Hispanic, the implication was that these cultures were at fault.[17] Compassionate though it undoubtedly was, Head Start did not escape the kind of implicit condescension that goes with reform movements. In most places it did not address the sore issues of the third of our antinomies—what it is like being poor and black or poor and Latino, leaving aside what it means to have your kids for part of the day at Head Start with its middle-class child-rearing ideals.

But I must take a detour now. All these developments were taking place in the decade after *Brown v. Board of Education*,[18] when affirmative action programs were still new and highly disputable. Head Start was seen as an extension of affirmative action—its very title affirms that. It was dedicated to stopping not the broader culture's system of racial discrimination, but one of its flawed cultures from depriving its children through faulty child rearing. It was, to be sure, a massive step forward in addressing a problem that had been ignored before. And it certainly was the beginning of a new consciousness that was, I believe, part and parcel of the same broad movement that outlawed school segregation and provided a window of opportunity for such remedies as affirmative action. Nevertheless, it was condescending. It failed to face the underlying issue of discrimination squarely.

But never underrate the power of antinomies to work themselves into public consciousness. By the early 1970s, research began "proving" that IQ gains from Head Start disappeared within a few years. Ghetto children seemed unable to sustain the initial Head Start boost once they got further into school. A Jensen and a Herrnstein came forward to reassert the old IQ-centered "inside-out" view of development: poor kids, particularly black kids, just didn't have the genetic endowment—the IQ—to benefit from Head Start or anything else.[19] And there were politicians willing to exploit these "findings" in an appeal to an increasingly squeezed lower middle class who, in any case, had fled to the suburbs to put big cities, high taxes, and poverty problems behind them. The big cities, which were losing their manufacturing industries and their middle-class tax base, were being saddled with increasingly impoverished ghettos and welfare costs and thus were less able to support Head Start projects. The unspoken message was that the costs of Head Start and other forms of aid to the less fortunate were generating tax costs that undermined the way of life of majoritarian, middle-class culture. Indeed, even federal financing of Head Start was questioned in this new period of middle-class urban austerity. The program survived, but it did not grow as much as it might have.

Head Start survived, I think, because it had created a new consciousness (or tapped a faith right under the surface of consciousness) that, by intervening in the developmental scene early enough, you could change the life of children later. I say this was a "faith," for during those years there was not much direct evidence that Head Start had "permanent" effects (or that it didn't). When the twenty-five-year results on Head Start began coming in, they showed that it had made an astonishing difference, even if it hadn't produced a mass miracle.[20] Kids who had been through the program were, by comparison to "controls," more likely to stay longer and do better in school, to get and to hold jobs longer, to stay out of jail, to commit fewer crimes, and the rest. In fact, it "paid": the cost of Head Start (even of fancier Head Start programs) was far less than economic losses from unemployment, cost of imprisonment, and welfare payments. It was "good for the society" in hard-nosed socioeconomic terms, even if it didn't turn the trick for each individual child. A working compromise was achieved that respected both sides of the first of our antinomies—even if the other two remained unresolved.

III

We have come through a long and troubled evolution in our conception of how to deal with the antinomies inherent in providing early care for children. In the process, we have gained much knowledge about what helps children grow effectively. Our conception of childhood has become richer and more complex. But for all our knowledge, for all that we know about the importance of self-initiated activity, of responsive social environments, and even of the construction of selfhood, we have still not quite managed to formulate an approach to early education that fits the complicated conditions in which we are living today. So let me turn my attention to these conditions, and let me take off from where Head Start got to.

Plainly, Head Start is not a magic elixir. Not because it is not always up to standard: that is easily fixed. It is not enough because it cannot on its own, as only a *starting* subculture, counteract the subsequent social alienation of poor black and Hispanic kids and their families—particularly when many of these are headed by a single parent, very often an unwed mother. There is too much in the society working against it. School after Head Start is rarely geared to getting inner-city kids to take school work as a viable option for getting out of poverty. After all, even when you hold IQ constant, the percentage of black youths who are unemployed is twice as high as the rate for the IQ-matched whites. As drug peddling and turf wars increase as one of the few viable lines of activity for blacks, homicide becomes the chief threat to life among black inner-city kids, and prison a residence for more than a third of them at some point between ages sixteen and twenty-five.

But what we have learned about learning in all this discouraging morass is anything but trivial: Even under the least favorable conditions—psychologically, fiscally, educationally—we still succeed in giving some children a sense of their own possibilities. We do it by getting them (and sometimes their parents) to collaborate in an enabling community. My own view is that experiments like Head Start give kids (and perhaps their mothers) a sense of a possible way through a poverty culture even when it seems to them to be blindly reproducing itself. I think that some version of the Head Start idea can also be extended into schooling in the years after preschool. But it is quite a different version from the one based on middle-class child rearing.

Let me describe the sort of thing I have in mind by means of a case history, exemplified by a school that ghetto children get to around ten or eleven years of age.[21] Some of the children in the school in question had the benefit of Head Start, most not. This school is in the Oakland, California, school system, part of a program financed by both federal and foundation funding, though the greater part of the costs are met by the city of Oakland. It illustrates vividly some of the principles that we have come to recognize as crucial for enabling children not just to build their skills, but to develop an effective sense of participating in an enabling community.

The Oakland project is directed by Ann Brown and has now become the hub of a consortium of schools spread all round the country. It easily achieves the usuals: raising reading levels, raising test scores, and all the other standard end-result things that school reform is supposed to achieve. Much more to the point is the kind of collaborative school culture it creates for its participating students and teachers alike.

The Oakland project follows a very few but very powerful principles, several of which were mentioned in Chapter 1: it is a collaborative community, a group in the real sense. And like most such, its members were engaged in producing a joint product, an *oeuvre*. When

I visited the school, the students were studying the aftermath of the *Exxon Valdez* oil spill in Alaska. Their aim was to come up with a Plan. And in the interest of their Plan they were willing to entertain all possible proposals, however "wild," knowing that others would listen and nobody would make fun of their ideas. One of the "hot ideas" during that visit, for example, was that you could get oil off birds using peanut butter as an "oil blotter." There was no mocking about it: they pushed the idea to its limits, arguing that peanut butter should be easy to get since "there's so much of it anyway." These children had learned to treat ideas respectfully, pragmatically, and actively. They were seriously engaged in trying to justify to a problem-solving community why "oil blotters" might be a great idea for rescuing birds caught in an oil spill, and in doing so they were "teaching" each other in the egalitarian sense—and, indeed, were part of a community whose aim was just such "teaching by sharing."

I firmly believe that approaches of this kind are extremely important not just because they aid learning generally, but because they provide examples of a culture-in-practice relevant for the rest of a student's life. It is as relevant for a middle-class child as for a child of poverty—particularly the latter, for it is a specific way to counteract the debilitating effects of alienation, helplessness, and aimlessness.

There is nothing new about all this. We have known for years that if you treat people, young kids included, as responsible, contributing parties to the group, as having a job to do, they will grow into it—some better than others, obviously, but all benefit. Even old people in nursing homes, if made responsible members of the community with duties to discharge, live longer, get sick less, keep their mental powers longer.[22] Korean immigrants in America score fifteen points higher in IQ than their fellow Korean immigrants in Japan, where they are scorned, segregated, and treated as "inferior," whereas in America the presumption is that they are "very bright." We need desperately to look more closely at what we mean by an "enabling" culture, particularly that part of the enabling culture represented by its schools.

Perhaps successful school cultures—like successful Head Start programs—should be considered as "countercultures" that serve to raise the consciousness and meta-cognition of their participants as well as enhancing their self-esteem. It is an interesting possibility. But if that were all there was to it, then we might expect school to be an effective activator only "on the spot"—effective in "jump starting" only school-related activity. But I think there's more to it than that. Let me offer an example of the spreading effect of such activating "countercultural" school matters. The Ministry of Education in Norway has been involved for several years in a program to reduce school bullying, a program rather typical of that compassionate country. At the outset, to be sure, just raising the topic had a releasing effect on discussion among the kids. But it got to parents as well. It probably was a topic that had been "in the closet" waiting for a legitimizing passport to enter more communal discussion. The topic of school bullying found its way into discussions of bullying in the mundane daily life of people in general.[23] School "countercultures" may not always start "revolutions," but they often do have the revolutionary effect of launching submerged topics into open discussion—as we know well from the uprisings of 1968, where the topics at issue were ones that had been ignored in school settings and then spilled out onto the unruly streets.

This is not unlike the lessons that Vivian Paley learned in her stunning study of nursery school kids who excluded other kids from their little cliques—her wonderfully titled You Can't Say You Can't Play.[24] Ethical precepts, she learned, do not easily or automatically become praxis. They need exemplification in daily practice. We Americans, for example, are awash in precepts about equality, and we have an Equal Protection Clause as the Fourteenth Amendment to our Constitution. But the history of our practices speaks more truly than our slogans. The children in Vivian Paley's classes were having their first "in practice" experience with what "equal protection" means in the cultural praxis of a school classroom—and they did not take easily to it, as I shall relate in a moment.

Consider this point. School provides a powerful opportunity for exploring the implication of precepts for practice. It is an extraordinary place for getting a sense of how to use mind, how to deal with authority, how to treat others. Look at it for a moment in light of the unusual perspective of the French social theorist Pierre Bourdieu,[25] whose ideas I introduced briefly in the opening chapter. Praxis takes place in any and all settings that provide a "market in distinctions," to recall his term. Such a market is anywhere that one "trades" some form of symbolic capital in return for some recognized distinction: approval, identity, respect, support, recognition. Markets in distinction are ubiquitous: not just in commercial markets or on the trading floor of the stock exchange, where the distinction is even more abstractly translated into money, but in the intimate settings of classrooms, dinner tables, and cliques. A clique of nursery school kids who exclude an "outsider" from their play are practicing exclusion of others in return for the distinction of being considered "insiders." And we all recognize that this is not extraordinary. Obviously there are in-groups and out-groups throughout life. But the issue is not only practice, but consciousness of what one is doing when one practices this form of exchange. If we are not aware of what and why and how we enter into such discriminative practices, we cultivate a mindlessness that, in the end, reduces our own humanity and fosters cultural division even when it is not intended. Excluding a kid from your playgroup is a prototype of the kinds of praxis we will later take for granted in our dealings with the world. It becomes what Bourdieu calls our "habitus," the stuff of daily life that gives shape to our biases and predispositions. For we seem to be more prone to acting our way into implicit thinking than we are able to think our way explicitly into acting.

It is through this process of becoming aware of practice that the good school and the healthy classroom can provide even the child of poverty, even the outsider immigrant child, some working vision of how a society can operate. In the instance of Vivian Paley's young nursery schoolers, her "rule" against mindless exclusion of other kids from your group does not assure that there will be an "even playing field," but (perhaps just as important) it gives children a lively sense of what an even playing field means and how one's praxis affects its "tilt." It is an antidote to mindlessness. And mindlessness is one of the major impediments to change.

IV

The three antinomies with which we started provide an appropriate coda to which we can return to conclude the discussion. Should education reproduce the culture, or should it enrich and cultivate human potential? Should it be based on cultivating differentially the inherent talents of those with the best native endowment, or should it give priority to equipping all with a cultural toolkit that can make them fully effective? Should we give priority to the values and ways of the culture as a whole, or give pride of place to the identities of the subcultures that comprise it?

The standard piety, of course, is that we honor both sides of each antinomy, or do something "midway between." A friend of mine once formulated what he jokingly refers to as "Jay's Law" to the effect that the real truth never lies midway between two contending ones. Perhaps he is right. But I think there is another route just as risky as "splitting the difference." It is to ignore them altogether—including the antinomies that relate to early education with which we have been concerned in this chapter. I think the brief history of our follies and small successes in early childhood education carries some interesting lessons for us.

The early deprivation-replacement metaphor of preschooling for the less advantaged was much too closely linked to the image of "feeding everybody up" to a standard that would bring out the best in all. It failed to take the self-reproducing reality of cultures into account. And it was based upon too passive an image of early human nature—rather like the classic *tabula rasa* theories of the soul. It failed as well to appreciate the enabling nature of human culture as a toolkit for active, questing children seeking greater mastery over their worlds.

The discovery of the importance of early human interaction and of the role of self-initiated, self-directed activity in the setting of interaction was an important step forward. But it should never have led researchers or educators to so ethnocentric a notion as "cultural deprivation." Such deprivation was interpreted narrowly as the absence of idealized, American middle-class, child-centered child rearing. It left too little room for the cultural identities and particularities of the varied ethnic and lower social-class children and families exposed to it. It left unexamined the nature of human groups and human cultures and the needs human beings have for guarding a sense of their own identity and tradition.

As we enter a new era marked by drastic, ever-increasing demographic changes in residence patterns, family patterns, ethnic awareness, and socioeconomic opportunity, we are having to rethink the antinomies of early educational practice. We are witnessing, particularly in the United States, a sharpened polarization between those who live in poverty, often segregated in ghetto-like neighborhoods and housing developments, for whom schooling no longer seems like a "way out," and those who (however insecure their long-term outlook) feel securely enough established in national and class identity to aspire for their children. The latter group, perhaps because they do not "own" their wealth in the classic capitalist sense, have come to recognize as never before that the education of their children is their best investment for the future. And they are keen to see an improvement in our educational practices. In between is what I would call the "demographic stream in jeopardy"—those who are struggling to achieve a more secure social-class status but are unsure whether the changes in the world's economic climate may land them among the poor and underprivileged.

I have argued that both from the point of view of the integrity of the larger national cultures with which we are inevitably concerned as well as from the point of view of the less advantaged subcultures that constitute them (including the three large demographic groupings just mentioned—the poor, the established, and the "in jeopardy"), we are in need of preschools that, virtually on a case-by-case basis, recognize the increased conflict imposed by our changing times. This increased pressure reflects itself in the force with which our three antinomies generate conflict within national cultures.

Consequently, I conceive of schools and preschools as serving a renewed function within our changing societies. This entails building school cultures that operate as mutual communities of learners, involved jointly in solving problems with all contributing to the process of educating one another. Such groups provide not only a locus for instruction, but a focus for identity and mutual work. Let these schools be a place for the praxis (rather than the proclamation) of cultural mutuality—which means an increase in the awareness that children have of what they are doing, how they are doing it, and why. The balance between individuality and group effectiveness gets worked out within the culture of the group; so too the balancing of ethnic or racial identities and the sense of the larger community of which they are part. And since school cultures of mutual learners naturally form a division of labor within them, the balance between cultivating native talent and enabling all to move ahead gets expressed internally in the group in the more humane form of "from each according to his or her ability." In such school cultures—and I have tried to describe one of them briefly—being natively good at something implies, among other things, helping others get better at that something.

I commented, half in jest, that with such a regimen of practice, schools in some interesting way become rather like countercultures—centers for the cultivation of a new awareness about what it is like living in a modern society. Some will doubtless object that such school atmospheres would be too "unstable" or even upsetting to some children. I would challenge this timid response. My counsel is not that we throw children in over their heads. It is only that we should give them an opportunity—as in the example I drew from Vivian Paley's work—to enter the culture with awareness of what it is about and what one does to cope with it as a participant.

Speaking now as an American, I can only remark that we would do far better to face the conjectures I have raised about early schooling than we would do by, for example, proclaiming rather airily that America will be first in science, math, and languages by the end of the decade. Nobody doubts that it would be desirable for us to compete in world markets, and that being first in one would help us to be first in the other. But what does it mean to be "first" if we do not address the countervailing ideal of developing human potential as fully as we can? And how does it speak to the sense of socioeconomic jeopardy into which families feel they have been put by the increasingly unjust distribution of wealth in the broader community? If the broader culture took on the challenge of becoming a mutual community, perhaps our boasts about our future prowess might be accompanied by the guarantee that making the country richer by working hard in school would not just make the rich richer and the poor poorer, but would result in a new pattern of distributing the national wealth more equitably. In a word, we would not simply be trying to reproduce the culture as it has been.

Are we willing enough, united enough, courageous enough to face up to the revolution we are living through? We probably have little better sense of where the culture is heading than did the French in 1789. And the changes may be even greater than in those days. In America, for example, there was a larger proportion of parents who had achieved high school educations in 1980 than there were parents with grade school educations a half-century before—more than eight in ten. At the turn of the century nearly half of America's families lived on farms, with all hands pitching in. Today, the figure is less than 5 percent. As for the family, the number of children in the median American family dropped to less than two per family this past year, down from nearly four in 1920. And perhaps the swiftest change of all: the number of children with mothers at work outside the home rose from one in ten in 1940 to six in ten in 1990—the same half-century in which the divorce rate increased from two per thousand marriages to about twenty-one per thousand. And in consequence, the percentage of kids living in mother-only households swelled from 6.7 to 20.0. The kids born into "Ozzie and Harriet" families (a first marriage with father working and mother at home)[26] now constitute about a quarter of American children—fewer than the one-third of children born into families at or below the poverty line.[27] And all these trends are more exaggerated for immigrant and black children.

I have no reason to believe that America is suffering greater changes than any other advanced nation. Or that our educational crisis is any graver than in most other countries—though I know it is exacerbated by many uniquely endemic problems like racism and American reluctance to face up to its declining economic position in the world. The only point I wish to make is that what is needed in America—as in most countries of the developed world—is not simply a renewal of the skills that make a country a better competitor in the world markets, but a renewal and reconsideration of what I have called "school culture." I have tried to characterize the new idea as creating communities of learners. Indeed, on the basis of what we have learned in recent years about human learning—that it is best when it is participatory, proactive, communal, collaborative, and given over to constructing meanings rather than receiving them—we even do better at teaching science, math, and languages in such schools than in more traditional ones.

No educational reform can get off the ground without an adult actively and honestly participating—a teacher willing and prepared to give and share aid, to comfort and to scaffold. Learning in its full complexity involves the creation and negotiation of meaning in a larger culture, and the teacher is the vicar of the culture at large. You cannot teacher-proof a curriculum any more than you can parent-proof a family. And a major task for any effort at reform—especially the participatory kind I've briefly outlined—is to bring teachers into the debate and into the shaping of change. For they are the ultimate change agents. It was a dedicated teacher corps that finally realized the ideals of the French Revolution—through nearly a century of dedication.[28]

Alas, not all advocates of reform recognize this truth. For in the years since *A Nation at Risk*[29] was published in 1983, when our national debate on education became a "public" media event, we have virtually closed our eyes to the nature, uses, and role of teaching. Not quite: we have sourly damned the teaching profession as unqualified, and concentrated on raising their licensing qualifications. Teaching has been treated as a necessary evil; would that we had computers that could do it. Thus we have probably alienated our most important ally in renewal.

There is nobody in America today who knows the temper of the American teacher better than Ernest Boyer, who conducted a study of their views in the five years following the 1983 publication of *A Nation at Risk*. This is what he concluded in the 1988 Annual Report of the Carnegie Endowment for the Advancement of Teaching:

> We are troubled that the nation's teachers remain so skeptical. Why is it that teachers, of all people, are demoralized and largely unimpressed by the reform actions taken [thus far]? . . . The reform movement has been driven largely by legislative and administrative intervention. The push has been concerned more with regulation than renewal. Reforms typically have focused on graduation requirements, student achievement, teacher preparation and testing, and monitoring activities. But in all these matters, important as they are, teachers have been largely uninvolved . . . Indeed, the most disturbing finding in our study is this: Over half the teachers [surveyed] believe that, overall, morale within the profession has substantially declined since 1983 . . . What is urgently needed—in the next phase of school reform—is a deep commitment to make teachers partners in renewal at all levels . . . The challenge now is to move beyond regulations, focus on renewal, and make teachers full participants in the process.[30]

I will end by noting that all that I have said implicates not only a transformation of school as a learning culture, but also the transformation of the role of the teacher in that learning culture—and, I suspect, in the culture at large. But that is a broader topic to which I shall return later.

4

▼

TEACHING THE PRESENT, PAST, AND POSSIBLE

It is surprising and somewhat discouraging how little attention has been paid to the intimate nature of teaching and school learning in the debates on education that have raged over the past decade. These debates have been so focused on performance and standards that they have mostly overlooked the means by which teachers and pupils alike go about their business in real-life classrooms—how teachers teach and how pupils learn.

It is all the more astonishing that this more intimate perspective has been so absent from the national debate, for, in fact, it has been a decade in which we have learned a great deal about learning and teaching in schools. Perhaps the leading figure in this advance has been Ann Brown, whose work I have mentioned in previous chapters. Taking my inspiration from her work with Joseph Campione, I want to reflect in this chapter on what we've learned from it. Accordingly, I want to begin by discussing four crucial ideas that have become much better understood thanks to their efforts. They are ideas we have already encountered in Chapter 1.

The first of these is the idea of *agency:* taking more control of your own mental activity. The second is *reflection:* not simply "learning in the raw" but making what you learn make sense, understanding it. The third is *collaboration:* sharing the resources of the mix of human beings involved in teaching and learning. Mind is inside the head, but it is also with others. And the fourth is *culture,* the way of life and thought that we construct, negotiate, institutionalize, and finally (after it's all settled) end up calling "reality" to comfort ourselves.

Thanks to Ann Brown's work in the Oakland schools, those children will never look at the world in the same way again—or at their fellow learners, or at the resources of knowledge and the uses to which those resources can be put, or at their place in a learning community. And neither will their teachers, to use a quaintly old-fashioned word. Those kids in Oakland learned so much more than just how to think about an environment. They learned empowering ways to use mind, including how to use technology for extending their powers. They learned to reflect on and get to the gist of what they knew lightly in order to teach it to others and to make further use of it themselves. And they acquired an enlivened sense of what a learning culture can be like. Obviously, performance "improved" among those kids: how could it *not?*

I want now to extrapolate those four ideas—agency, reflection, collaboration, and culture—to an aspect of what we teach that has been too little discussed, possibly avoided as a hot potato. It is the subject closest to life, closest to how we live. In school jargon it usually gets referred to as social studies, history, and literature. You could just as easily call these the human Present, Past, and Possible, the three great P's. My message is that teachers and students can be just as tough-minded in understanding these tender-minded topics as they can about quadratic equations or the conservation of mass—and we had better be in the interest of survival. To achieve such tough-mindedness in the human studies demands somewhat different skills, different sensibility, and more courage, for consideration of the human condition arouses contrary passions. But such passions cannot be sanitized by scattering them over self-contained "subject matter" oases, as we are learning at a high cost.

As a prologue to the issue at hand, let me describe a recent visit made to me by two high officials of the educational establishment in Russia. I thought I was in for another discussion of the usual: early Bruner on teaching the structure of a discipline (usually mathematics) or on devising a spiral curriculum. But that was not it at all. What do we do now, they asked, about teaching Russian history of the last century, including the seventy-five years of the Communist regime? Teach it as just one big mistake? As Russia hoodwinked by Party opportunists in the Kremlin? Or can the past be reconstrued to make sense not only of the past and its tragedies but of how the future could be shaped? "You," one of them said, "have been writing about history and culture as narrative, about the need for constant updating and reconstrual of past narratives. So how do we get a new generation to reflect upon and reconstrue their history? How do we keep from fooling ourselves again?" The discussion went on past midnight—better to have fresh readings, say, of Dostoevski's *Notes from the Underground* or Gogol's *The Inspector,* than "exposing" official histories of "The Revolution"? The next morning I thought, how come we're not asking questions like that? Because we "won"? Should that mask our failures and blindness—not a moment of official mourning for the tens of thousands of oppressed Iraqi civilians killed in Desert Storm, never mind how just our cause? No public pondering about the richest country in the world generating poverty at a rate second to none? Is that "winning"?

II

Let me begin with the theme of "reflection": making sense, going "meta," turning around on what one has learned through bare exposure, even thinking about one's thinking. Since the seventeenth century, the ideal of how to understand anything is to *explain* it causally by a theory: the ideal of science. A theory that works is altogether a miracle: it idealizes our varying observations of the world in a form so stripped down as to be kept easily in mind, permitting us to see the grubby particulars as exemplars of a general case. Explanatory theories work, moreover, however you feel about them, or (at least presumably) whatever your personal perspective toward the world. It matters not a fig that Newton's laws of color came to him the summer when Cambridge, where he was then resident, was threatened by the Plague. So he left town and finished his work elsewhere. The object of his theory was to *explain* the mixing of colored light, and the conditions of its discovery are irrelevant. The laws of color, we say, are "eternal" and "context-free."

Now think about the fact that only a half-century after the Supreme Court decided that "separate but equal" was *not* racial discrimination (in *Plessy v. Ferguson*), the Court dismissed that "finding" as invalid, replacing it with the opinion in *Brown v. Board of Education*. So how do the Court's interpretive procedures differ from Newton's explanatory ones?

Scientific explanations "die" of being unparsimonious or for lack of generality or derivational depth. But that's a very highbrow and specialized way to die. Newton's law is still right about white light being a mixture of all spectral colors. This model of explanation is so robust that then contemporary philosophers, yearning for certainty, anointed it as the *only* way to true understanding. "Cast all else unto the flames," advised David Hume, "it is naught but sophistry and illusion."

What then of shifting judicial opinions and historical accounts, what then of whether Eugene O'Neill's *Long Day's Journey into Night* captures something deep about a decaying American middle class? And is Blake only fanciful when he writes: "The dog starved at his master's gate / Spells the downfall of the state"? Sophistry and illusion? But with anti–illusionist positivism overshooting itself in the latter nineteenth century, the humanities were on the defensive (with psychology, of course, caught in the middle). History, the human sciences (the old *Geisteswissenschaften*), and literature were not quite serious, up for grabs rather than subject to proof. They explained nothing, but only "enriched the mind."

Then, while the hard-nosed science professors were decrying the softness of the "soft subjects," Europe marched off to war once again—acting out the historical–social studies–literary stories that were presumed only to be "enriching the mind." Surely we could do better at understanding ourselves and our mad lurchings. Poison gas and Big Berthas might be the deadly fruits of verifiable science, but the impulse to use them grew out of those stories we tell ourselves. So should we not try to understand their power better, to see how stories and historical accounts are put together and what there is about them that leads people either to live together or to maim and kill each other?

In the first quarter of this century, something crucial happened to thinking people. Let us call it "the interpretive turn." The turn first expressed itself in drama and literature, then in history, then in the social sciences, and finally in epistemology. It is now expressing itself in education. The object of interpretation is understanding, not explanation; its instrument is the analysis of text. Understanding is the outcome of organizing and contextualizing essentially contestable, incompletely verifiable propositions in a disciplined way. One of our principal means for doing so is through narrative: by telling a story of what something is "about." But as Kierkegaard had made clear many years before, telling stories in order to understand is no mere enrichment of the mind: without them we are, to use his phrase, reduced to fear and trembling.

Understanding, unlike explaining, is not preemptive: one way of construing the fall of Rome narratively does not preclude other ways. Nor does the interpretation of any particular narrative rule out other interpretations. For narratives and their interpretations traffic in meaning, and meanings are intransigently multiple: the rule is polysemy. Narrative meanings, moreover, depend in only a trivial way on truth in the strict sense of verifiability. The requirement, rather, is verisimilitude or "truth likeness," and that is a compound of coherence and pragmatic utility, neither of which can be rigidly specified.

Since no one narrative construal rules out all alternatives, narratives pose a very special issue of criteria. By what standards can competing narratives or competing interpretations of a narrative be adjudged as "right" or "acceptable"? For one thing, alternatives may derive from different perspectives. But that surely is not enough: some narratives about "what happened" are simply righter, not just because they are better rooted in factuality, but also because they are better contextualized, rhetorically more "fair-minded," and so on. But what is even more crucial, alternate narrative accounts may show comparable awareness of the requirements of narrative itself. And there are such requirements, as we shall see in a moment. In a word, narrative accounts can be principled or not, even though such principledness does not rest on stark verification alone, as with scientific explanations. Any constitutional lawyer worth her salt can tell you how Mr. Justice Taney's way of construing history in the famous *Dred Scott* decision was excruciatingly tunnel-visioned, unmindful of competing perspectives, and therefore lethal in consequences. His opinion wasn't right even from a pro-slavery perspective. It was shoddy, among other reasons, for its failure to take into account the alternative framings in terms of which like "cases" (and cases are always stories) had been narrativized in the past. He blundered, and helped unleash the bloodiest and most bitter war in our history.[1] Bad narrative interpretation in high places is poison.

Now let me come to my point. Just as the underlying method of explanation in science can and must be taught with care and rigor, so too can the interpretive and narrative methods of history, social studies, and even literature be taught with care and rigor. But they rarely are, too often being seen either as "gotcha" exercises in finding *the* preemptive story, or as rhetorical exercises in pushing a partisan point of view. Neither has much to do with what, in fact, good historians, social scientists, and literary theorists *do* when they're doing their business. When Simon Schama tells the story of how General Wolfe was "constructed" after the French and Indian War, you learn something about how to think history: history as a discipline of understanding the past rather than as an account of "what simply happened." History never simply happens: it is constructed by historians. It is a lame excuse to say that children can't do it. I have seen the interpretive approach to history developed at the Learning and Development Research Center at Pittsburgh, where kids were learning to *be* historians rather than consumers of potted "correct" histories or rooters for shoddy partisan accounts: neither just "getting the facts right" nor wallowing in rhetorical self-indulgence.

There is always some worry that the pragmatic epistemology of the interpretive turn will undermine values: the "Is nothing sacred?" critique. What is sacred is that *any* well-wrought, well-argued, scrupulously documented, perspectivally honest construal of the past, the present, or the possible deserves respect. We all appreciate that, nevertheless, we must decide between competing accounts, competing narratives. That is political and social reality. But that does not condone suppression: after all, that's what the major amendments to our Constitution are all about.

Let me be clear on one crucial point before leaving the topic of reflection. A respectful tough-mindedness toward alternative "stories" about how things are, how they might have come to be that way, and where they might be going is in no sense antithetical to scientific thinking. Scientific explanations are adjuncts to narrative interpretation and vice versa: after all, stories deal with the human meanings of theories too. Some theoretical efforts in the social sciences, indeed, are enriched by, even elucidated by responsible narratives. How did three-quarters of the nation's wealth get into the hands of less than a quarter of our population? That's an interesting story begging for an explanatory theory more discriminating than Darwin's. Indeed, Carol Feldman has shown beautifully how story making can help a child discover where a theory (rather than a story) is needed.[2]

III

Let me turn now to the issues of agency and collaboration. They need to be treated together, else learning is made to seem either too solo or not solo enough. Again, we need a little background. In the classical empiricist tradition that formed our Anglo-American ideology about "learning," mind was an impressionable surface (a wax tablet in Locke's account) on which the world wrote its message. Order was created by the mind keeping track associatively of which things went together in the impinging world. Continental rationalists supplemented this solo, passive version of learning with the idea of "right reason": the human appreciation of logical relations, particularly a sensitivity to logical contradiction. In both rationalist and empiricist accounts, things happened pretty automatically and quite unassisted by others. There wasn't much room in either picture for active agency or collaboration.

The agentive view takes mind to be proactive, problem-oriented, attentionally focused, selective, constructional, directed to ends. What "gets into" mind is more a function of the hypotheses in force than what is bombarding the sensorium. Decisions, strategies, heuristics—these are key notions of the agentive approach to mind. Even the mental life of human infants has been found to be far more agentive than we ever expected—thanks to a whole generation of research, as recounted briefly in Chapter 3.

And what we are also finding is that a *solo* agentive view of mind is wildly off the mark—probably a projection of our Western individualistic ideology. We do not learn a way of life and ways of deploying mind unassisted, unscaffolded, naked before the world. And it is not just sheer language acquisition that makes this so. Rather, it is the give and take of talk that makes collaboration possible. For the agentive mind is not only active in nature, but it seeks out dialogue and discourse with other active minds. And it is through this dialogic, discursive process that we come to know the Other and his points of view, his stories. We learn an enormous amount not only about the world but about ourselves by discourse with Others. Agency and collaboration are rather like yin and yang.

In the Oakland project, Ann Brown has joined agency and collaboration together in the design of classroom culture. Kids not only generate their own hypotheses, but negotiate them with others—including their teachers. But they also take the role of teacher—offering their expertise to those with less. This is how it is *structurally*. You argue with your benchmates about the best ways to get oil off a polluted sea bird caught in the *Exxon Valdez* spill, or how it could have happened in the first place, and you learn about explanatory and interpretive accountability in the process. Kids are tougher critics than teachers. There's even a classroom ethnographer reporting back periodically on how the collaborative effort is progressing.

Now let me return to the agenda of the three P's: learning how to construe interpretively the human Present, Past, and Possible, and particularly how to do this by the responsible use of narrative. How do agency and collaboration figure in this picture? To begin with, skill is the instrument of agency acquired through collaboration. Without skill we are powerless. So too for the skills and the know-how of narrative construal. Though we know the rudiments of narrative from a tender age (just as we know the rudiments of discourse and dialogue), there is a long way to go to reach adult narrative maturity. And this is what I want to consider now.

As a starter, we seem to construct stories of the real world, so called, much as we construct fictional ones: the same forming rules, the same narrative structures. We simply do not know, nor will we ever, whether we learn about narrative from life or life from narrative: probably both. But nobody questions that learning the subtleties of narrative is one of the prime routes to thinking about life—much as a grasp of the associative, commutative, and distributive rules helps us grasp what algebraic thinking is. So let me try a quick summary.

At a minimum, a "story" (fictional or actual) involves an Agent who Acts to achieve a Goal in a recognizable Setting by the use of certain Means. What drives the story, what makes it worth telling, is Trouble: some misfit between Agents, Acts, Goals, Settings, and Means. Why is Trouble the license for telling a story? Narrative begins with an explicit or implicit prologue establishing the ordinariness or legitimacy of its initial circumstances—"I was walking down the street minding my own business when . . ." The action then unfolds leading to a breach, a violation of legitimate expectancy. What follows is either a restitution of initial legitimacy or a revolutionary change of affairs with a new order of legitimacy. Narratives (truth or fiction) end with a coda, restoring teller and listener to the here and now, usually with a hint of evaluation of what has transpired. In all these stages—the establishment of initial legitimacy, the management of restitution or overthrow, and the hinted evaluation of the coda—narratives are profoundly and inescapably normative—though this normativity may be heavily masked as conventional reality. Note also that narrative, whether fictional or "real," is played out on a dual landscape: a subjective one in the consciousness of the protagonists, and an "objective" or "real" one that the narrator informs the listener about, though protagonists in the tale may not know about it—such as Oedipus not knowing, though you do, that Jocasta, his chosen wife, is his blood mother.

A word about the more cognitive side of narrative thought or the narrative construction of reality. As the great Vladimir Propp put it,[3] a narrative structure is composed of a set of grammar-like rules for ordering characters and events sequentially in a fashion such that the events and characters, to use Propp's language, become "functions" of the overall plot structure. A "false hero" trying to do a true hero out of his rightful rewards is a representation of the world that makes sense only by virtue of being nested in a particular kind of narrative structure. There are two things about these narrative structures that are particularly fascinating. The first is that there are so few of them: magisterial literary theorists like Northrop Frye claim there are only four of them: tragedy, comedy, romance, and irony.[4] Yet stories are endlessly varied, which can only mean, of course, that narrative genres must be highly abstract, almost algebraic. Battles between false and true heroes are the stuff, for example, of drama-narratives as different as the Lincoln-Douglas debates, *Wuthering Heights,* Ibsen's *A Doll's House,* and the adversarial oral testimony of Thurgood Marshall and John W. Davis in *Brown v. Board of Education.* Finally, at least according to Propp, all narrative genres revolve around a desired resource that is in short supply, often only implicitly indicated.

Armed with even this small grasp of the formal structure of narrative, it is astonishing how much more disciplined we become in clarifying what a "text" is claiming to be about—"we" including not just "lit crit" buffs, but psychologists, lawyers, and especially kids. Yet I have scarcely mentioned the rhetorical side of narrative: such as the narrator's link to the story, why she is presumed to be telling it, with what authority, what motive, in what selected frame. J. L. Austin reminded us decades ago that stories are *the* medium for offering our excuses. But *all* stories, even when not about why I'm late again, are justifications told from the perspective of a norm. More to the point, where narrative negotiation is concerned, skilled narrators and beholders can and do learn to make life easier by helping each other understand how their stories are put together, from what perspective, and so forth. The omniscient narrator is only a fictional convention: in life he is likely to be a menace to the traffic of narrative negotiation. No story can be locked within the limits of a single horizon. Novelists taught us this first: Flaubert, Kafka, Joyce, Calvino—not to mention Laurence Sterne in *Tristram Shandy*. Then historians followed, then anthropologists.[5] Like novelists, they tell us or tease us about the point of view from which they select and construct their "facts." And by doing so with honest self-criticism and as a joint community, they vastly enrich our sense of the possible.

It is a perverse idea that teachers and students cannot deal with narrative matters with comparable skill and openness and with a comparable gain in self-awareness. Nobody needs to "go to war" over the multiple meanings, multiple perspectives, multiple frames that can be used in understanding the human Past, Present, and Possible. Collaborative narrative construal is not a zero-sum game. Making sense jointly need not be *hegemony,* just shoving the story version of the stronger down the throats of the weaker—even when tense political issues are at stake. Just as feminist, third-world, and minority fiction has opened our horizons, so too can history and social commentary written honestly, construed wisely, and debated openly create a richer democratic world. That same kind of negotiating might even save psychometric assessment from falling into the kinds of anti-feminist and nativistic traps that scholars like Cynthia Fuchs Epstein and James Deese have so persuasively illuminated in their recent work.[6] I see debate and negotiation, again openly pursued, as the enemy of hegemony—whether related to gender, race, ethnic origin, religion, or just brute force.

But let me be clear: I do not see the outcome of this process of fair-minded joint construal as producing a single list of "American values" chiseled in granite. Indeed, I think the very idea of "American values" smacks of intellectual and moral timidity—the same kind of timidity that insists that stories always turn out with the same endings. The objective of skilled agency and collaboration in the study of the human condition is to achieve not unanimity, but more conscious-ness. And more consciousness always implies more diversity.

IV

My final topic in this chapter is culture. I share the view of many anthropologists today that it is no longer a very useful fiction to conceive of "a culture" as an established, almost irreversibly stabilized way of thinking, believing, acting, judging. Cultures have always been in the process of change, and the rate of change becomes greater as our fates become increasingly intermingled through migration, trade, and the rapid exchange of information. In an ironic sense, the best way to describe contemporary industrialized cultures may be by reference to the procedures they have in place for absorbing change reasonably, constrained by a lively awareness of broad goals—such as freedom, accountability, equality of opportunity and responsibility, and even equality of sacrifice. Different cultures manage these matters differently. What they all have in common is the dilemma of imper-fection: keeping faith in the ability to change for the better while knowing that a final and settled end can never be attained. In our own professedly egalitarian society, for example, we have a staggeringly lopsided distribution of wealth and earnings—52,019 people with annual incomes over $1 million a year in 1990 in a country whose median annual income is under $30,000: a sixfold increase in the number of fat-cat earners in a decade! We all sense this as a problem. Kids may not know the figures, but they also sense it in the air, as on the "real" agenda.

But for reasons of delicacy, perhaps, or expediency, this is a topic that gets left out in school. Enough such leavings out, and school begins to present so alien or so remote a vision of the world that many learners can find no place in it for them or their friends. This is true not just of girls, or blacks, or Latinos, or Asians, or other kids we target for special attention as potentially at risk. There are also those restless, bored kids in our sprawling suburbs who suffer the pandemic syndrome of "What am I doing here anyway? What's this to do with *me?*" They all know something is left out either from seeing it played out on the street or on the ubiquitous television screen. The resulting disenchantment with the educational establishment expresses itself in so many and such varied forms as to be mind-boggling—and we *are* boggled, boggled at the power of street culture, at the increasing fear of suburban kids about going into the city, at the anomie in middle-class children. But I am equally impressed at the success of some schools and teachers in combating it.

Now, school is a culture itself, not just a "preparation" for it, a warming up. As some anthropologists like to put it, culture is a toolkit of techniques and procedures for understanding and managing your world. When I mentioned earlier that a more searching examination of narrative structure can help students understand the stories they construct about their worlds, it was in that procedural sense that I intended my remarks. And obviously the bare-handed procedures I talked about can be augmented by newly available technologies for helping with the interpretive tasks that students need to master—retrieval blockbusters like CD-ROM, analytical ones like Hypercard, ordering devices for putting things into different branching structures, and the like. It is clear that kids learn quickly to use these technical aids and to share their results with others.

But prosthetic technology is not the point, even if it is crucial to what a culture is about. What *is* the point is the procedure of inquiry, of mind using, which is central to the maintenance of an interpretive community and a democratic culture. One step is to choose the crucial problems, particularly the problems that are prompting change within our culture. Let those problems and our procedures for thinking about them be part of what school and classwork are about. This does not mean that school becomes a rallying place for discussion of the culture's failures. But just as Ann Brown in her Oakland classroom used the ghastliness of the oil spill of the *Exxon Valdez* to probe issues of the human habitat, so should we begin our probing into the human condition—Past, Present, and Possible—with the Troubles that keep that topic as current today as it ever was. How, for example, did we get from the original "all men are created free and equal" to the lopsidedness of our system of distributing wealth? Remember what I said earlier: Trouble is the engine of narrative and the justification for going public with a story. It is the whiff of trouble that leads us to search out the relevant or responsible constituents in the narrative, in order to convert the raw Trouble into a manageable Problem that can be handled with procedural muscle.

All this is nothing new. This is what a culture is all about—not just anthropological prose-poems about patterns, but a mode of coping with human problems: with human transactions of all sorts, depicted in symbols. Good teachers of literature, history, and social studies have known this "trouble feature" of narrative forever. Those two Russian gentlemen with whom I spent that long, soul-searching evening were having their noses rubbed in it by circumstances. I, for my part, would like to see us face up to the responsibility of narrative accounting as well, and we are in a much better position to do so. Besides, I see the challenge of narrative as a means to bring together the study of society, of human nature, of history, of literature and drama, even of law, in the interest not so much of out-competing our trade rivals as of overcoming our own shortsightedness.

Some readers may wonder why literature and drama play such a large part in my account. Narratives, for all their standard scripts about life, leave room for those breaches and violations that create what the Russian Formalists used to call *ostronenyie:* making the all-too-familiar strange again. So while the "storying" of reality risks making reality hegemonic, great stories reopen it for new questioning. That's why tyrants put the novelists and poets in jail first. That's why I want them in democratic classrooms—to help us see again, afresh.

5

▼

UNDERSTANDING AND EXPLAINING OTHER MINDS

In the preceding chapter I made a case for interpretive narrative as an appropriately disciplined mode of thought for construing the present, past, and possible human condition. In the process of doing so, I touched glancingly on the differences between *explaining* and *interpreting*. Now I want to address those differences more directly, for they are crucial not only to a more abstract philosophy of knowledge but also to the conduct of classroom teaching and learning.

But it is a vast topic, and like most such, it needs to be approached by reference to some more particular subject lest it dissipate into the rarefied air of logical analysis. Good fortune and the hard work of many psychologists have provided us with an exemplary topic in the light of which to examine the difficult distinction that concerns us—namely, how young children learn to interpret what others are thinking, feeling, intending, and above all, what they mean by what they say. For understanding other minds is par excellence an interpretive process, and it is at the heart of the task of making sense of what an anthropologist says about the Trobriand islanders, or what a historian tells us about the Industrial Revolution. It is no less important in the classroom: teachers understanding what their pupils are thinking and vice versa.

Now the psychologist's prototypical question is whether the process of interpretation can be explained *scientifically*. If it can be, then interpretation is, as it were, just another "fact of nature" like other facts of nature that are subject to scientific explanation. In which case, it can be "reduced" to conventional science—just another difficult topic to be tamed scientifically.

I have always held that although there is a link between explaining and interpreting—between the ways of a biologist and the ways of a historian—the two modes of making sense cannot be reduced to each other. They are fundamentally different.

Then recently Janet Astington and David Olson wrote a thoughtful article on the subject in which they attacked my separatist views on the matter, an article intended for a major scientific journal in the field of human development. They argued, if I may simplify somewhat, that if one held a priori that developmental psychology could not achieve an explanation of how children learned to interpret other minds, then it would fail as a science. But more important, they asserted that the new work on the development of children's theories of other minds proved that I was mistaken about the impossibility of achieving a scientific explanation of interpretation.

Astington and Olson sent me a prepublication copy of their article, for we frequently exchange ideas and manuscripts, and at the same time the editor of the scientific journal for which it was destined wrote to ask whether I would like to write a commentary on it for publication in the issue of the journal in which it was to appear. The present chapter is, in effect, the commentary I prepared—one of several to appear with the Astington-Olson paper. But it is more than an "answer" to them. For I used the occasion as an opportunity to reply not only to their concerns about whether we could explain the growth of children's theories of mind, but also to address the general issue of how interpretation and explanation differ.

▼

Janet Astington and David Olson have done us a favor by articulating a common complaint against those who insist that there is an irreconcilable difference between causal-explanatory and interpretive-hermeneutic approaches to how we understand our own and others' minds. The first of these, the explanatory, aims to elucidate the necessary and/or sufficient conditions that enable us to recognize a mental state: for example, a lesion in the hypothalamic amygdala destroys our ability to recognize facial expressions of emotion, and the amygdala's functioning is therefore a "cause" of our ability to recognize emotions.[1] The interpretive way is after-the-fact and typically context-dependent, and therefore "historical": Was the massive killing in the Balinese village of Pare at the time of the Indonesian revolution[2] a reflection of the anxiety-ridden social system discussed in Geertz's famous Balinese Cockfight,[3] or was it attributable to the politics of anti-colonial revolution sweeping the Third World in the 1960s? The amygdala can indisputably be said to play a causal role in the recognition of facial emotion. But the best we can do is to find a reasonable way of interpreting how the people in Pare made sense of their situation. In the latter case, one reasonable interpretation does not preclude others.

Astington and Olson wisely propose to limit this classically vexing issue of explanation versus interpretation to the "new field" of children's theories of mind, a particularly emblematic topic, for it is a product of the cultural revolution that has generated much debate on the issue of interpretation and explanation. It has always been supposed, moreover, that it is the *object* of study that determines which of the two approaches is appropriate to it. Generally, human action that is believed to be mediated by *meaning* is regarded as the domain of interpretation. Meaning, according to the classical mantra, cannot be explained causally.

Causal explanation, on the other hand, is categorial rather than particular, and based on the testing of propositions whose verifiability does not depend upon a contextual setting or upon the meaning-making processes of participants in the action. In old-fashioned terms, causal explanations deal only in material, efficient, and formal causes.

Not only is meaning banned from the consideration of causation, but so too are teleological explanations that presuppose meaning. Again, that at least is the canonical mantra.

Now let us look at the "new field" of theories of mind. Note first that it is neither "new" nor can it, save by fiat, be called a "field." Anthropologists have been studying preliterate peoples' beliefs about other minds for over a century.[4] Indeed, France's leading school of historians, the *Annales* group,[5] takes as its central mission the study of "mentalities," which includes what people at any given time and place made of each others' minds. One *Annales* historian[6] even wrote a very good book on adults' changing theories of children's minds over history. As for *children's* theories of mind, and their development, virtually every developmental linguist of the last century (with the conspicuous exception of some committed believers in an autonomous Chomskian "language organ") has taken children's theories of mind as crucial to the acquisition of language, and has attempted to infer their nature from observation—Grace de Laguna[7] being perhaps the most elegant exponent.

All of this work has been unselfconsciously interpretive. It continues today. I can find no better representative of this interpretive tradition than an earlier study by Janet Astington[8] in which she investigated how children come to understand "commissive" speech acts such as predictions, intentions, and promises—sentences like *I promise you that it will be a sunny day on your next birthday*. The youngest children in her sample were unable to appreciate that such an expression was "wrong," and Astington argued that such an error could be "explained" by the children's failure to grasp that what they thought (as judged by what they said) is not related to what happens in the world later. Being able to understand this relationship is, of course, a central "felicity condition" on promising[9]—you can't promise what you can't deliver.

Is Astington's conclusion an interpretation, or is it a causal explanation? It surely rests upon a gloss of what promising *means* to a child. Even if that fact makes it interpretive, it does not in the least discourage further efforts to explain the phenomenon by the use of well-controlled experimentation. Do children who promise no rain on your birthday nevertheless recognize, for example, the distinction between a broken and a fulfilled promise made to them by their parents? Suppose they do. Is the first finding now to be considered context-specific? And what if it is? We can now set out to "explain" the nature of the context effects we observe. Can we say that the function of "explanatory research" is to convert what was formerly an interpretation into what eventually may become an explanation? Is the only value of interpretation that it provides the raw material for later testable hypotheses leading to explanation? Caution, please!

We know full well, from Dunn,[10] that even quite young children are upset by broken promises made to them by those on whom they depend—despite their well-known difficulty in grasping the difference between false and true beliefs. So, like Chandler, Fritz, and Hala,[11] we have to incorporate into our theory of developing minds some distinction between the kinds of situations where promises may get made or broken: participatory versus non-participatory, agentive versus recipientive, and so forth. We can then submit each of these new conditions to a hypothesis amenable to empirical test. What typically emerges at the end of the long day—given that children's meanings vary by context—is an interesting patchwork of observations and reproducible experimental results that is partly explanatory in a causal sense and partly interpretive. This kind of patchwork is beautifully represented in the major synoptic book on the subject: Janet Astington's distinguished *The Child's Discovery of the Mind*.

Perhaps, then, there is something that is in principle hybrid about the study of children's developing theories of mind, inasmuch as it appears to entail both causal explanation and interpretation. But let us take another approach to the matter.

II

Consider a second question. What do we mean by the child (or anybody) *having* a "theory of mind"? What is the relation between having a theory of mind and responding to others in a way that seems to presuppose that others have particular theories of mind—without there being any consciousness of anything like a theory? Is there not an important distinction to be drawn between a tacit presupposition that guides a response, and a theory? Now, actually shaking out a quilt, the way most of us do it, "presupposes" some consideration of the "spring of the air." That was the fact of the matter even before the great Boyle achieved renown for his "discovery" of that physical phenomenon. Our practices often presuppose knowledge that is plainly not accessible to us by means other than praxis. Most people have no "theory of grammar" despite speaking in well-formed sentences. It requires the mighty labor of linguistics to discover the "rules" of grammar. And so, as Astington and Olson note, we must heed Wittgenstein's warning that rules of grammar do not explain how people speak, nor "cause" them to speak in a certain way.

So what are we to make of the difference between the tacit presuppositions that guide our intersubjective practices, and the theories that provide an explicit descriptive calculus for explicating them after the fact? Norbert Weiner, for example, propounded and understood a theory of cybernetics that "explained" the nimbleness of Martina Navratilova, though she could doubtless make a monkey of him on the tennis court, with or without understanding his theory. Indeed, reliance on an explicit theory of mind, often encountered among gifted autists,[12] leads to a certain telltale, unnatural awkwardness in their interpersonal interactions. Apparently, a theory in the explicit sense is no substitute for tacit presuppositions about how people's minds work.

Mastering the presuppositions that guide our unreflective interactions with others is probably much like learning a language. The two are highly dependent upon participating in the local context, or even the micro-context, of a culture.[13] We are discovering a good deal about how children acquire their presuppositions or biases about other minds, and at any one moment it is hard to know whether our knowledge is fully explanatory or interpretive. We are even discovering some innate neurophysiological mechanisms that predispose children to acquire some of these presuppositions—like the tendency to follow another's line of regard,[14] which in turn is aided by the tendency to "latch on" to others' eyes, which may be further explained by the operation of a cortical center that is activated uniquely by eye-like configurations.[15] And there may even be some larger-scale, more complex psychological adaptations that predispose the young of our species to respond as they do in typically cultural interactions.[16] I refer, of course, to treating a child (or, by extension, treating an enculturated young pygmy chimpanzee) *as if* her intentional states were being taken into account—her beliefs, desires, and so on. This way of being treated, then, seems to lead children to behave as if both they and the person treating them that way *had* mental states.[17] This interactive routine seems to be the road to mutual intersubjectivity, ontogenetically and perhaps phylogenetically as well.

Many of the tacit presuppositions guiding intersubjective transactions seem surprisingly incorrigible, even surprisingly inaccessible to conscious reflection. This does not imply, however, that they are based upon strongly predetermined or innate biological adaptations. For early-acquired cultural presuppositions also become notoriously automatized and inaccessible to reflection and introspection. So accustomed do we become to treating others "as if" they have intentional states that we come to take it for granted that they do. We even develop conventionalized notions about what our own mental states are like and how they are experienced by others. For example, we come to take it for granted that thinking is effortful, and that we and others are not "thinking" unless there are accompanying signs of effort. Rudolf Arnheim once sent me a pair of photographs intended to represent "thinkers"—one the well-known muscular bronze of Rodin, the other an exquisite wooden Japanese figure from the sixth century. Arnheim had just read a piece I had written describing a discussion with a Zen master concerning the nature of thinking. Arnheim's accompanying comment reads: "You might like to compare the delicately hesitant, most Japanese reasoning of this wooden figure of the sixth century with our massive thought efforts à la Rodin." Apparently, effort was not the external mark of thinking for sixth-century Japanese.

Cultures are famous for cultivating conventions both for expressing and for "reading" mental states—like the show of concentrated effort in "thinking." These conventions can be found not only in a culture's myths and visual arts, but also in daily routines and even in linguistic usage. This conventionalization is well known in painting, the famous example being the image of the running horse in Western art, with its front and rear legs thrust longitudinally forward and backward from the body. It was not until Muybridge's famous serial photographs,[18] shot to settle a wager on the subject that Leland Stanford had made with a friend, that it was discovered that such fore and aft extension of the legs is impossible in the galloping horse. Yet Remington's cowboys galloping along on their orthopedically impossible horses *still* seem to us like the apotheosis of high-speed motion. So, too, does Rodin's muscular figure seem lost in thought. The most I can read into that hesitant sixth-century figurine is that its model is wrapped in aesthetic contemplation.

Matters of this kind are made even more vivid by a recent paper by Flavell, Green, and Flavell,[19] entitled "Young Children's Knowledge about Thinking." It is principally about children's "theories of mind" in the top-down sense—for example, what children think "thinking" really is, which is probed in this study by asking children questions about the matter point-blank. Such an article would have been virtually unimaginable in an SRCD Monograph before the cognitive revolution. Paul Harris, one of the two commentators on the monograph, offers this succinct précis of its findings:[20] "Young preschool children are surprisingly mentalistic in their conception of thinking; at the same time, they are surprisingly ill-attuned to the ongoing process of thinking." Children do indeed describe thinking as something that goes on "inside their heads," though they cannot give much of an account of what is taking place there. Well, what *is* taking place there? In spite of their prompts and leading questions, Flavell and his colleagues seemed unable to make children "see" that thought is experienced as a "stream of thought" whose successive contents are held together by contingent links between them. It is this "ongoing process" to which, in Harris's terms, children are ill-attuned. Granted that "stream of thought" is an elegantly expressed Jamesian turn of phrase, and that it is the standard stuff of textbooks, is it really just there for anybody to *see,* so long as they are "attuned" to "reality"?

Even James Joyce, who depicted the famous stream of thought in his later writings, had to struggle very hard to create a form of writing that could produce the impression of such a stream.[21] For in fact the stream of thought is a *theory* of thought, and not a natural kind to be observed. Indeed, it has not even been widely subscribed to in the history of the subject. Dennett[22] believes thought is shot full of blank pauses which we fill in. Fodor[23] believes that the processes that take place inside the thought module are inaccessible to observation altogether. And psychologists of the Würzburg school[24] were convinced by their studies that thoughts were imageless *(unanschaulich Denken)* and not to be observed at all. And what of Immanuel Kant, who conceived of thought as imposing space, time, causality, and moral exigency on the raw stuff of sensing? The only "ill-tunedness" of the young subjects in the Flavell experiment was really to the cumbersome Herbartian theory[25] of flowing associations, a cumbersomeness that even shows through William James's graceful turn of phrase.

The fact of the matter is that we do not have much of an idea of what thought *is,* either as a "state of mind" or as a process. Indeed, "thought" as it is usually discussed may be little more than a way of talking and conversing about something we cannot observe. It is a way of talking that functions to give "thought" some form that is more visible, more audible, more referable, and more negotiable.[26] It may simply be one of those "oeuvres," discussed in Chapter 1, that we create after the fact.

Janet Astington, who is the other commentator on the Flavell monograph, puts it well: "A major problem is that, considered simply as ongoing mental activity, *thinking* does not have any behavioral indices. It is therefore difficult for children to acquire knowledge of it, and for researchers to investigate children's knowledge about it."[27] Indeed, as Flavell and colleagues also note, children conceive of thinking as an effortful, voluntary mental process associated with problem solving. Rodin lives again! Astington remarks: "In ordinary language use, we might compare the terms *think* and *breathe*. Both . . . [go] on all the time, but unnoticed and not talked about, except in marked cases"[28]—such as when the doctor tells you to "breathe in," or when a parent tells you to "think about" where you might have left your locker key. The "theory of thinking" embodied in the use of "cultural conversation" seems to shape and categorize experience itself, defining thinking in terms of certain effortful experiences of a particular kind. Learning such terms as *think, believe, pay attention, remember* is, then, learning a theory of mind. Indeed, Astington quotes Harris as asking in an earlier publication, "'Does the community offer the child a way of talking, a gloss, that provides instruction in how to conceptualize mental states?'"[29] And she answers his query like the interpretivists she and Olson have to be: "I think that language is fundamental to children's conceptualization of the mental world. This means that any attempt to assess young children's understanding has to be supremely sensitive to the way the children themselves might talk about these things."[30]

But reference to self and to the states of self requires far more than a lexicon of self-reference, even more than the shifter requirements that govern pronominal discourse (I am "I" when I am speaking; I am "you" when you are).[31] For self is also defined and delineated in situated speech by its location in discourse and by the role it plays in the social world in which the participants believe themselves to be operating.[32] Many languages are even marked syntactically and lexically to take such matters into account. It was such considerations as these that led Markus and Kitayama[33] to conclude that the Japanese "self" was a more relational one than the American. Indeed, many anthropological linguists contend that self and its states are indexed in discourse according to the speaker's and/or listener's position in a social context.[34] Self-situating in Japanese is made particularly clear by the presence of lexical pairs whose use in that language requires contextual decisions—such contrastive pairs as *uchi* and *soto* (inside vs. outside), *omote* and *ura* (background vs. "up front"), *giri* and *ninjoo* (feelings vs. obligations), *honne* and *tatamae* (inner life vs. surface duties)—all of them variants on the inner world of self in contrast to one's outer world.[35] To *use* these words requires that the child appreciate not only words but his contextualization within the society around him. And this, of course, is necessarily an interpretive task, a search for meaning in praxis. I am sure that Astington and Olson would have no difficulty with cultural examples of this kind—and such examples can be vastly multiplied both within and beyond Indo-European languages.[36]

III

So what's the problem? Why are Astington and Olson so worried about interpretivism? Granted that interpretivism is a somewhat embarrassing partner for the searcher after causal explanation, are the consequences of their occasional liaison as troublesome as Astington and Olson foresee it being? Will it end with the study of developing theories of mind divided between interpretivist humanists on the one side, studying the acquisition of cultural conventions, and neuropsychologists on the other, seeking to establish causally that, say, an intact amygdala is necessary for recognizing somebody's emotional state? On this view, psychologists are locked out of the feast altogether, with not so much as a finder's fee to show for their discoveries. Have psychologists nothing to offer as explanations of the interpretive activities of their young subjects—or of their not so young colleagues trying to explain the interpretations of these same young subjects? Theirs is much too gloomy a view and seems to me a little unrealistic about how psychological science progresses.

Plainly, Astington and Olson do not deny interpretive processes to children. But they nonetheless claim that, somehow, we will not be able to account for these interpretive processes causally. Or, more precisely, they believe we will be left with a cultural interpretive approach on the one level and a biological account on the other. But they conflate this matter by drawing too sharp a distinction between brain sciences and psychology, and do not take fully enough into account what is meant by a cultural analysis.

Nearly eighty years ago, Alfred Kroeber,[37] in a celebrated article on "The Superorganic," had this to say: "The distinction between animal and man which counts is not that of the physical and the mental, which is one of relative degree, but that of the organic and the social. . . . The beast has mentality, and we have bodies; but in civilization, man has something that no animal has."[38] Or more succinctly later: "Bach, born in the Congo instead of Saxony, could not have produced even a fragment of chorale or sonata, though we can be equally confident that he would have outshone his compatriots in some manner of music."[39]

In a word, one can go some way in explicating man's *capacity for culture* by reference to causal processes, psychological or biological.[40] Within the psychological domain, we explore processes like, say, the capacity to delay gratification, while in the conventional cultural domain we look for possible public communal rituals that can support such delay. The first example is explanatory, the second interpretive. Within the domain of culture itself, explanation is infeasible—why, for example, the alto recorder is in an e-flat rather than a c register. I believe that the two modes of knowing are irreducibly different but complementary. But this difference between them, I would insist, makes no practical difference. It is a difference that looms large only when we wish to relate them epistemologically.[41]

Let me illustrate with an example. Suppose, to take a reasonable case, we find that the development of some aspect of children's theory of mind is nicely correlated with their attendance at preschool—that attending preschool is correlated with the ability to distinguish between true and false belief. We say, interpretively, that it must have something to do with what school "means" to children. Is it: (a) Because school holds the child explicitly accountable for his own use of mind? (b) Because the child has more concentrated interaction with like-aged peers at school than at home? (c) Because the child must interact with relative strangers in school whose ways of behaving he cannot so easily predict, thus forcing him to work harder at figuring out what makes them tick mentally? or (d) Because school provides a standardized lexicon referring to the true and false beliefs that one encounters? Note that each of these hypotheses is designed to tame interpretation by forcing it into a propositional form characteristic of causal explanation. Given some ingenuity, we usually succeed at such taming. Cognitive science would be arid without such intervening interpretive assists, given that meaning making is so central a feature of cognition in the symbolic world of culture.

For all that, the two processes, interpretation and explanation, cannot be reduced to each other. Explanation does not exhaust interpretation, nor does interpretation exhaust explanation. Indeed, it is probably the tension between the two that keeps research on developing theories of mind from becoming a set of shallow experimental routines, or becoming as hermeneutic as, say, literary theory. Yes, interpretation does offer candidate products for "taming" by those in search of causes. And, yes, experimental findings that might yield insight into causes, like the discovery of the false belief divide, do provide food for the interpretivist's interpretations. But the two approaches are fundamentally different, and play different roles in the search for knowledge.

I don't believe that Astington and Olson disagree with this. Let me quote them:

> What needs to be explained is the beginning of children's efforts at interpretation of their own and others' talk and action. As we suggested, that interpretation should be seen by the psychologist as a cultural way of viewing, not just the functioning of a mental organ, [but the] patterns of persons acting in a world, indeed patterns of actions in which the child may already be a participant. Yet, as we also suggested, these patterns of social interaction ultimately have to be explained in terms of the sets of concepts available and by appeal to the processes involved in the child's acquisition, elaboration, and reorganization of concepts.[42]

I agree. But let's see what this means in actual practice.

Consider three characteristics of the interpretive view, all related to how we make sense of what young subjects say in response to our queries about their theories of mind. (1) In interpretation, all statements (including ones about other human beings and their minds) are taken to be relative to the perspective from which they are made. What we make of another's remarks will depend on whether we see her as a friend, a rival, or a stranger, which in turn depends on how those terms are used in our subcommunity. (2) What subjects say, moreover, depends upon how participants construe the relationship between the questioner and the answerer. Some children in our culture, for example, respond to out-of-the-blue, point-blank questions from adults as "teacher-like" and as a signal for an adult-like response, or, failing that, they fall back on their version of a "child response." Thus, what a child says about other minds, or about his own mind, is bound to be discourse-dependent. Nor is this truism limited to childhood. Geoffrey Lloyd[43] tells us that ancient Chinese mathematicians supposed that mathematical problems were resolved by rhetorical debate, whereas their classical Greek counterparts thought deduction governed—each conforming to the approved mode of discourse and theory of mind of their culture. (3) Finally, what one says about anything depends on the "situatedness of the discourse." *I object* means something quite different at the family dining table than in a court of law. To infer the mental state of another requires more than a theory of mind: it also requires a theory of culture. Lacking the guiding presuppositions required by speech acts, how could we understand what somebody has in mind when they say, "Would you be so kind as to pass the salt?"

Perspective, discourse, and context: surely nobody believes, and surely not Astington and Olson, that you can make sense of what people tell you about their beliefs concerning mind without taking this triad into account. But as I have said repeatedly, being interpretive does not imply being anti-empirical, anti-experimental, or even anti-quantitative.[44] It simply means that we must first make sense of what people tell us in light of the triad before we start explaining it. And even at that, our explanation will not exhaust the interpretive possibilities. The crux of the matter is that both processes are necessary. As I have tried to argue elsewhere,[45] the two are mutually enlightening, but not reducible to each other. Nonetheless, it seems that Astington and Olson would like it otherwise.

IV

Need there be only one way of knowing, one to which all others must be reduced? Since I think not, I should finally say how I think we manage to live with both interpretation and explanation. An example: the early appearance of mother–child joint visual attention can probably be explained causally, and probably there are even some psychobiological assists to the child's early sensitivity to somebody pointing. After that, as already remarked, treating the child as if you knew what was on his mind, and expecting him to know what was on yours, makes possible his progress toward developing a workable theory of mind.[46] There is probably some universal psychological readiness for this form of parent–child interaction. But how we go about showing that we are treating each other in this way will vary from culture to culture.[47] How further meanings are constructed within this important psychobiological format will depend mightily upon the interactive arenas of one's culture,[48] what Bourdieu calls "symbolic markets."[49] These are the settings in which the child comes to master culturally canonical usage, and they are greatly in need of study.[50]

Let me offer one last assurance to Astington. I am not a flat-out relativist just by virtue of granting an irreducible role to interpretation.[51] I have long since taken heed of Hilary Putnam's caution that absolute statements about *all* knowledge being relative to perspective are self-contradictory.[52] From my interpretivist perspective, reliance upon verifying context-free, causal propositions to achieve explanation simply indicates that a causal-explanatory perspective is in force. Nor am I grudging in my admission that such a perspective works brilliantly in helping us predict and control the inorganic physical world—and, indeed, certain aspects of the human world. But I do not believe that we will ever *explain causally* what William Blake meant in 1802, or what we now take him to have meant then, by his famous lines on the dubious universality of Newtonian science:

> May God us keep
> From single vision & Newton's sleep.[53]

6

▼

NARRATIVES OF SCIENCE

My remarks in this chapter take their inspiration from Robert Karplus, who was a key figure in the curriculum reform movement of
the late 1960s and 1970s. His ideas about how to teach science were
not only elegant but came from the heart. He knew what it felt like
"not to know," what it was like to be a beginner. As a matter of
temperament and principle, he knew that not knowing was the
chronic condition not only of a student but of a real scientist. That is
what made him a true teacher.

What he knew was that science is not something that exists out
there in nature, but that it is a tool in the mind of the
knower—teacher and student alike. Getting to know something is an
adventure in how to account for a great many things that you
encounter in as simple and elegant a way as possible. There are lots
of different ways of getting to that point, and you don't really ever
get there unless you do it, as a learner, on your own terms. All one
can do for a learner en route to her forming a view of her own is to
aid and abet her on her own voyage. The means for aiding and
abetting a learner is sometimes called a "curriculum," and what we

have learned is that there is no such thing as *the* curriculum. For in effect, a curriculum is like an animated conversation on a topic that can never be fully defined, although one can set limits upon it. I call it an "animated" conversation not only because it is always lively if it is honest, but also because one uses animation in the broader sense—props, pictures, texts, films, and even "demonstrations." So the process includes conversation plus show-and-tell plus brooding on it all on one's own.

Robert Karplus's film on the "reversibility" of physical phenomena was a wonderful example of a prop. Rather than answering a question, it opens one—the great meta-question of whether you can describe something in nature without specifying the frame of reference or position from which you view it. "Obvious" distinctions like up-down, right-left, moving-stationary suddenly become nonobvious—as they are in physics. Not only does the film make everybody think (which in itself is a glorious pedagogical outcome), but it also livens the conversation. Well, the two are not so very different: thinking comes very close to being an internal conversation, and conversation can't be much good unless in some degree you are thinking aloud in the midst of it. That is what these days has come to be called, after Bakhtin, the "dialogic imagination." I shall have more to say about it presently.

I'd like to take a moment, before getting into my main topic, to contrast the spirit of the "curriculum reform" movement in which Karplus was so deeply involved with the present wave of school reform—what for lack of a better expression I shall call "assessment reform," or perhaps I should call it "governors' reform."

I have no objection in principle to creating better measuring instruments in order to find out how well our students are doing in science, in mathematics, in literature, in reading. For that matter, I don't even object in principle to assessments of how well our teachers are doing their jobs. If you think that the poor performance of our educational establishment is due principally to a failure in teacher evaluation or in student assessment, then such a reform movement would be appropriate enough. Our state governors in solemn conclave proclaim that, by the turn of the century, we will "turn things around" and be tops in the world in science and mathematics. And just what is it that is to be turned around? Assessment procedures and "standards"? If only that, then we will succeed only in fueling our internal indignation about how little geography our students know, how badly they read, how sorely lacking they are in mathematical skills, how deficient they are in understanding what science is about. Surely, that is a curiously indirect route to improving matters, indirect in the sense that indignation just *might* conceivably lead us to do something further about how we conduct our schools and the process of education generally. It might even, conceivably, lead to a different message on public lips about financial support for schools and schooling. Schools are surely as important as the savings and loan industry that we proposed to "bail out" with a three hundred billion dollar handout. It might even lead us to question why, for example, we have made such an exclusive fetish of improving our record in science and mathematics rather than, say, concentrating our efforts as well on teaching our students about the politics and economics of the revolutionary world changes we are living through, or about why human nature risks its neck in the interest of freedom in Tiananmen Square in Beijing, or in East Berlin, in Prague, in Bucharest, in Vilnius. I am not against providing the nation with scientifically and mathematically literate workers so that we can outperform the Japanese or the new Europe in world markets—as if that aim alone could ever inspire either teachers or students. We forget at our peril that the great advances in Eastern Europe (and soon, we hope, in South Africa and in the Republic of China) were led not so much by mathematicians and scientists (although they were there too) but by playwrights, poets, philosophers, and even music teachers. What marks a Nelson Mandela or a Václav Havel is human wisdom and philosophical depth. And so it was too with Thomas Jefferson; his vision was possible because he stood on the philosophical shoulders of John Locke and the learned men of the French Enlightenment.

Of course we need standards and resources to make our schools work well in solving the myriad tasks they face. But resources and standards alone will not work. We need a surer sense of what to teach to whom and how to go about teaching it in such a way that it will make those taught more effective, less alienated, and better human beings. The nation's teachers have been struggling to carry out this daunting task and, under the circumstances, have been doing it with courage and skill against enormous odds. We in the universities and in scientific and cultural institutions have been giving them precious little help. I am not proud to admit that much of the most strident recent criticism has come from such self-appointed guardians of the culture as Alan Bloom, who longs bitterly for an imaginary past while immured in his ivory tower. Teachers and schools, let it be said, did not create the conditions that have made American education so difficult. They did not create an underclass. Nor could they have undermined the research and development mission of competitive American industry anywhere as effectively as the greedy takeover tycoons of the 1980s, fueled by junk bonds. Nor did they, like the money-churners and real-estate speculators, create the disgraceful condition of homelessness on one side and consumerism on the other, both now afflicting our economy and our sense of purpose. Nor the drug problem, which Washington now proposes to solve not by capping the flow of drugs into the country or by destroying our home-grown drug cartels but, ironically enough, by giving over the prevention task to the schools.

What we need is a school reform movement with a better sense of where we are going, with deeper convictions about what kind of people we want to be. Then we can mount the kind of community effort that can truly address the future of our educational process—an effort in which all of the resources of intellect and compassion that we can muster, whatever the price, are placed at the disposal of the schools. That is what Robert Karplus stood for in the domain of science—that human beings would be the richer for understanding the physical universe. He did his part by trying to help teachers do their task better. All the standards in the world will not, like a helping hand, achieve the goal of making our multicultural, our threatened society come alive again, not alive just as a competitor in the world's markets, but as a nation worth living in and living for.

II

Now let me turn to the main topic of this chapter—narrative as a mode of thinking, as a structure for organizing our knowledge, and as a vehicle in the process of education, particularly in science education. In order to do so, I must take a step back to consider some fundamentals.

A long time ago, I proposed the concept of a "spiral curriculum," the idea that in teaching a subject you begin with an "intuitive" account that is well within the reach of a student, and then circle back later to a more formal or highly structured account, until, with however many more recyclings are necessary, the learner has mastered the topic or subject in its full generative power. In fact, this was a notion that grew out of a more fundamental, more obvious view of epistemology. I had stated this more basic view in the form, almost, of a philosophical proverb, to the effect that "Any subject can be taught to any child at any age in some form that is honest." Another way of saying the same thing might be to say, "Readiness is not only born but made." The general proposition rests on the still deeper truth that any domain of knowledge can be constructed at varying levels of abstractness or complexity. That is to say, domains of knowledge are *made,* not *found:* they can be constructed simply or complexly, abstractly or concretely. And it can easily be demonstrated within certain interesting limits that a so-called "higher-level" way of characterizing a domain of knowledge encompasses, replaces, and renders more powerful and precise a "lower-level" characterization. For example, the intuitive statement "the further out a weight is from the fulcrum of a lever, the more force it will exert" is contained, as it were, in the more powerful and precise Archimedean rules about how levers operate. And Archimedes, in turn, is replaced and contained by the rules of levers as described by quadratic equations. The kid who understands the intuitive rule of the lever and applies it to the playground seesaw is well on his or her way to becoming Archimedean, just as Archimedes was on his way toward that Renaissance algebraist who recognized that expressions in the form $(x^2 + 4x + 4)$ could be equated to the multiplicative pair of the form $(x + 2)(x + 2)$. All of which could tell you some canny ways of placing weights on a beam so that they would balance. A ten-year-old once said to me, having discovered how all of this mathematical abstraction can guide one to making a beam balance, "This gadget knows all about algebra." I tried to dissuade him, to convince him that it was *he* who knew the algebra, not the balance beam. But I doubt whether I succeeded. That insight might come later up the curriculum spiral, perhaps in graduate school, or perhaps, with the luck of some good teaching, in the very next grade.

The research of the last three decades on the growth of reasoning in children has, in the main, confirmed the rightness of the spiral curriculum, although it has also provided us with some cautions. There are stages of development that constrain how fast and how far a child can leap ahead into abstraction. Piaget's views are always to be taken seriously in this regard, but they too must be regarded with caution. The child's mind does not move to higher levels of abstraction like the tide coming in. Development depends also, as Margaret Donaldson has so beautifully demonstrated,[1] upon the child's practical grasp of the context or situation in which he or she has to reason. A good intuitive, practical grasp of a domain at one stage of development leads to better, earlier, and deeper thinking in the next stage when the child meets challenging new problems in that domain. As a teacher, you do not wait for readiness to happen; you foster or "scaffold" it by deepening the child's powers at the stage where you find him or her now.[2]

I am fully aware that what I've been saying is old hat to working teachers. They have grasped all of this intuitively ever since Socrates in the *Meno* set forth the first version of the idea by illustrating how that slave boy could, starting from innocence, quickly grasp the main ideas of plane geometry. But it helps to push our understanding to another level. I still get a lot of mail from teachers; years back it used to average ten letters a week. Most of it was to cheer me on for going public with what every teacher already knew. But there was also a steady trickle of doubting Thomases who dared me to try to teach calculus or Mendeleev's periodic table in nursery school. Well, five-year-olds are delighted with the story of the tortoise and the hare. And you can go easily on from there to the joke-story that is embodied in Zeno's paradox—there's still halfway to go, wherever you are, so how do you ever get there. Invariably, given the superiority of intuition, young kids think Zeno's paradox is "silly." But it bothers them. Have you ever heard a six-year-old tell a friend about Zeno's paradox? He does it like a shaggy dog story (which it is, of course). And that now brings me to the heart of the matter—narrative.

Let me say a little about stories and narratives generally. For it is very likely the case that the most natural and the earliest way in which we organize our experience and our knowledge is in terms of the narrative form. And it may also be true that the beginnings, the transitions, and the full grasp of ideas in a spiral curriculum depend upon embodying those ideas into a story or narrative form. So what is a narrative? Fortunately, we are aided by a decade of lively research on this problem, and from a variety of sources—linguistics, literary theory, psychology, philosophy, even mathematics.

I'll begin with some obvious points. A narrative involves a sequence of events. The sequence carries the meaning: contrast "The stock market collapsed, the government resigned" with "The government resigned, the stock market collapsed." But not every sequence of events is worth recounting. Narrative is discourse, and the prime rule of discourse is that there be a reason for it that distinguishes it from silence. Narrative is justified or warranted by virtue of the sequence of events it recounts being a violation of canonicity: it tells about something unexpected, or something that one's auditor has reason to doubt. The "point" of the narrative is to resolve the unexpected, to settle the auditor's doubt, or in some manner to redress or explicate the "imbalance" that prompted the telling of the story in the first place. A story, then, has two sides to it: a sequence of events, and an implied evaluation of the events recounted.

What is particularly interesting about a story as a structure is the two-way street that it travels between its parts and the whole. The events recounted in a story take their meaning from the story as a whole. But the story as a whole is something that is constructed from its parts. This part/whole tail-chasing bears the formidable name "hermeneutic circle," and it is what causes stories to be subject to interpretation, not to explanation. You cannot explain a story; all you can do is give it variant interpretations. You can *explain* falling bodies by reference to a theory of gravity. But you can only *interpret* what might have happened to Sir Isaac Newton when the legendary apple fell on his head in the orchard. So we say that scientific theories or logical proofs are judged by means of verification or test—or more accurately, by their verifiability or testability—whereas stories are judged on the basis of their verisimilitude or "lifelikeness." Indeed, one of the reasons why it is so difficult to establish whether a story is "true" or not is precisely because there is a sense in which a story can be true *to* life without being true *of* life. For those who have concerned themselves with such arcane matters as the theory of meaning, this means that stories can make sense but have no reference. It is much harder to construct "fictional science," not to be confused with science fiction, simply because it is immediately caught up in issues of verifiability with respect to a specifiable possible world. And that, after all, is what *real* science is about.

Science uses as its apparatus of exposition such means as logic or mathematics to help it achieve consistency, explicitness, and testability. One of its favored weapons is the hypothesis which, if well formed, will be "frangible"—easily found to be false. However derivationally deep any scientific theory may be, its use should lead to the formulation of falsifiable hypotheses, as Karl Popper would say. But you can falsify an awful lot of hypotheses, historians of science make clear, without bringing down the theory from which they have been derived. Which has suggested to many in recent years that grand theories in science are perhaps more story-like than we had expected.

A few other points about stories are relevant here. Stories, notably, are about human agents rather than about the world of nature—unless the world of nature is conceived "animistically" as human-like. What marks human agents is that their acts are not produced by such physical "forces" as gravity, but by intentional states: desires, beliefs, knowledge, intentions, commitments. It is intrinsically difficult to "explain" exactly why it is that human agents, impelled by intentional states, do as they do or react to each other as they do—particularly in the unexpected or non-canonical situations that constitute stories. This reinforces the requirement of interpretation in understanding stories. As does one other thing: stories are the product of narrators, and narrators have points of view, even if a narrator claims to be an "eyewitness to the events." Now this is also the case where science is concerned, although the language of science, cloaked in the rhetoric of objectivity, makes every effort to conceal that view except when it is concerned with the "foundations" of its field. The famous "paradigm shifts" that occur during scientific revolutions reflect this cover-up situation, since they betray the fact that the so-called data of science are constructed observations that are designed with a point of view in mind. Light is neither corpuscular nor wavelike; waves and corpuscles are in the theory, in the mind of the theory makers and holders. The observations they devise are designed to determine how well nature fits these pieces of "fictional science."

It has been a curious habit of Western thought since the Greeks to assume that the world is rational and that true knowledge about that world will always take the form of logical or scientific propositions that will be amenable to explanation. It was thought until quite recently that theories, made up of such propositions, would be found to be true or false by virtue of whether they corresponded to that world. Nowadays we quite properly ask how it is that we can ever know what *the* world is actually like, save by the odd process of constructing theories and making observations once in a while to check how our theories are hanging together—not how the world is hanging together, but our theories. The more advanced a science becomes, the more dependent it becomes upon the speculative models it constructs, and the more "indirect" its measurements of the world become. My physicist friends are fond of the remark that physics is 95 percent speculation and 5 percent observation. And they are very attached to the expression "physical intuition" as something that "real" physicists have: they are not just tied to observation and measurement but know how to get around in the theory even without them.

Constructing "speculative models" at the highest levels of science is, of course, highly constrained by the mathematical languages in which advanced theories are formulated. They are formulated in that way, of course, so that we may be as explicit as possible. Through explicitness, logical contradictions can be avoided. But the mathematics has another function: a well-formed mathematics is also a carefully derived logical system, and it is the full derivational power of the mathematics that the scientist is out to exploit. After all, the object of a mathematicized theory in physics is not just description, but generativeness. So, for example, if the algebra of quadratic functions describes what might be happening in the domain of levers and balance beams, then the application of such *general* algebraic rules as the associative, distributive, and commutative laws should (with luck) lead to previously unimagined predictions about levers, fulcrums, balance beams, and so forth. When that happens, it is science heaven and a time for prizes.

But as every historian of science in the last hundred years has pointed out, scientists use all sorts of aids and intuitions and stories and metaphors to help them in the quest of getting their speculative model to fit "nature" (or getting "nature" to fit their model by redefining what counts as "nature"). They will use any metaphor or any suggestive figure or fable or foible that may luckily come to hand. Niels Bohr once confessed the story of how he had arrived at the idea of complementarity in physics—illustrated, for example, by the principle that you cannot specify both the position and the velocity of a particle simultaneously and therefore you cannot include both in the same set of equations. The general idea had first struck him as a moral dilemma. His son had stolen a trinket from the local notions shop, but some days later, stricken with guilt, he had confessed the theft to his father. As Bohr put it, although he was greatly touched by this moral act of contrition, he was also mindful of his son's wrongdoing: "But I was struck by the fact that I could not think of my son at the same moment both in the light of love and in the light of justice."[3] This led him to think that certain states of mind were like the two aspects of one of those trick Gestalt figure-ground pictures where you can see either the duck or the rabbit, the vase or the profiles, but not both at the same time. And then some days later, as if the idea were blossoming, it occurred to him that you could not consider the position of a particle as stationary in a particular position and at the same time as moving with a velocity in no particular position at all. The mathematics was easy to fix. It was grasping the right narrative that took the hard work.

To come directly to the point, let me propose that we characteristically convert our efforts at scientific understanding into the form of narratives or, say, "narrative heuristics." "We" includes both scientists and the pupils who inhabit the classrooms in which we teach. This would consist of turning the events we are exploring into narrative form, better to highlight what is canonical and expected in our way of looking at them, so that we could more easily discern what is "fishy" and off-base and what, therefore, needs to be explicated. Here are a couple of examples, one from the frontier, one from the classroom. A physics colleague lamented to me some years ago that what was wrong with contemporary physical theory was that it conceived of most events as entirely in the extremely short-term nanosecond range, which made no sense since the physical world went on forever. So, he asked, what kind of "story" could you tell about an enduring universe? I jokingly suggested to him that he should invent a kind of hypothetical physical glue, a substance that went on and on in time, call it, say, glueterium. "Brilliant, brilliant," he said, for reasons still unclear to me. Several years later he told me that the idea of glueterium had been a turning point in his thinking. My second example comes from a classroom discussion. The topic was "atomicity," the smallest thing of which other things might be made, which is as old a topic as you can get. The discussion grew lively when it reached the point where it got to "cutting up" matter into smaller and smaller pieces until, as one of the children put it, "they've got to be invisible." Why invisible? somebody asked. "Because the air is made of atoms"—which produced a general pause. A kid took advantage of the pause to ask, "Does everything have to be made of the same atoms?" "Well, so how could the same atoms make stones and water both?" "Let's have different kinds of atoms then—hard ones and soft ones and wet ones." "No, that's crazy: let's have them all the same, and they can make up into different shapes like Lego or something." "And what happens when you split an atom?" "Then the whole thing goes Boom!" Echoes of the early Greek philosophers: not Thales but Empedocles prevailed.

What happens when the discussion takes that turn? Well, to put it as bluntly as possible, the focus of attention shifts from an exclusive concern with "nature-as-out-there" to a concern with the *search* for nature—how we construct our model of nature. It is that shift that turns the discussion from dead science to live science *making*. And once we do that, we are able to invoke criteria like conceivability, verisimilitude, and the other criteria of good stories. Gerald Holton, the distinguished historian of science and a keen observer of the scientific *process,* comments that scientists from earliest times have relied on just such narrativizing to help them, using metaphors, myths, and fables along the way—snakes that swallow their own tails, how to lift the world, how to leave traces that can be followed back, and so on.

Let me put it in somewhat different language. The process of science making is narrative. It consists of spinning hypotheses about nature, testing them, correcting the hypotheses, and getting one's head straight. En route to producing testable hypotheses, we play with ideas, try to create anomalies, try to find neat puzzle forms that we can apply to intractable troubles so that they can be turned into soluble problems, figure out tricks for getting around morasses. The history of science, as James Bryant Conant tried to show us,[4] can be dramatically recounted as a set of almost heroic narratives in problem solving. His critics liked to point out that the case histories that he and his colleagues had prepared, while very interesting, were not science but the history of science. And I am not proposing that we should now substitute the history of science for science itself. What I *am* proposing, rather, is that our instruction in science from the start to the finish should be mindful of the lively processes of science making, rather than being an account only of "finished science" as represented in the textbook, in the handbook, and in the standard and often deadly "demonstration experiment."

I know perfectly well that good science teachers (and there are many, though there can never be enough of them) in fact do just what I have been proposing: place the emphasis on live science making rather than upon the achieved remains of, so to speak, already accomplished science. But in the spirit of Robert Karplus, I want to make a few suggestions about how we in the scientific community can help each other—rather than merely laying down the law about standards and about the linking of salaries to teacher qualifications. For I believe that there is what one might call a "soft technology" of good teaching that would be an enormous help in the classroom, a technology that would place the emphasis back on the process of science problem solving rather than upon finished science and "the answers." I'll conclude with a few examples and perhaps a principle or two.

The first suggestion might even qualify as one of those principles. It says: "The art of raising challenging questions is easily as important as the art of giving clear answers." And I would have to add, "The art of cultivating such questions, of keeping good questions alive, is as important as either of those." Good questions are ones that pose dilemmas, subvert obvious or canonical "truths," force incongruities upon our attention. In fact, much of the best support material produced by the science projects of the curriculum reform movement of the 1960s was of this order. Let me mention a couple of them, both of them produced by the Physical Science Study Committee. One was a "frictionless puck," a squat can of dried ice with a hole in its bottom, such that thawed carbon dioxide seeped through, causing the puck to float frictionlessly atop its cushion of gas on a pane of window glass. On that surface, under those conditions, bodies set in motion seemed virtually to stay in motion just as counterintuitively as required by Newtonian laws of motion. It is only a neat little hardware store trick, but it leads to endless questions about the "ideal conditions" required by general physical laws, how you figure out ideal conditions, what you might mean by such things as "perfect vacuums" and "frictionless planes," and so on. It gets a narrative conversation going in much the same way as Sir Alan Bullock got a conversation going a few years ago with the Queen of England on the occasion when she as Royal Patroness was to come to the annual dinner of the Tate Gallery. Sir Alan, as Chairman of the Board, was her host. He is a mighty historian and was then Vice Chancellor of the University of Oxford. Queen Elizabeth is notorious for her dislike of small talk, so Sir Alan decided he would find a question that would be deeply non-trivial while not being politically too controversial. He hit on the perfect one. "Ma'am," he asked, "when did the Royal Family decide to become respectable?" "Well," she said, "it was during Victoria's reign, when it was realized that the middle class had become central to Britain's prosperity and stability." And the conversation went on for the better part of an hour. Able historian that he was, Sir Alan had realized that the "Royal image" was a construction, a stipulation, an ideal condition for a theory of royalty. The moral of the story: always look an "ideal condition" in the mouth if you want to find out how the world works.

The other demonstration was a ceiling-hung pendulum with a large can of finely ground sand at its terminus, with a tiny hole in the middle of the can's bottom, and with wrapping paper spread on the floor beneath it. The notable thing about this gadget is that it leaves a trail of its movements—trajectory length, damping effects, Lissajous figures for its eccentric excursions, the lot. Now, the objective in making any scientific instrument (whether for research or teaching) is to enable the scientist/learner to observe or describe or measure events in nature that before were too small or weak, too big and ubiquitous, too fleeting or not fleeting enough, to observe or describe. I think the idea of the "tin can pendulum" had originally been hit upon by Frank Oppenheimer at the Exploratorium in San Francisco. It is perfect for exploring an otherwise inaccessible world of forces and symmetries: you can dream up and do experiments at the rate of a dozen an hour. I have seen a group of twelve-year-olds at a summer session in Cambridge learn more fundamentals in an afternoon through such experiments than many kids learn in a term from a standard text.

The recording pendulum has a lesson that goes with it, which runs something like this: "If one picture is worth a thousand words, then one well-wrought guess is worth a thousand pictures." A well-wrought guess, of course, is usually and rather grandly called "a hypothesis." What is important about a hypothesis (or a well-wrought guess) is that it derives from something you already know, something generic that allows you to go beyond what you already know. That "something generic" is what I used to call the "structure" of a subject, the knowledge that permitted you to go beyond the particulars you had already encountered. The structure is, so to speak, in the head. Being able to "go beyond the information" given to "figure things out" is one of the few untarnishable joys of life. One of the great triumphs of learning (and of teaching) is to get things organized in your head in a way that permits you to know more than you "ought" to. And this takes reflection, brooding about what it is that you know. The enemy of reflection is the breakneck pace—the thousand pictures.

In some deep sense, just as Mies van der Rohe said of architecture, we can say of learning, and in particular science learning, that "less is more." And that again has a narrative tang to it. The story is how you can get the most out of the least. And the denouement is learning to think with what you've already got hold of. I believe that this truism lies at the heart of every good curriculum, every good lesson plan, every learning-and-teaching encounter. So when it comes time for the bureaucrats to set their standards and to make up their tests for monitoring how we are doing, they ought to adopt this one as their primary standard. They will have to construct better tests than the ones we have now. And when the time has come again for us to help each other in devising or constructing curricula in science, I hope this ideal will shine over the effort.

7

▼

THE NARRATIVE CONSTRUAL
OF REALITY

What, in fact, is gained and what lost when human beings make sense of the world by telling stories about it—by using the narrative mode for construing reality? The usual answer to this question is a kind of doxology delivered in the name of "the scientific method": Thou shalt not indulge self-delusion, nor utter unverifiable propositions, nor commit contradiction, nor treat mere history as cause, and so on. Story, according to such commandments, is not the realistic stuff of science and is to be shunned or converted into testable propositions. If meaning making were always dedicated to achieving "scientific" understanding, such cautions might be sensible. But neither the empiricist's tested knowledge nor the rationalist's self-evident truths describe the ground on which ordinary people go about making sense of their experiences—say, what a "cool" greeting from a friend meant, or what the IRA meant by not using the word "permanent" in its 1994 cease-fire declaration. These are matters that need a story. And stories need an idea about human encounters, assumptions about whether protagonists understand each other, preconceptions about normative standards. Matters of this order are what enable us to get successfully from what somebody said to what he meant, from what *seems* the case to what "really" *is*. Although the scientific method is hardly irrelevant to all this, it is certainly not the only route to understanding the world.

Are narrative construals, then, just about particulars, idiosyncratic accounts fitted to the occasion? Or are there also some universals in the realities they construct? I want to argue in this chapter that there are indeed universals, and that these are essential to life in a culture. To make my point, I want now to sample nine such universals of narrative realities in order to address my opening question about what is gained and what lost by using such construals in forming a conception of "reality."

We might begin by asking why, rather suddenly, so many of us in psychology have become so interested in the narrative construction of reality. Was it the new postmodernism that finally provoked psychologists into rejecting stimulus-response linkages as the "causes" of behavior? Probably not. For the malaise that led to the new interest in the narrative construction of reality long predates the rise of anti-foundational, perspectivally oriented postmodernism. Sigmund Freud probably had more to do with it than Derrida or Foucault, if only by proposing a "psychic reality" that seemed more driven by dramatic necessities than by states of the objective world.[1] And the New Look, by particularizing our views about how the world is literally perceived to enhance personal meaning, had a comparable effect.[2] More recently, it was probably the rebellion against Piaget's generalized rationalism—that mental development consisted in logical leaps forward nurtured by general experience with the environment. Mental development turned out to be much more domain-specific than that: learning how a seesaw works, for example, does not by any means lead automatically to understanding what makes a balance beam work—though the two are governed by identical physical principles and are described by the same algebraic rule. So what's the problem?

Piaget's appeal to décalage—why principles did not always transfer from domain to domain—seemed to please nobody. The new mantra (following the discovery that domain specificity was the rule rather than the exception in logical development) was that the achievement of knowledge was always "situated," dependent upon materials, task, and how the learner understood things.[3] It was perhaps John Seeley-Brown and his colleagues who put the matter most succinctly when they proposed to speak of intelligence as not simply "in the head" but as "distributed" in the person's world—including the toolkit of reckoning devices and heuristics and accessible friends that the person could call upon.[4] Intelligence, in a word, reflects a micro-culture of praxis: the reference books one uses, the notes one habitually takes, the computer programs and databases one relies upon, and perhaps most important of all, the network of friends, colleagues, or mentors on whom one leans for feedback, help, advice, even just for company. Your chance of winning a Nobel Prize, interestingly, increases immeasurably if you have worked in a laboratory with somebody who has already won one, not just because of "stimulation" or "visibility," but because you have shared access to a richer distribution network.[5]

So it is probably as true of the sciences as of messy daily life that the construal of meaning is not from some Apollonian "view from nowhere."[6] The young child, even when engaged in understanding the world of nature, ought not really to be stereotyped as a "little scientist"[7] unless one leaves room for the narrative quirkiness of life in the worlds described in James Watson's *Double Helix,* in Richard Feynman's memoirs, or in Abraham Pais's masterful studies of Albert Einstein.[8] Indeed, if you make science classrooms more like the quirky worlds of working scientists—full of the humor of wild hypotheses, the exhilaration of unconventional procedures—the dividends in better performance are quickly evident.[9] Learning to be a scientist is not the same as "learning science": it is learning a culture, with all the attendant "non-rational" meaning making that goes with it.

In sketching out nine ways in which narrative construals give shape to the realities they create, I have found it impossible to distinguish sharply what is a narrative mode of *thought* and what is a narrative "text" or discourse. Each gives form to the other, just as thought becomes inextricable from the language that expresses it and eventually shapes it—Yeats's old dilemma of how to tell the dancer from the dance. As our experience of the natural world tends to imitate the categories of familiar science, so our experience of human affairs comes to take the form of the narratives we use in telling about them.[10]

▼

And now to the nine universals of narrative realities.

1. A structure of committed time. A narrative segments time not by clock or metronome, but by the unfolding of crucial events—at least into beginnings, middles, and ends. It is irreducibly aspectual in the grammarian's sense of that term. Narrative time, as Ricoeur has noted,[11] is "humanly relevant time" whose significance is given by the meanings assigned to events by either the protagonists in the narrative or the narrator in the telling—or by both.

Some close students of narrative, like William Labov, locate this inherent temporality of narrative in the meaning-preserving sequence of clauses that make up narrative *discourse* itself.[12] But while this is a useful linguistic point, it may obscure something deeper in the nature of narrative as a mode of thought. The temporal sequence of clauses certainly preserves meaning in a sequence like "The king died; The queen mourned." But there are other conventionalized ways of expressing personal durativeness other than strict clausal sequencing—like flashbacks and flashforwards, temporal synecdoche, and so on. As Nelson Goodman insists, there are many means for representing the sequence of human events in a narrative.[13] In narrative painting, for example, a beholder imposes sequential structure without the benefit of sequenced clauses; in the films of Robbe-Grillet, like *Last Year at Marienbad,* prolepsis and analepsis cunningly play with sequence while actually violating it. What underlies our grasp of narrative is a "mental model" of its aspectual durativity—time that is bounded not simply by clocks but by the humanly relevant actions that occur within its limits.

2. Generic particularity. Narratives deal with (or are "realized" in) particulars. But particularity seems only to be the vehicle of narrative realization. For particular stories are construed as falling into genres or types: bad-boy-woos-nice-girl, bully-gets-his-comeuppance, power-doth-corrupt, whatever. From Aristotle to today, thoughtful students of narrative and drama have puzzled over the chicken–egg question of whether genres "generate" particular stories, in the sense of leading us to construe sequences of events according to their generic prescription, or whether genres are mere afterthoughts that occur to tidy academic minds.

Two arguments predispose me to take genres as generative of their particulars. The first is the commonsensical one that certain stories just seem alike, versions of something more general, however particular they may be. Stories inevitably remind people of ones just like it. Are different versions of the bad–boy–nice–girl tale simply instances of a natural kind, much as Golden Delicious, Granny Smiths, and Cox's Pippins are versions of the natural kind *apple*? So what kinds of categories *are* genres?

The second argument addresses that problem. It is that the characters and episodes of stories take their meanings from, are "functions" of, more encompassing narrative structures. Stories as wholes and their constituent "functions" are, in this sense, tokens of more inclusive types. The bad–boy–woos–nice–girl script requires filler episodes, and a range of them will serve appropriately. The "tempting of the nice girl" can be accomplished by presenting her with a lavish gift, by telling her of your Rolls Royce, by referring to famous friends, and so on down the list. The lavish gift itself can be exotic orchids, a box at the opera, or even an endless golden thread. The particular of a narrative is achieved by its fulfilling a generic function. And it is by this "function filling" that narrative particulars can be varied or be "filled in" when omitted.

It is all well and good for Alastair Fowler to say that a "genre is much less a pigeonhole than a pigeon."[14] That may be the reaction of a literary theorist faced with carping critics in a typical boundary dispute about "types" of genre. For the rest of us, genres have an astonishing, almost preternatural "reality." But *where* is that reality? In what sense does it exist?

A genre is usually characterized as either a kind of *text* or as a way of construing a text. Mary McCarthy wrote short stories for magazines in several genres—mostly in what Northrop Frye called the genre of "irony."[15] She then organized the stories into a book, sequencing them according to the age of the female protagonist, presumably herself. Between the stories she added commentary about her own life, and published the lot as an autobiography entitled *Memories of a Catholic Girlhood*. Had she shifted genres? Thereafter (and doubtless to her dismay) readers almost invariably greeted each new story she published as a fresh installment of her autobiography rather than as fiction. But this is a risky game, for I know that reading a text as factual self-revelation is almost incommensurate with reading it as a fictional story.[16]

So what then *are* genres, and *where* are they? How do we reconcile their varied faces? On the one hand, a genre "exists" in a text—in its plot and its way of telling. On the other, it "exists" as a way of making sense of a text—as some sort of "representation" of the world. But are genres not also "in the world"? Are there not conflicts of loyalty, spirals of greed, corruptions of power? Well, not quite. For any story, any narrative reality can be "read" in various ways, converted into any genre: comedy, tragedy, romance, irony, autobiography, whatever.

It is not surprising then that what writers *write* and how they are *read* do not always go in parallel. Edna O'Brien shocked her Irish readers with her early novels. She wrote them in protest against women's plight; they read them as salacious explorations of infidelity. Today these novels are hailed even in the respectable Dublin press as reflecting a new and pioneering sensibility toward women caught in the grip of our changing times, and O'Brien's public readings are packed with the applauding daughters of mothers who were shocked in earlier times.[17] For narrative construal is deeply affected by cultural and historical circumstances. In that respect, Alastair Fowler is right about genre being more a pigeon than a pigeonhole. Or as Clifford Geertz puts it, genres get blurred.[18]

This is not to say that particular genres are written into the human genome or even that they represent cultural "universals." But the existence of genres *is* universal. No natural language that has been studied is without them: ways of conducting discourse, ways of construing the topics involved in the discourse, speech registers and even idiolects characteristic of the discourse, often a specialized lexicon as well.[19] We would not know how to begin construing a narrative were we not able to make an informed guess about the genre to which it belonged. Genres, I would conclude, are culturally specialized ways of both envisaging and communicating about the human condition.

Where does this leave the unrepentant realist who wants to cling to the view that genres—whether taken as construals or as modes of communicating—also reflect a "reality" in the world? Well, in a way his plight would have amused Borges and other "magic realist" writers. For the would-be realist becomes a comic victim of the literary designs of others, a dupe. But even at that, he is protected by a universal of culture. Even the most sophisticated cultures cannot resist the siren call of the genres they construct: "reality" by fiat or even by statute is made to imitate our literary genres. We people our world with characters out of narrative genres, make sense of events by assimilating them to the shape of comedy, tragedy, irony, romance.

3. Actions have reasons. What people do in narratives is never by chance, nor is it strictly determined by cause and effect; it is motivated by beliefs, desires, theories, values, or other "intentional states." Narrative actions imply intentional states. Experimental narrative sometimes depicts action in a way that ruptures this connection between action and the intentional states that are its background—a literary trick sometimes used, for example, by Michel Leiris.[20] But even "anti-narrative" fiction counts on the fact that the reader will recognize it as a departure from the expected, as off the track. When physical events play a role in a story, they do so as "setting"; they are interesting for the effects they have on the acts of protagonists, their intentional states, their moral circumstances (as when a storm at sea leads to the cowardice of Lord Jim when he deserts his pilgrim ship). As Baudelaire put it, "The first business of an artist is to substitute man for nature."

But intentional states in narrative never fully determine the course of action or the flow of events. Some element of freedom is always implied in narrative—some agency that can intrude on a presumed causal chain. Agency presupposes choice. Even when agency is reduced to near zero—as in Beckett's novels and plays or in the "anonymist" novel of Jules Romains, *The Death of a Nobody*—its effect is achieved by contrast to narrative expectancy. Perhaps it is the ever-present intrusive possibility of human choice that pits narrative against the notion of causality in the human domain. Intentional states do not "cause" things. For what causes something cannot be morally responsible for it: responsibility implies choice. The search in narrative is for the intentional states "behind" actions: narrative seeks reasons, not causes. Reasons can be judged, can be evaluated in the normative scheme of things.

4. Hermeneutic composition. What does it mean to say that the comprehension of narrative is hermeneutic? For one thing, it implies that no story has a single, unique construal. Its putative meanings are in principle multiple. There is neither a *rational* procedure to determine whether any particular "reading" is necessary as logical truths are necessary, nor an *empirical* method for verifying any particular reading. The object of hermeneutic analysis is to provide a convincing and non-contradictory account of what a story means, a reading in keeping with the particulars that constitute it. This creates the famous "hermeneutic circle"—trying to justify the "rightness" of one reading of a text not by reference to the observable world or the laws of necessary reason, but by reference to other alternative readings. As Charles Taylor puts it, "We are trying to establish a reading for the whole text, and for this we appeal to readings of its partial expressions; and yet because we are dealing with meaning, with making sense, where expressions only make sense or not in relation to others, the readings of partial expressions depend on those of others, and ultimately of the whole."[21]

Since the meanings of the parts of a story are "functions" of the story as a whole, and, at the same time, the story as a whole depends for its formation upon appropriate constituent parts, story interpretation seems irretrievably hermeneutic. A story's parts and its whole must, as it were, be made to live together. And when a story captures our interest, we cannot resist the temptation to make its parts do so. That is what creates narrative's hermeneutic compulsion.[22]

Some literary theorists and philosophers of mind argue that we resort to hermeneutic procedures only when a text or the world it depicts is "confused, incomplete, cloudy . . ."[23] We are certainly more aware of falling into the interpretive mode under these circumstances. But is it really the case that interpretive thinking is forced upon us by poor illumination? A certain kind of facile narrative even seduces us into thinking that it is simply about "the world as it is," with no interpretation needed. The famous Martian invasion "created" by Orson Welles's *War of the Worlds* simply channeled interpretation by a brilliant exploitation of ready-made hermeneutics.[24] The broadcast was a triumph in what Roland Barthes calls the "readerly text." "Readerly" texts work by triggering routinized, well-rehearsed narrative structures; "writerly" ones by provoking the hearer into creating ones of his own—the reader as coauthor.[25] Both are hermeneutic. Automatized interpretations of narratives are like "default settings" on a computer.

Another hermeneutic feature of narrativized reality is the itch it creates to know "why" a story is being told now under "these" circumstances by "this" narrator. Narratives are rarely taken as "unsponsored texts" cast our way by fate.[26] Even when the reader takes them in the most "readerly" way, he rarely renounces his right to question the narrator's motive for telling or his own privilege of interpreting what has been told in the light of it. Narrative construals of reality lead us to look for a "voice"—despite authorial efforts to seem objective and dispassionate, like the omniscient narrator.

Hilary Putnam has proposed two principles that bear on this point. The first, the Principle of Benefit of Doubt, "forbids us to assume that . . . experts are factually omniscient"; the second, the Principle of Reasonable Ignorance, forbids us from holding that "any speakers are philosophically omniscient (even unconsciously)."[27] We judge their accounts accordingly. Although Putnam is not speaking specifically about narrative construals of reality, his principles are particularly relevant. There must be more like them. For instance: "Every narrator has a point of view and we have an inalienable right to question it."

5. Implied canonicity. To be worth telling, a narrative must run counter to expectancy, must breach a canonical script or deviate from what Hayden White calls "legitimacy."[28] Breaches of the canonical are often as conventional as the scripts that they violate—tales of the betrayed wife, the cuckolded husband, the fleeced innocent, and so forth. They are the stuff of "readerly" narratives. The "narrative reality" of the world is either canonical or is seen as a deviation from some implied canonicity.

But convention and canonicity are prodigious sources of boredom. And boredom, like "necessity" in the proverb, is also a mother of invention. Some even argue that it is the effort to overcome boredom that creates the "literary impulse,"[29] that the function of literary language itself is to make the all-too-familiar strange again.

Given the safeguards of verification built into the logical–propositional mode of construing reality, it is the narrative mode that serves best in creating a sense of freshness and excitement. The innovative storyteller consequently becomes a powerful cultural figure provided his stories take off from conventional narrative canons and lead to our seeing what had never before been "noticed." The shift from Hesiod to Homer, the advent of "inner adventures" in Laurence Sterne's *Tristram Shandy,* the advent of Flaubert's perspectivalism, of Joyce's epiphanies of the ordinary, or of Beckett's psychic reductivism—any of these can serve as examples of the power of such narrative invention. Each in their way tempts a new genre into being: Flaubert begets Italo Calvino or Roger Barnes or Malcolm Bradbury or David Lodge; Joyce begets Beckett; and one can even see reflections of long-gone Sterne in the contemporary novels of Don DeLillo or John Updike and in the plays of John Guare. Eventually new genres become old banalities. And so goes the construal of history: ideologically motivated revisionisms are often tempting by dint of their sheer freshness. Whatever covert populist ideology may have motivated the *Annales* historians in France, their volumes on the history of everyday life are refreshing for their contrast to "kings-cabinets-and-treaties" histories from which they diverge. Without readers being complicit with writers, none of this would happen.

In effect, then, narrative reality links us to what is expected, what is legitimate, and what is customary. But there is a curious twist to this linkage. For the canonical linkage of narratively constructed realities risks creating boredom. So through language and literary invention, narrative seeks to hold its audience by "making the ordinary strange again."[30] And so, while the creator of narrative realities links us to received conventions, he gains extraordinary cultural power by making us consider afresh what before we took for granted. And our way of construing narrative realities—our openness to hermeneutic skepticism—makes us all the more ready to go along with the storyteller's fresh version.

6. Ambiguity of reference. What a narrative is "about" is always open to some question, however much we may "check" its facts. For its facts, after all, are functions of the story. Narrative realism, whether "factual" as in journalism or "fictional," is a matter of literary convention. Narrative creates or constitutes its reference, the "reality" to which it points, so that it becomes ambiguous in a way that the philosopher's reference does not. The atomic "single definite referring expression" is thwarted by the necessarily "functional," Proppian way in which narrative manages reference.

This anomalous state of things led Roman Jakobson to distinguish two "axes" of language—a horizontal and a vertical. The vertical axis is illustrated by placement of a word in a top-down/bottom-up hierarchy: country–city–neighborhood–block–address, England–London–Bloomsbury–Such Street–27b Such Street. The horizontal Jakobson axis is given by the place of a word and by its role in a sentence. So, knife–fork–plate–glass–claret–conversation form a horizontal axis constructed around an utterance dealing with a dinner party. One could say, then, that the horizontal axis is a somewhat meandering line through a conventional scenario, in the way that "board" becomes an element in one scenario that fits with "carpenter" and, in another, with "corporation."

Every time one refers to something in the context of a sentence, its reference becomes "horizontally" ambiguous. And that is probably why a dictionary is not of much help in deciding whether "board" is a piece of timber or a level of corporate authority. All of this anomaly is what makes some of us uneasy at Frege's easy distinction between "reference" and "sense" as the two aspects of meaning when applied to narrative.[31] For narrative construals marinate "reference" in "sense" to the point where the former becomes only a way through which the latter expresses itself: Moby Dick is a whale and the book by that name is a tale about hunting for him. So why is he a *white* whale? Melville confided to Hawthorne that the book's secret was that Moby Dick "stood for" stifling "white" Christianity; thus the hunter-whaler "Pequod" was manned by a heathen crew.[32] So what is *Moby Dick* about?

Is this only the case for "fiction"? Surely not. Consider the handling of news stories. Particularly when they are complex as, for example, most public scandals are, they eventually get converted into a canonical form. But usually not until the "facts" have been marinated to fit it—however extended the process may be. Why did the Prime Minister of Ireland, when he was Minister of Trade and Industry, suddenly change his mind about providing publically financed insurance to cover beef shipments sent to Iraq by one Mr. Larry Goodman, a very rich and very suspect business operator? How could Albert Reynolds, the Prime Minister in question, have spent public money in that way when "everybody in the know" knew that the beef in question was not even of Irish origin but from other countries in the European Union? So over the next year, the story grows more and more contingent, more hemmed around by circumstances, less linked to canonical patterns familiar to the ordinary consumer of stories—the voter. Indignant boredom sets in: "What is this all about?" people begin to ask. Not even a special "Beef Tribunal," chaired by a highly respected Justice of the Irish Supreme Court, seemed able to give narrative shape to the scandal. The Prime Minister announces to the press that he has been "completely exonerated" by the Tribunal's ambiguous report. The Opposition objects. Narrative chaos reigns.

But narrative reality claims the last word. A few days later, the Irish papers run a story listing the fees paid to solicitors retained by the Beef

Tribunal to conduct its investigation. They were very high, even as lawyers' fees go. The smell of corruption and cover-up becomes unbearable. A narrative structure emerges. Never mind that it is an oversimplified version of betrayed trust in high places. By now, a truly "postmodern" condition prevails. Within months, Ireland has a new Prime Minister, though no clear version, at least no official version, of the "real" facts was ever given. It was not so much the facts that brought the old Prime Minister down. Given the set of circumstances and the legal fees, this *had* to be a tale of corruption in high places. Narrative necessity required it. Now we can await the turn of the historian. Was the Prime Minister "really" a dupe, a fool, or a knave? This is how it is in the complex world of narrative realities.

7. *The centrality of trouble.* Stories pivot on breached norms. That much is already clear. That places "trouble" at the hub of narrative realities. Stories worth telling and worth construing are typically born in trouble.

Recall Kenneth Burke's celebrated account of the dramatic "pentad," which consists of an Agent, Action, Scene, Goal, and Instrument. An imbalance in the conventional "ratio" between any of these leads to the Trouble that is the "engine" of the narrative. Nora in *A Doll's House,* for example, is a rebellious Agent in an inappropriately bourgeois Scene. But Burke's pentad now seems epistemically thin in this age of skepticism. He emphasizes plight, *fabula,* as if it were given. His dramatism is morally and ontologically concerned with a cultural world whose arrangements are settled: they "exist." But his *Grammar of Motives* is a product of the 1920s.

For in the last half of our century, dramatism has become epistemic, gripped not just by "what happens" but by the puzzle of how in a turbulent world we come to know or to construct our realities. "Troubles" now inhere not only in a mismatch between a protagonist and her setting, but also in a protagonist's internal struggle in construing that setting at all. Flaubert's early and "revolutionary" perspectivalism gradually becomes more explicit in Julian Barnes's *Flaubert's Parrot;* Italo Calvino makes interpretation itself the "trouble" in his *If on a winter's night a traveler.* In another genre, Michel Foucault writes of the construction of history and of "the archaeology of knowledge," or Eric Hobsbawm of the "invention" of traditions. A Broadway play from the early 1990s is about a young black man who exploits the "correctness" of a well-placed and sophisticated New York couple by impersonating a college friend of their son's and builds a "scam" around it. Whereupon the playwright, John Guare, is sued by a young black man who alleges the play was slanderously based on a "real-life" episode reported in the press in which he was involved. "Cover-up" becomes an emblematic concept; "smoke and mirrors" a popular metaphor. The "inward turn" of the novel becomes an inward turn on life itself.

The shape of narrative trouble is not historically or culturally "once for all." It expresses a time and circumstance. So the "same" stories change and their construals change in sympathy, but always with a residue of what prevailed before. One "consolation of narrative" may be its very sensitivity to changing norms. If its archetypal sameness consoles, then the other side of the coin may be its chimerical quality.

8. *Inherent negotiability.* Coleridge's dictum that we suspend disbelief in listening to a story was intended for fiction. But it carries over into "real life" as well. We accept a certain essential contestability of stories. It is what makes narrative so viable in cultural negotiation. You tell your version, I tell mine, and only rarely do we need litigation to settle the difference. We easily take competing story versions with a perspectival grain of salt, much more so than arguments or proofs. Judy Dunn's remarkable book on the growth of social understanding in children makes plain that narrative negotiation starts early and is ubiquitous.[33] It may be this readiness to consider multiple narrative construals that provides the flexibility needed for the coherence of cultural life.

9. *The historical extensibility of narrative.* Life is not just one self-sufficient story after another, each narratively on its own bottom. Plot, characters, and setting all seem to continue to expand. We attempt to stabilize our worlds with an enduring pantheon of gods who continue to act in character, though circumstances change. We construct a "life" by creating an identity-conserving Self who wakes up the next

day still mostly the same. We seem to be geniuses at the "continued story." Ronald Dworkin proposes that precedents in law are like continued stories.[34] We impose coherence on the past, turn it into history.

So how do we cobble our narratives together to assure their unlimited continuity? And how much continuity *do* we require? Such continuity is no problem for the hard sciences. They fall back on "universal principles": the law of gravity is forever, so long as there is mass and space. But "history" is full of quirky particulars that follow each other and are seen to follow *from* each other.

Why is historical causality so irresistible? Take a classic example. Pope Leo III crowns Charlemagne Holy Roman Emperor at the Vatican on Christmas day in 800 in the presence of the great and powerful of what was then Europe. Inevitably, some think of it as a first step on the way toward the European Union a millennium later. It is astonishingly easy for us to move forward or backward in time from that long-ago Christmas day—backward to Pope Leo's concern with the steady Muslim advance and with the Vatican's need to cultivate allies to stem it; forward to the Thirty Years' War and the Treaty of Westphalia that ended it. Never mind the vast literature on the dangers of historicism. Even the well versed can't resist the temptation.

One thing that makes this expansibility of history (and autobiography) possible is the conception we seem to have about "turning points," pivotal events in time when the "new" replaces the "old." I want to explore this a little now, for I think "turning points" are a crucial ingredient in this feature of narrative reality.

Hayden White helps us here.[35] Following the French *Annales* historians, he distinguishes historical *annales, chroniques,* and *histoires.* An *annale* is made up of selected events roughly fixed in date, as say, in the *Annals of St. Gall:*

709 Hard winter. Duke Gottfried died.
710 Hard year, deficient in crops.
712 Floods everywhere.
714 Pippin, Mayor of the Palace, dies.

718 Charles devastated the Saxons.
721 Theudo drove Saracens from Aquitaine.
725 Saracens came for the first time.
731 Blessed Bede, the presbyter, died.
732 Charles fought the Saracens at Poitiers.

The list is constructed of "happenings," the rest of the time being when "nothing happened." So the annalist's selected events are themselves little turning points in history—candidate turning points in an implicit history. Pippin's death earns a place in the St. Gall annals: strong men matter in palace politics. The St. Gall annalist, like his colleagues since, is a trouble collector, always sensitive to Labov's "precipitating events." They may upset the narrative apple cart, create the conditions for the overthrow of a legitimate state of things.

Hence the *chronique:* its function is to explore such possibilities. *Chroniques* accrue event-sized narratives into life-size ones. They would make it clearer why Pippin mattered, perhaps by dealing with the narrative of a reign. A good example is the delegitimizing of European power by Napoleon, with the Congress of Vienna as a restoration of legitimacy. In the telling of that *chronique,* the "restoration of legitimacy" theme is even helped by such details as Count Rosomovsky being the Russian ambassador to the Congress—the patron of Beethoven's "deathless" middle quartets! They too were turning points.

The trouble with extended *histoires* is that it is hard to fit them to the human shape of narrative. *Histoires* are supposed to give coherence and continuity to *chroniques.* But that involves many difficulties. For *histoires* go beyond lifetimes, beyond the reach of the usual protagonists struggling their way out of Trouble. How to narrativize a dynasty? Or Marx's transition from feudalism to capitalism to socialism? It is not surprising that history in the large moves toward sociology. And by the same token, philosophers of history regularly propose that history be treated as a science governed by "covering laws," again rather like sociology,[36] only to be rejected by fellow historians who insist that the leap from *chronique* to *histoire* is not to be confused with getting over the chasm between the humanities and the sciences, between interpretation and explanation.[37]

This is no matter to be settled here. Clio, the Muse of Poetry, remains the Muse of History, though her reign may be threatened. The point I would make, rather, is that we seem inevitably to convert impersonal, non-narrative *histoires* into more narrative guises. That is why I began the discussion with Pope Leo III crowning Charlemagne Holy Roman Emperor in the Great Hall of the Vatican on Christmas Day in the year 800 in the presence of a company of nobles such as was rarely seen in the Europe of that day, a "Europe" that surely did not exist in the minds of any in attendance at that glittering event. And having then recounted that Pope Leo's act might have been motivated by the "Saracens'" advance into Europe (the annalist of St. Gall also makes mention of them being "turned back" at Poitiers), and having thus evoked the idea of "alliance," it becomes almost impossible to resist a search for some narrative protagonist who "carries" that "idea" forward—perhaps Napoleon, caught in the romantic notion that the best allies are those you have conquered, or the fine gentlemen of the Congress of Vienna promulgating a gentlemanly notion of "balance of power."

The accrual of history is an extraordinary narrative enterprise, shot through with alien elements not easily tamed into Proppian "functions." It seems to be dedicated to finding some intermediate ground where large-scale, almost incomprehensible forces can be made to act through the medium of human beings playing out a continued story over time.

W. T. Stace proposed two philosophical generations ago that the only recourse we have against solipsism (the unassailable view that we cannot prove the existence of a real world, since all we can know is our own experience) is that human minds are alike and, more important, that they "work in common."[38] One of the principal ways in which we work "mentally" in common, I would argue, is by the joint narrative accrual of history. For history, in some modest and domesticated way, is the canonical setting for individual autobiography. It is our sense of belonging to this canonical past that allows us to frame our self-accounts as, somehow, impelled by deviation from what was expected of us, while still maintaining complicity with the canon. Stace's concern with solipsism seems terribly old-fashioned two generations later. We would more likely be concerned today with whether the accrual of narrative into history leaves us dominated or alienated or locked in an embrace with those who wrote histories in the past. But whatever the contemporary version, it is still plain that the expansibility of narrative into history poses a special problem in understanding narrative realities.

▼

The "narrative construal of reality," the topic of this chapter, is surprisingly difficult to dissect—difficult in a rather unique way. Narrativized realities, I suspect, are too ubiquitous, their construction too habitual or automatic to be accessible to easy inspection. We live in a sea of stories, and like the fish who (according to the proverb) will be the last to discover water, we have our own difficulties grasping what it is like to swim in stories. It is not that we lack competence in creating our narrative accounts of reality—far from it. We are, if anything, too expert. Our problem, rather, is achieving consciousness of what we so easily do automatically, the ancient problem of *prise de conscience*.[39]

The three classic antidotes for this peculiar kind of unconsciousness of the automatic, of the ubiquitous, are *contrast, confrontation,* and *metacognition*. Listening to two contrastive but equally reasonable accounts of the "same" event is a homely example of the first. It leads us to examine how two observers could "see" the same things happening and come away with such different stories of what went on. It wakes us up. Novelists, playwrights, and filmmakers classically use this device to "raise the consciousness" of their readers and viewers—from Sophocles' *Oedipus Tyrannus* to Thomas Mann's *Felix Krull*. And there have been more than a few analyses of the textual devices that writers use to achieve this "waking up by contrast," among the most recent and brilliant of which is Michael Riffaterre's short volume on "fictional reality."[40]

Confrontation is a strong but risky medicine for unawareness. Its active ingredient is thwarted expectation, finding that your narrative version of reality clashes with what subsequently transpires or with the reality claims of others. Confrontation may eventually require adjudication of conflicting narratives, as in the adversary process embedded in virtually all advanced legal systems, but it is so fraught with the perils of conflict that it requires a threat of coercion to be useful. Indeed, confrontation is more likely to arouse anger and resentment than to raise consciousness. Even so, there are privileged forms of confrontation—in intimate friendship as well as in psychoanalysis—where *prise de conscience* is the objective of the whole exercise.

Which brings us to metacognition. In this form of mental activity, the object of thought is thought itself. But metacognition can also be directed at the language codes in terms of which thoughts are organized and expressed—as in the Riffaterre volume just mentioned, or as in Roman Jakobson's discussion of the metalinguistic function of language itself.[41] Metacognition converts ontological arguments about the nature of reality into epistemological ones about how we know. While contrast and confrontation may raise consciousness about the relativity of knowing, the object of metacognition is to create alternate ways of conceiving of reality making. Metacognition, in this sense, provides a reasoned base for the interpersonal negotiation of meanings, a way to achieve mutual understanding even when negotiation fails to bring consensus.

But it is usually the case that discussions of narrative reality lead not to reflections on the negotiation of meaning within the human community, but to the indignant rejection of "stories" as sources of human illusion. Stories, for all that they require verisimilitude, cannot produce the Truth. Truth-finding is the prerogative of science and logic alone—the paradigmatic mode of knowing.[42] No sensible human being would deny that the methods of science have vastly increased man's power of predicting and controlling his environment, particularly his physical environment. But need the once prevalent "anti-illusionism"[43] of science still beset us, still lead us to reject all forms of narrative reality as "just stories"? We are finally in a time when the intolerant puritanism of "scientific method" is recognized as no less ideologically narrowing than the religious dogmas that it set out to destroy.

So the conclusion to this chapter takes a surprising turn—though it has been voiced earlier and will recur later. We devote an enormous amount of pedagogical effort to teaching the methods of science and rational thought: what is involved in verification, what constitutes contradiction, how to convert mere utterances into testable propositions, and on down the list. For these are the "methods" for creating a "reality according to science." Yet we live most of our lives in a world constructed according to the rules and devices of narrative. Surely education could provide richer opportunities than it does for creating the metacognitive sensitivity needed for coping with the world of narrative reality and its competing claims. Is it so bizarre, given what we now know about human thought, to propose that no history be taught without historiography, no literature without literary theory, no poetry without poetics? Or that we turn our consciousness to what narrative construal imposes on the world of reality that it creates? This chapter has been a small effort in that direction.

8

▼

KNOWING AS DOING

The point of departure for the ideas in this chapter was a conversation I had in 1983 with Sylvia Scribner about "the psychology of work." At the time, I recall, I was having trouble understanding the general line of reasoning she was pursuing. I had always taken "the psychology of work" to refer to problems of fatigue, absenteeism, and job satisfaction. But Scribner's account didn't fit my stereotype: she was describing how one figured out how dairy workers went about delivering milk and other products to stores and restaurants around Manhattan. The requirements of their jobs, she was trying to tell me, were shaping their problem solving, how they thought, and especially how they formulated problems. She saw this work as an extension of Vygotskian cognitive psychology.

I did not see her point at all. It seemed to me that either she had just rediscovered "the division of labor" à la Durkheim, or was reinventing the old French idea of *la déformation professionelle,* the curious way in which one's work shapes the psychic reality one called "the world." But she maintained that what she was driving at was quite different from either of those matters, though she took both of them as givens that were preliminaries to her own work. I still could not see why anybody would be interested in how milkmen figured out the right number of bottles of milk and cream and yogurt they needed for their deliveries.

In the months following I thought about our conversation a lot, and in the end the thinking did me some good. Sylvia Scribner may even have succeeded in forcing me to discover yet again that what seems most obvious psychologically may obscure some of life's most important secrets. And the secret, of course, is that mind is an extension of the hands and tools that you use and of the jobs to which you apply them.

As it turns out, that conversation was a frontal exposure to a very central issue in understanding how a culture provides a rebus (in the classical sense) for cognitive activity and cognitive growth. *Rebus* in its classical sense derives from the Latin *res,* and it denotes how *things* rather than words can control what we do. Our learned ancestors surely understood the expression *non verbis sed rebus,* explaining in things not words, understanding by doing something other than just talking. Or as the great Ella Fitzgerald put it in a jazzier way, "When you're talking about it, you ain't doing it." And much of what is involved in being a member of a culture is doing what the "things" around you require—tending the garden, paying the bills, repairing the downspout. Frequently, indeed, we know how to do those things long before we can explain conceptually what we are doing or normatively why we should be doing them. That's what Sylvia Scribner was trying to explain that day in 1983, only I was not grasping what she was trying to get across to me. So I want to begin this discussion by considering how work or activity or, more generally, *praxis* provides a prototype of culture.

At the beginning of Vygotsky's *Thought and Language* is an epigraph taken from Francis Bacon: *Nec manus, nisi intellectus, sibi permissus, multam valent; instrumentis et auxilibus res perficitur.*[1] When I had the privilege of writing an introduction to Vygotsky's penetrating book in 1962, I managed almost completely to intellectualize the meaning of Bacon's motto and Vygotsky's intention in using it as an epigraph.

What Bacon says, to give a rough translation, is: "Neither hand nor intellect by themselves serve you much; tools and aids perfect (or complete) things." I naturally took this to mean that tools and aids serve the same kind of function in shaping the famous "stream of thought" that words do. But I was reckoning without the rebus. I think Vygotsky (and probably Bacon) had a quite different message in mind. Those instruments and aids that complete things are by no means serving the same role in shaping mind as the lexicon and grammar that shape our thoughts. They were referring to the instruments and aids by which, in the first instance, we *define* our work, even before we complete it. Let me give some primitive examples.

The oar and oarlock invent the rower; the catenary sail creates the up-wind sailor; the spirit level begets the horizontal measurer. At a more superordinate level, the assembly line gives birth to affordable automobiles; the law of torts brings into being phenomena like "attractive nuisances" and "willful negligence." The theory of rowing or the aerodynamics of the fore-and-aft sail are still poorly understood. And try to explain to a New York cab driver what is meant by negligence deemed in law to be willful. So, not surprisingly, there was a rebus for building the pyramids a millennium before there was a theory of mechanics. What Francis Bacon and Lev Vygotsky were trying to say is that *praxis* most typically precedes *nomos* in human history (and, I would add, in human development). Skill, to put it another way, is not a "theory" informing action. Skill is a way of dealing with things, not a derivation from theory. Doubtless, skill can be improved with the aid of theory, as when we learn about the inside and outside edges of our skis, but our skiing doesn't improve until we get that knowledge back into the skill of skiing. Knowledge helps only when it descends into habits.

Now all of this so far seems, if not quite trivial, at least rather low-level. Our model of skill is one that is managed fairly far downstream in the course of information processing. We say, indeed, that skill is "habitual," to use another word that reeks of familiarity but really deserves to glow with mystery. Or we locate it in the brainstem or even put it in the ventral roots of the spinal cord. But there are two crucial reasons for taking a critical look at this demeaning view, reasons which I shall call *conventionalization* and *distribution*. Both of them implicate culture massively, so much so, indeed, that each is specified normatively in the law, a matter to which I shall return presently.

Conventionalization refers to the fact that our ways of doing things skillfully reflect implicit forms of affiliating with a culture that often go beyond what we "know" in an explicit form. And these forms of affiliation provide deep sources of uniform cultural reciprocity without which a culture would soon be cast adrift. Let me give a rather subtle example that takes us beyond such conventions as "driving on the right." It is not enough that we greet others; we must also use a common and complementary set of specifications for doing so. One day I went walking with an Italian friend in the Alpine foothills above the village where she has spent her summers since childhood, and I noted that when we met others on the paths up in the hills, she greeted them with a ritual nod and wave, men and strangers included. I followed suit, of course. When we came back down and were near the village again, I continued in the same vein. "No, no," she said, "not when we're already on the outskirts." She was hard put to explain this when pressed. Then finally (as if in a burst of insight) she said: "Well you see, of course, it must be that a stranger has a different significance in the hills than in the village—like he might attack you up there so you want to be sure you express good will." "Hmm," she continued, "I'd never thought about it before. Interesting, eh?"

Interesting indeed. An entirely cultural distinction between "safe at home" and "in danger away" was written into a mere greeting ritual. And a clever woman with advanced degrees in both art history and psychology had "never thought about it before." So I told her about what in New York we call "street smarts." It is what most New Yorkers have as a working substitute for "urban sociology," and what has led such thoughtful students of the human condition as Harold Garfinkel, Pierre Bourdieu, and Erving Goffman to brood about culture as implicit praxis and not only as conscious awareness of rule structures and the like.[2] And when we were driving back to Milan from the hills the next day, I tried to explain the point to my friend's husband, who is a distinguished architect. He laughed and said, "But that's what a good part of your practice as an architect is all about, doing something and then trying to figure out why you thought it necessary." I'll come back to this point about praxis in a moment, but let me say first what I mean by *distribution*.

There has been much discussion of this topic in recent years, following the now classic paper by Seeley Brown and colleagues on distributed intelligence.[3] The gist of the idea is that it is a grave error to locate intelligence in a single head. It exists as well not only in your particular environment of books, dictionaries, and notes, but also in the heads and habits of the friends with whom you interact, even in what socially you have come to take as given. In the previous chapter I mentioned Harriet Zuckerman's finding that your chances of winning a Nobel Prize increase enormously just by virtue of the fact that you have worked in the laboratory of somebody who has already won one. And this is obviously not just because the association gives you some "pull" or makes you more visible. It has to do also with your having entered a community in whose extended intelligence you share. It is that subtle "sharing" that constitutes distributed intelligence. By entering such a community, you have entered not only upon a set of conventions of praxis but upon a way of exercising intelligence.

But do not think that this rule holds only for the exalted domain of Nobel laureates. It prevailed in the same way in the hills above and at the edges of the little village in Italy where we were walking that day—not just for me and my friend, but all those who were complicit in acting as we did. Not only did we share conventions, but the sharing embedded us in a world of practice that went beyond each individual, practice whose very operation depends upon being distributed communally. I think of these practices as connected sets of rebuses—things to be looked after; I'll return to this point later in discussing the more extended idea of an "oeuvre," a concept mentioned in the opening chapter.

II

I want now to look briefly at an old, almost classical issue in cognitive psychology, for it will help me return more systematically to the discussion of cultural psychology as practice. It is the issue of representation. Some years ago, several of us at the Center for Cognitive Studies at Harvard brought out a book entitled *Studies in Cognitive Growth*.[4] It argued, in a rather oversimplified way, that there were three ways in which humans represented the world or, better, three ways of capturing those invariances in experience and action that we call "reality." One was by enaction; a second through imagery; and a third through constructing symbolic systems. You represented the world in action routines, in pictures, or in symbols, and the more mature you became, the more likely you were to favor the after end of the progression than the starting end. At the time we thought that the course from enactive through iconic to symbolic representation was a progression, although I no longer think so. But I do still find it useful to make a threefold distinction in modes of representation, although not on developmental grounds.

The first mode, the enactive, is crucial in guiding activity, and particularly what we call skilled activity. More generally, it is this mode that imposes means–end or instrumental structures on the world. If I had to rename it now I would call it the *procedural* mode. It was this procedural feature, I think, that led Sir Frederic Bartlett in his last book, *Thinking*,[5] to see "thinking" (conceived principally as problem solving) as very closely related to skill, *motor* skill at that, noting that they shared such common features as preparatory phase, point of no return, and so on. But mental problem solving is not what I meant by enactive representation, even granting that problem solving resembles complex motor skills. "Work" or directed activity is involved. It provides the needed rebus.

I'll say only a brief word about iconic representation, one that may prove useful in a moment. I confess I missed some of its significance the first time around. And it was Eleanor Rosch who first awoke me to my oversights.[6] For images not only capture the particularity of events and objects, they give birth to and serve as prototypes for *classes* of events, and then provide benchmarks against which to compare candidate instances for membership in those classes. And so, very early on, before thought ever becomes operational in the Geneva sense, our power to render the world in terms of typical images and similarities provides us a kind of preconceptual structure by which we can operate in the world.

Surely nothing more needs saying about the third mode, symbolic representation of the world—not that we have achieved full understanding, but only that it is somewhat overcooked compared with the other parts of the meal before us. So I'll return to my earlier concern with action, procedure, and cultural psychology.

I will draw my examples from the law, for I am much involved in research on jurisprudence these days and I have found interesting ways of reopening classic psychological issues by reference to classical issues in the law. The first thing that anybody learns from observing a law school or law courts or lawyers is that they live in the heart of Procedure Land. Writs need to be filed, and they must take a certain form; briefs must register complaints (which must also be of a standard form) and responses to the complaints must similarly be filed; depositions must be taken under a certain kind of oath; and so forth. If the case is litigated, pleading follows an adversary process and Uniform Rules of Evidence prevail. And so on and so on. The procedures are sometimes in plain violation of prevailing good sense, like the rule proclaiming that matters of fact and points of law are totally independent of each other, a view that few physicists or philosophers have believed for a century. Nonetheless (and again procedurally), juries deal with the former, judges with the latter, and appellate courts do not concern themselves altogether with factual issues.

The great student of jurisprudence Robert Cover has argued that law arose in the first instance not (as early legal realists would have us believe) as a canny way of substituting cool procedures for the hot acts of revenge that might otherwise have been committed by the kin of the injured party, but rather as an extension of joint action.[7] Hebrew law, in its jurisgenic phase, was an extension of the action of groups that worshipped together, shared a common God and community, and felt connected by bonds of family. Such a system of jurisgenic law did not require abstract concepts like justice and rights. It required little more than practice—as in the hills around the Italian village where I walked. Abstract concepts were developed, Cover argues, only after the destruction of the first Temple and with the beginning of the first Diaspora that followed it. In that phase, the community having been scattered, the collective representation that was law had to be transformed from a way of living into a code defining justice, fairness, and rights. Skilled doing was transformed into more abstract knowing.

But even after that, law never fully abandoned its old links to action. In spite of its formalization into rules and procedures, the law hangs on to one crucial talisman of its origin in conventional action and its distribution. In Anglo-Saxon law we call that talisman *stare decisis:* that in reaching a decision on a particular case now, the court will abide by decisions made for similar cases in the past. Law is tied not to deductive principles but to precedent—to what we did before, how we settled it before, or, to use the standard phrase of English common law, how it is "when the mind of man runneth not to the contrary." And we manage those precedents not by the enunciation of high principles but by exemplification in concrete action. For example, in the landmark case of *Euclid v. Ambler Realty* in 1926, the zoning powers of the village of Euclid were upheld by Mr. Justice Sutherland on the ground that principalities have always enjoyed the right of exercising police power (for which there is no dearth of citations from the past), and police power implies the right to regulate local disorder, of which zoning is an example. The good Justice's decision includes mention of everything from traffic and intruders to roaches and smoking chimneys, which are as compelling in this context as a smoking gun in a murder trial. From any rational point of view, *Euclid* as it came out was the father of the lily-white segregated suburb, of restrictive covenants, of the lack of affordable housing in decent surroundings. By protecting the extension of familiar police powers, *Euclid* managed to weaken the equal protection clause of the Fourteenth Amendment. It prevails today, and the present Supreme Court would probably refuse to hear a zoning case that challenges it.

Ways of doing are not easily changed when they become institutionalized not only in law but also in the habits of those who have come all too unconsciously to depend upon the more heavily sedimented procedures of law. Like *stare decisis* itself, they provide a sometimes heavy but needed consistency to our culture. If you read Michel Foucault's remarkable *Discipline and Punish* you will be struck by the degree to which the practice of punishment preceded the theory, but also by the effort that was made, once theory came into being, to construct one that fit practice.

One final word about iconic representation and the world of images. I suspect that the most powerful technique for arousing one of those action-related modes of dealing with the world is through depiction: using a Willy Horton, or a Biafran baby with a belly distended from kwashiorkor. For images are not only prototypes of categories, but also stopped action frames in narratives. When human action finally achieves its representation in words, it is not in a universal and timeless formula that it is expressed but in a story—a story about actions taken, procedures followed, and the rest.

Which brings me full cycle back to Sylvia Scribner's milkmen in their New York dairy, sorting out their deliveries of milk, cream, yogurt, and butter. They were engaged collectively (and expertly) in an "oeuvre" in the sense in which that term was discussed in Chapter 1—the usage given to it by Ignace Meyerson. The oeuvre in question—delivering dairy products in a huge city, the nearest supplier of which is at least fifty miles distant—is composed of hundreds of small "things," small rebuses, ranging from the highly technical (providing regular tuberculosis testing for cows, for example) to the highly traditional (providing the products in canonical containers in traditional colors and flavors, and at a traditional time of day). You could probably write a passably complete account of modern urban culture by giving the full procedure and rationale for milk delivery. And it would be interesting to conjecture why, for example, milk and dairy delivery to homes in New York was done by horse-drawn "milk wagons" long after suitable motorized vans had taken over home delivery of other products. Was it an expression of our Western distinction between the raw and the cooked, to which Claude Lévi-Strauss first brought our attention?[8] Did the horse as the delivery agent reinforce the imagery of the "raw," or was there an efficiency motive: horses following the milkman without the fuss of being "started up" and driven?

Delivering milk and dairy products, like practicing law or medicine, is tied into procedures whose execution in effect creates the work of those involved in it. Sylvia Scribner was quite right in seeing this complex pattern as central to the psychology of work. As in many things, she was ahead of her time. What she envisaged was a *cultural* psychology of work.

9

▼

PSYCHOLOGY'S NEXT CHAPTER

PART 1: THE STUDY OF MAN

Can a cultural psychology such as I've espoused in the preceding chapters simply stand apart from the kind of biologically rooted, individually oriented, laboratory dominated psychology that we have known in the past? Must the more situated study of mind–in–culture, more interpretively anthropological in spirit, jettison all that we have learned before? Some writers, like Harré or Gergen, propose that our past was a mistake, a misunderstanding of what psychology is about.[1] While not intending to defend the positivist excesses of our forefathers—as I hope I made clear in a previous book[2]—I would like to urge an end to the kind of "either-or" approach to the question of what psychology should be in the future, whether it should be entirely biological, exclusively computational, or monopolistically cultural.

But I do not want to make my case on the basis of deductions from metaphysical or methodological principles. To understand mind is a pursuit so embedded in pragmatic considerations as to be beyond such philosophical inquiry, useful though the inquiry may be. What I want to do instead in this final chapter is to show one way in which psychology can, by devoting its attention to certain critical topics in a variety of ways, illustrate the interaction of biological, evolutionary, individual psychological, and cultural insights in helping us grasp the nature of human mental functioning. This "next chapter" in psychology, as I call it in the title, is about "intersubjectivity"—how people come to know what others have in mind and how they adjust accordingly. It is a set of topics that, in my view, is central to any viable conception of a cultural psychology. But it cannot be understood without reference to primate evolution, to neural functioning, and to the processing capacities of minds. Before we get to our task, however, there are preliminaries to be got out of the way.

Let me begin by noting that the study of mind poses difficulties that inhere not only in its subject matter per se, but in its method. As Noam Chomsky remarked in his Locke Lecture some years ago,[3] we seem not to possess the natural mental categories for explicating our own minds, or at least not anywhere to the same degree that we possess categories for explicating the physical world—those necessary categories of time, space, causality, and even logical necessity that provide the intellectual skeleton of the physical sciences. Our mental states, for example, seem not to be bound even by the canon of non-contradiction: we can love and hate simultaneously and are often not sure whether this is really a contradiction. And the measures we formulate for the physical world seem to fit poorly to those that characterize our subjectivity: subjective time and space do not neatly correspond with Newtonian clocks and meter sticks.

For all that, psychology in its "modern" version chose to model itself on the methods of physics. Our first psychological "laws" were about psychophysics—concerned with the systematic ways in which subjective magnitudes measured psychologically deviated from magnitudes measured physically. Our forebears were in search of the "dimensions of consciousness" as deviant but systematic counterparts to the "dimensions of nature." And within limits (albeit narrow ones), this approach yielded interesting results. On the practical side, it opened up interesting questions about man-machine relations, for example, and on the theoretical side it suggested some possible approaches to the issue of how mind and brain related to each other.

But its successes also generated its failures. "Classical" psychophysical psychology had no place for "folk psychology." Yet a culture's folk theories about the nature of human nature inevitably shape how that culture administers justice, educates its young, helps the needy, and even conducts its interpersonal relationships—all matters of deep consequence. In a certain way, the ordinary conduct of life, social life particularly, requires that *everybody be a psychologist,* that everybody have theories about why others are acting as they do. Call it ethnopsychology or folk psychology, but without beliefs about other minds and their *modus operandi,* we would be lost. And often, of course, these implicit theories reflect a culture's ideals and aspirations. Thus, the human sciences in their very nature face a daunting challenge: to formulate a view of man that is sometimes incongruent with folk psychology, but what is even more serious, incongruent with our cultural ideals. Yet the human sciences are also a part of the culture that sustains them. So it is of the utmost importance that psychology offer its views about man in a fashion that is sensitive to those ideals yet nonetheless reflects an honest standard that is beyond bias and selfishness.

But to underline the importance of a culture's folk psychology as a shaper of human behavior is *not* to deny that we are a natural, biological species, *Homo sapiens,* and cannot be fully understood without reference to our evolution and biology. Yet human biology per se gives us only indirect and partial knowledge about the behavior of our species. A good example came my way recently, when my attention was brought to a new paper in *Nature* entitled "Impaired Recognition of Emotion in Facial Expressions Following Bilateral Damage to the Human Amygdala."[4] It reports the testing of a patient with a very rare case of Urbach-Wiethe disease, which destroys the amygdala while sparing the hippocampus and other related neocortical structures around it. The amygdala, of course, is a part of the brain involved with "emotion." The study's chief finding was that the lesions produced by this degenerative disease virtually destroyed the patient's capacity to recognize the facial expressions of such emotions as fear and anger, while seeming to affect *not at all* her capacity to recognize the identity of photographs of people whom she knew, though she had not seen some of them in years. Like all neurological studies, this one told me nothing definitive about mind. What it gave me, however, was a useful hint. If the business of recognizing the emotional state of a fellow human being is carried out in a different place in the brain from where it carries out the business of identifying who that human being is, then I must ask a question. What function is served by that kind of anatomical separation? Is it that we must first know *who* it is before we judge whether that person is angry or not? If we did not know the "who" first, independently of the "what," we would be unable to take context into account with the "what"—whether it is my best friend or my worst enemy who appears angry. Recognizing someone's identity, of course, unlocks access to context. To adapt, we must know the context in which the anger is occurring. Direct signals from "nature" (like facial expressions *eo ipso*) rarely trigger an adaptive response by themselves, though they may sometimes do so, to be sure. My line of reasoning, it is clear, does not get me to a "clinching" conclusion, but it makes use of a powerful hint—the anatomical separation of two kinds of brain processes. Without such hints, our hypotheses about mental functioning would be even poorer than they are.

I can match the amygdala example with another from the field of primate evolution and development that is even richer, one even closer to my own research. As we know, prolonged eye-to-eye contact is a feature of infant-caretaker interaction, one that appears just before infant-caretaker joint attention to objects. It is also known that prolonged eye-to-eye contact is virtually absent in our nearest kin, the chimpanzee.[5] But with good reason. Below man, anything longer than momentary eye contact precipitates attack and threat behavior by the dominant animal—especially in Old World monkeys and baboons.[6] Which in turn is a reminder that we should be careful about prolonged eye-to-eye contact with human strangers in strange places, like the subway: it will always be overinterpreted. If one is about to propose a general theory about the role of eye contact in human intersubjectivity, one had better be mindful of this troublesome bit of primate evolutionary history.

I want to discuss now a subtle anomaly in the evolution of our species *Homo* that leads to a second challenge in the study of human nature and the human condition. It has to do with the evolution of culture itself as a mediating process in the human response to the world. Culture imposes revolutionary *discontinuity* between man and the rest of the animal kingdom. And it is this discontinuity that creates the difficulty in extrapolating directly from our evolutionary biology to the human condition. What is this revolutionary turn that human evolution has produced? I am going to argue that, just as we cannot fully understand man without reference to his biological roots, so we cannot understand man without reference to culture.

Let me try to characterize the "cultural turn" in human evolution from two perspectives. The first, the "individualistic" perspective, is this. Culture rests psychologically on a symbolic capacity in man for grasping "standing for" relationships that transcend either mimesis or indexicality in the sense that, say, a totemic animal "stands for" my clan. In a culture, things stand for other things in a way that goes beyond smoke standing for fire or Gilbert Stuart's famous portrait standing for George Washington. A culture seems to be a shared network of communal "standings for." And as members of our species, we live in that network as well as in nature. We form our allegiances and construct our communities around this sharing.

This individualistic perspective on human cultural evolution leads inevitably to the view that human "meaning making" and its negotiation are at the core of the cultural turn. As a species, we adapt to our environment in terms of what things, acts, events, signs are taken to *mean*. Meanings infuse our perceptions and thought processes in a way not to be found elsewhere in the animal kingdom. What does it "mean," we ask, that Oedipus tears out his eyes when he discovers what he has done? Or, to revert to the amygdala, what does it mean when my *son* looks angry, in contrast to mine *enemies* (and what does it mean, besides, that the Psalmist tells me that an invisible Lord "preparest a table" for me in the presence of those enemies)? Without meaning making, there could be no language, no myth, no art—and no culture. I'll consider later what language itself contributes to meaning making, for the relation between them is not a one-way street.

The second perspective on the cultural in evolution is more collectivist, and emphasizes a *transactional* turn as crucial to the human way of life. The most primitive thing about this turn is that not only do we *represent* the world in our own minds (replete with meanings), but we respond with preternatural sensitivity to the way that world is represented in the minds of others. And by virtue of that sensitivity we form a representation of the world as much from what we learn about it through others as from responding to events in the world directly. Our worlds, then, are vicarious to a degree unthinkable in any other species. Obviously, successful speciation anywhere in the animal kingdom depends upon conspecifics responding adaptively to each other's reactions, but the human case goes beyond that. We respond to each other's proximity by appropriate spacing, to each other's warning calls and mating releasers, but also to each other's mental states and representations of the world. From birth, literally, we seem to be guided in our responses to our conspecifics by what has come to be called a "theory of mind," a guiding but changing folk epistemology.

Not only do we partake, so to speak, of each other's minds, but we have "superorganic" ways (to borrow Kroeber's contentious term again)[7] of preserving knowledge from the past. We seem to institutionalize knowledge in folklore, in myth, in historical records, eventually in libraries and constitutions, and now on hard disks. And in storing it we shape it to fit the myriad requirements of communal living, squeezing it into the shapes required for dictionaries, legal codes, pharmacopoeia, holy books, and the rest. In some deeply puzzling way, this stored knowledge, replete not only with information but with prescriptions for how to think about it, comes to shape mind. So, in the end, while mind creates culture, culture also creates mind.

Thus, the complex phenomenon we so glibly refer to as "culture" seems to impose constraints on how mind works and even upon the kinds of problems we are able to solve. Even so primitive a psychological process as generalization—seeing the similarity between things—is corseted by culturally sponsored construals of meaning rather than by the churning away of an individual nervous system. For centuries, the ancient Mayans had beautifully balanced prayer wheels. Yet they made their dogs pull loads on cross-sticked travois whose pointed ends dragged clumsily on the ground. They seemed unable to "think wheel" in any general way: wheels were prayer, period. Why didn't it occur to them to attach a small wheel to the dragging end of the travois? Was it the theocratic thrall in which prayer wheels held them? Well, then, why did the people of the Olduvai Gorge spend thousands of years using digging sticks for digging up roots before adapting them as drills to poke holes into the dirt for planting seedlings? What makes slaves of us—our culturally shaped ways, William James's habit mechanisms, or the two working in the hand-in-glove that constitutes the interaction of mind and culture?

When I was much younger, I had the good fortune to meet the great Louis Leakey, just back from digging in East Africa. Not much for small talk, he asked me at once what I, as a psychologist, made of his group's having discovered a perfect, carefully stowed, highly polished, unused stone hand chopper at the famous Olduvai site just mentioned. Did I think the Olduvaians had hit on the idea of a bureau of standards at which, as it were, a perfect stone hand chopper was stored for copying, like the famous platinum meter stick in Paris? Impossible, I said (for I was a very serious as well as a very brash thirty-year-old); it is inconceivable that in such technologically primitive times man could have separated a tool from its situated use to that extent. More likely, I continued, the perfect hand chopper was an object of quasi-religious reverence, a piece of sympathetic magic to help assure good outcomes to all who used hand choppers, whatever they used them for and however imperfect they might be. "How interesting," said Leakey, courtly and courteous to the end. I had never even seen a hand chopper in the flesh!

My reflections on this episode bring me to my third general point. Just as you cannot fully understand human action without taking account of its biological evolutionary roots and, at the same time, understanding how it is construed in the meaning making of the actors involved in it, so you cannot understand it fully without knowing how and where it is *situated*. For, to paraphrase Clifford Geertz,[8] knowledge and action are always local, always situated in a network of particulars. I think what I said to Louis Leakey was absolutely correct, but too specialized. It is practically impossible to understand a thought, an act, a move of any sort from the situation in which it occurs. Biology and culture both operate locally; however grand the sweep of their principles, they find a final common path in the here and now: in the immediate "definition of the situation," in the immediate discourse setting, in the immanent state of the nervous system, local and situated.

▼

It will surely not come as a surprise, then, that I now shall argue that the psychology of the future must, virtually as a condition of its fruitful existence, keep its eye on both the biological and the cultural, and do so with proper regard for how these shaping forces interact in the local situation. Do not be consoled by the false claim that psychologists already do so and have always done so. It is simply not so: sociotropes and biotropes still think they are involved in a zero-sum game; most mind-modelers would sooner be caught without their computers than be caught with historical interpretations; and all of them seem to delight in establishing separate divisions of the American Psychological Association where they can have the comfort of speaking only to their like-minded constituency. Psychology, alas, seems to have lost its center and its great integrating questions. I think it has given up prematurely, so in Part 2 of this chapter I propose to explore one exemplary subject-matter area, along with the bio-socio-situational methods that might lead us to do better in the future.

II

But first, there are two related matters that need clarification. One of them has to do with the relation of mind and culture, and the other is related to what I mean by the local or "situated" nature of human functioning.

Human functioning in a cultural setting, mental and overt, is shaped by the culture's toolkit of "prosthetic devices." We are a tool-using, tool-making species par excellence, and we rely on "soft tools" as much as on digging sticks and stone choppers—culturally devised ways of thinking, searching, planning. Given this reliance on prosthetic devices, it seems absurd to study human mental processes in isolation from them, in a glass vat, in vitro. Whatever we devise as the pure, culture-free in vitro case for studying the "basics" of some mental process will always turn out to be a choice driven by theoretical preconceptions. Pure memory, pure thought, pure perception, simple reaction time—these are fictions, occasionally useful, but fictions nonetheless. We typically proceed in such work by choosing a particular in-the-vat experimental paradigm, experimental study of which yields the "true" or untrammeled picture of it. Anything added to that paradigm, even a prosthetic device, is then given the status of a "variable" or a "source of variance."

The study of that most encultured of mental processes, human memory, provides a chilling example of this approach. I do not mean to disparage Ebbinghaus, the founder of this approach to memory research. His in-the-vat paradigm of human memory was memorizing nonsense syllables presented in fixed order one at a time on a memory drum at a rate sufficiently fast to prevent subjects from falling back on the usual memory crutches like rhyming schemes, rhythms, and the rest. Is human memory really shaped by evolution to operate free of those crutches—those rebuses discussed in the preceding chapter? Is my "real" memory for, say, tomorrow's appointments only what I can recall without my diary?

Recently I read David Olson's *The World on Paper,*[9] which reviews and reflects upon the impact of literacy in Western culture. Print affects profoundly how and what we go about remembering—if only by virtue of preserving a text, a prosthetic substitute for rote memory. And we know from the classic study by Ann Brown that even young subjects, once they view "what is to be remembered" as a text, begin "going meta"—considering not only *what* is to be remembered but *how* one might organize it to make sense of it. Very quickly children go from being like Ebbinghaus's subjects to being like Bartlett's. But does that make their memory less "real" or basic or pure? What about Bartlett's clever Cambridge undergraduate subjects in his famous study of *Remembering?*[10] Is that how remembering *really* is? Can we generalize from these clever undergraduates to Everyman Everywhere? Not before we read Shirley Brice Heath comparing romancers and literalists in her famous study of the kids of Trackton and Roadville.[11]

Do I have to give up theorizing scientifically about memory if I give up the idea of the paradigmatic purity of memory as studied in one particular situation? Can't I use the laboratory to investigate how memory works under especially interesting conditions that one might not find in daily life? Only in a laboratory would we ever have discovered our near-perfect capacity to recognize pictures and designs to which we are exposed at a rate of over a hundred per minute[12]—an interesting finding for a variety of technical reasons having to do with differentiating recognition and recall. What characterizes a good laboratory is that it is trying to elucidate *something particular* about a phenomenon, something related to other phenomena that also have to do with particulars. Is there ever an experiment that strips memory to its "natural" form? Is recognition "purer" than recall, and what kind of question is that altogether?

This is all reminiscent of the wrong turning in the debate over whether there are "limits" on immediate memory. Of course there are. Is it the "magic number 7"? Yes, if you are memorizing strings of zeros and ones. If you learn how to convert these strings into octal digits (clusters of three at a time), twenty-one becomes magic—seven octal digits. Is it a question of seven slots now filled with octal gold rather than digital dross? If so, how many slots do you need for a hundred lines of *Paradise Lost?* Or how many things do you "remember" by knowing that $S = \frac{1}{2} gt^2$?

All of which is not to say that there are no universals in mental functioning, no "psychic unity of mankind." It is surely a misbegotten claim (see Shweder, for example),[13] even an ideological agenda, that leads one from the premise that since each culture is unique, therefore psychic universals must be bogus. This is akin to arguing that since Bach's *Goldberg Variations* and a contemporary jazz improvisation are both unique and self-contained in their own terms, there are no universals of music. A theory of music that cannot contain both is deficient or even misbegotten. I find it difficult to grant that millions of years of evolutionary selection produced no underlying uniformities. Obviously the "magic number 7" tells us something fundamental about the universal limits of the human nervous system; it simply does not tell us enough. What the yards of bibliographical references on the subject of limits do tell us is that it is vain to think of culturally unique ways of managing memory as so many "add-ons" to some pure or basic form of memory. "Basic mental processes" are not something to which "other processes" are added. Complex processes, rather, have an integrity in their own right and must be understood as reflecting evolutionary, cultural, and situational interactions.

Rather than thinking of culture being "added" to mind or as somehow interfering with the mind's elementary processes, we do better to think of culture as *in* mind—to borrow the title of a book by Bradd Shore.[14] We would then assume the task of exploring the range of situated, culturally defined behaviors of which our species is capable, and try to build our theories in a fashion that sees them in their relation to each other as a putative human repertory. This is radically different from the reductionist, add-on approach that psychology has grown up with. I shall try to illustrate this point in Part 2 of this chapter.

But before I do, I would like to add one final argument. It is that the more general approach I am espousing is in principle more sensitive to the moral demands that exist for the human scientist—his or her role as participant in the culture in contrast to the role of being omniscient high-priest and purveyor of the Real Truth about the Human Condition. Let me turn briefly to that now.

III

My discussion is inspired in some measure by a recent, thoughtful article by D. C. Geary in the *American Psychologist*.[15] While his paper is specifically aimed at the issue of mathematics learning in and out of school, it is more generally directed to the interaction of biologically "primary" (as he calls them) psychological dispositions and biologically "secondary" ones. The former, as it were, come naturally; they can be found in all human cultures and even in biological orders lower than man in the evolutionary scale. Primaries are cognitive dispositions that have developed principally in response to evolutionary demands, and their expression in action aids adaptation to the natural world for navigating, getting about in a habitat, and so forth. Indeed, the exercise of these dispositions often leads to positive affect and, one might suppose, reinforcement. Judgments of numerosity, of "greater than" and "less than," and other "skeletal competencies" (to use Gelman and Gallistel's term)[16] fall into this category. Secondaries require transforming primary intuitions into a more formal, perhaps more conscious representation—into maps, graphs, formulas, pictograms, and the like. These do not come as naturally as primaries; they are limited or even spottily distributed among enculturated humans; and they typically require the expenditure of effort plus some external social compulsion, such as that imposed, say, by schools or organized elders. Every particular culture, in consequence, faces the decision as to which of the so-called secondary dispositions should be cultivated by its members to qualify them for full cultural competency and its rights and privileges.

Now plainly, this is my oversimplification of the necessarily oversimplified argument in Geary's brief article. The weakness of his argument is, of course, that his biological primaries are often overstretched abstractions from concrete, situated behaviors which, in any case, also require a degree of enculturation for them to be expressed in the human cultural setting. Even that most ubiquitous of biological primaries, interpersonal aggression, is typically forced into some sort of Marquis of Queensbury pattern to be minimally permissible. As Geertz would say, where humans are concerned there is no natural mind.[17] But leave that grave conceptual difficulty aside for a moment, for Geary's picture is thought-provoking and useful. There is no question that some cognitive dispositions are more easily and more pleasurably expressed in action—even in enculturated form.

What I find particularly useful is Geary's emphasis on the decision that all cultures must make about which "biologically secondary" dispositions to cultivate and to enforce for qualification, whether through schools or other disciplinary means. Few would doubt the importance of such decisions. But fewer still would fail to recognize that such decisions are, in their very nature, based on implicit values and ideals, ones not always readily accessible to the consciousness of those making them. They are decisions that reflect some sort of cultural consensus or some view of a reigning elite within the culture. Once put into force, by whatever means, these decisions are *policies,* cultural policies: for example, that all children must master the e-flat alto recorder, or grasp the principles of elementary mathematics, or learn to read maps in the Mercator projection, or learn to write in grammatically well-formed sentences. As with so much else in human culture, the objective behind such policy decisions is lost over time, and performance itself becomes the object: habits become motives. And the habitual patterns become institutionalized by means as varied as testing services, employment criteria, and traditional ways for promoting nostalgia.

Take the institution of school itself, school in Western cultures. Partly to enforce educational aims, partly to utilize scarce instructional resources, school was arranged as a setting in which a pupil gives over control of her attention to a teacher who decides what shall be its focus, when and to what end. This arrangement probably reflected not only a familistic ideal but also a folk psychological notion about how to transmit knowledge from someone who had it to someone who didn't. There is nothing any more or less "natural" about this conception of school than about many others that might come to mind. Besides, schools don't exist in nature.

Cultural policy decisions inevitably create unforeseen outcomes and shortfalls. It is typically the cultural critics, whatever other hat they may be wearing, who speak up. And they rarely invoke natural science. Theirs are normative arguments: kids aren't learning enough, or are acting up, or are getting lazy. Now, typically, the psychologist or educational researcher is called in. What he is asked to do is what self-styled scientists usually don't like to admit to doing: *policy research,* devising ways of getting to desired ends by uncertain means. And if he is not attuned to the importance of "situatedness" in learning, he will get nowhere.

Now, need educational research, even "policy research," be any less "basic" than any other kind of psychological research? Is it less basic, say, than two generations of research on rat or pigeon learning that ended by offering schools a "basic model" to guide their understanding of how children learn arithmetic or geography or the intricacies of *Silas Marner?* I will argue that the study of situated learning in pursuit of particular goals in a particular cultural setting constrained by biological limits is the stuff not only of good policy research but good psychological science.

PART 2: THE CHALLENGE OF INTERSUBJECTIVITY

In Part 1 of this chapter I did my best to make the case for a radical reconsideration of how psychology must study the life of mind. In brief, psychology must not only address the constraints on mental activity imposed by man's biological evolution, but also must bear constantly in mind one overwhelming discontinuity in that evolution: the emergence of human culture through which man creates a symbolic representation of his encounters with the world. I argued further that as a result of this enculturation of human mental activity, mind cannot in any sense be regarded as "natural" or naked, with culture thought of as an add-on.

In commenting on the encultured human mind, I noted two ways of approaching the shift from primate to human symbolic functioning. The first emphasized the individual human capacity for grasping symbolic "standing-for" relations through an arbitrary symbolic code. The second approach was more transactional, more "intersubjective," and focused on how humans developed the capacity to read the thoughts, intentions, beliefs, and mental states of their conspecifics in a culture. For human evolution is marked by just such a development. It is greatly facilitated by the continued growth of networks of mutual expectation—the mark of encultured human beings living in communities. These networks are in part constituted and, in any case, powerfully amplified by the use of a common language and a body of traditions that stabilize and institutionalize mutual expectations.

My intention now is to explore the emergence of intersubjectivity in our species—both phylogenetically and ontogenetically. In the course of this exploration, we shall even consider what happens when intersubjectivity is interfered with by a human pathology. As a matter of methodological principle, I want to approach this subject in a way that keeps *concurrently* clear not only (1) the systematic nature of the phenomenon in question, but (2) its ontogenetic growth in individual human beings in particular settings, as well as (3) its cultural-historical transformations over time, and (4) its phylogenetic history or evolution. I will try to show that an insight or discovery achieved along any of these four tracks is bound to produce insights or at least hypotheses along one or more of the others.

II

How do we "know" other minds, what kinds of theories do we develop or acquire to help us know others' mental states, how does this presumed capacity develop and mature, what are its evolutionary origins, and how has cultural history shaped it? A big order! Fortunately, there has been a decade-long explosion of work that can help us, work to which I have referred in earlier chapters.

The work began, as so frequently happens, with a series of odd findings in several ordinarily sealed-off bodies of literature. Why they cohered into a common enterprise I will leave to future historians of science, though I suspect that the so-called cognitive revolution may have encouraged this just by making it respectable again for psychologists to talk about "the mind." In any case, what resulted was a convergence of work on the infant mind, on autism, on children's developing theories about how others' minds work, and on enculturation in chimpanzees.

1. The infant mind. The new infancy research began when developmentalists decided, in light of the cognitive revolution, to have a fresh look at mental life in infancy—leaving aside St. Augustine's claims about ubiquitous infant "imitation," Locke's about the tabula rasa, and William James's about the newborn's "blooming buzzing confusion," all of which soon disappeared like mist with the rising sun. Colwyn Trevarthen, originally a zoologist but by then working at a cognitive studies center, was among the first to remark upon the extraordinary synchrony between a young infant's gestural and vocal patterns and his mother's.[18] It could not be accounted for, he observed, by a simple, step-at-a-time "serial matching" of infant reaction to mother followed by mother reaction to infant, and so on. It seemed, rather, to resemble that higher-order control that Lashley had proposed as essential to all iterative or recursive patterns occurring in finite time spans,[19] as in performing music or speaking a lexico-grammatical language. But in the mother–infant situation, *two* organisms were involved in creating this extended synchrony, like Nureyev and Margot Fonteyn, say, performing a *pas de deux* in "Swan Lake," each seeming to know at every step what the other was up to.

To account for what might be going on, Trevarthen borrowed the term "intersubjectivity" from the Scottish philosopher MacMurray.[20] Soon after, Daniel Stern,[21] a child psychiatrist working on infant-mother bonding, was struck by the same phenomenon, and dubbed it infant-mother "attunement." And before long a cottage industry sprang up around this intriguing subject, to which gravitated a variety of other observational studies born in other research traditions—from the Bowlby-Ainsworth-Main studies of infant separation,[22] from psychoanalysis,[23] from studies of infant recognition of the facial expression of emotion that began with Darwin,[24] and from elsewhere as well. An early, closely controlled study by Scaife and myself showed that young infants followed an adult's line of regard to search for an object on which to fixate,[25] such search being contingent on the adult and child first being in eye-to-eye contact.

The Scaife-Bruner study set off a cascade of experimental work on the phenomenon of "joint attention," centering on the question of how the infant "knew" what another person was attending to. The cascade still continues, as evidenced by a recent collection of research articles on joint attention under the editorship of Moore and Dunham.[26] A lot of challenging findings have emerged, including the following: (1) there is a unit receptor in the human cortex dedicated to processing eye-to-eye perceptual contact, which speaks to its biological underpinning; (2) while non-human primate infancy seems to be marked by no comparable preference for eye-to-eye contact, there is good evidence that even youngish monkeys will guide their search of a terrain by checking the line of regard of any animal who, on previous trials, had known where food was hidden;[27] (3) primate social behavior is often observed to be based upon an intent to deceive conspecifics in a rather Machiavellian way,[28] which suggests that they have a theory of mind of some kind; but (4) eye-to-eye contact beyond a certain minimal duration releases agonistic and threatening behavior in mature male Old World monkeys, notably among baboons—and, indeed, it is rarely taken lightly even in humans.[29] This is only a sampling of the "new" infancy research and what it has led to.

2. *Childhood autism*. Following Kanner's earlier, widely read book,[30] autism had been considered an acquired deficit in social responsiveness rooted in faulty interaction between mother and child (a view still firmly held by some orthodox psychoanalysts). What had been known for many years, of course, was that autistic infants, unlike normal ones, avoided eye-to-eye contact with caretakers, did not follow the line of another's pointing or regard, and seemed to live, as

folklore puts it, in "a world of their own." Notably, autists were very retarded in language development, and this retardation showed up early in their unwillingness or inability to enter into those prelinguistic interaction "formats" in which the early transition from preverbal to verbal communication is nurtured.

It was through the work of Beate Hermelin, Alan Leslie, and Simon Baron-Cohen, building on earlier insights of Hermelin and Neil O'Connor, that the old conception of autism was revolutionized.[31] They argued (and demonstrated persuasively) that at the root of this puzzling and disturbing syndrome was a deficit in or even an absence of a "theory of other minds." It was this deficit that kept autists from being socially responsive, and not some early difficulties in mother–infant interaction. Such difficulties were more often produced by the deficit rather than producing it. And autists had related difficulties, such as an absence of pretend play.[32]

The spate of research that followed on this truly radical reformulation (again attested to by dozens of books and articles and special journal issues) and the many refinements that have emerged since the original work need not concern us here—save perhaps one line of inquiry that bears directly on our general bio-cultural concern. Carol Feldman and I were among several investigators to note that autistic children seem conspicuously deficient in telling or comprehending narratives or stories.[33] To understand a narrative, of course, one must grasp the intentions and expectations of protagonists, the engine of a narrative usually being the thwarting of those intentions by circumstances and their rectification in the denouement. Whether it is an absence of narrative comprehension that produces a deficit in "theory of mind" or vice versa need not concern us now—though it poses an interesting conjecture. The point is that without a grasp of narrative, the autistic child is cut off from one of the principal sources of knowledge about the human world around him, particularly relating to human desires, intentions, beliefs, and conflicts. And as Happé and Sacks have recently so vividly illustrated,[34] even gifted autists, those suffering from Asperger's syndrome, so-called, are forced into reliance on wooden algorithms and formulas in order to comprehend what people have on their minds or simply have in mind. They seem stiff and "unnatural" in their social-emotional lives, as if they had learned life much as one might learn mathematics. If these findings stand up to future scrutiny, we have learned something crucial about how the intimate aspects of culture are transmitted—namely, through narratives, though many had suspected something of that order before.

3. Theories of mind. I now turn to work directly on the growing normal child's theories of others' minds. Work on this topic grew to some degree out of the complaint (in which I joined) that Piaget's widely known classic work had made it seem as if the growing child achieved her knowledge of the world by direct hands-on contact with it, rather than, as was ordinarily the case, by learning about it through others. For we even learn much of what we "know" about the physical world by hearing others' beliefs about it, not by poking about in it directly. Well then, how do we understand what others believe? That question tapped another constituency, not just among philosophers, perennially concerned with the issue of valid knowledge, but among psychologists in their "baby labs." A child before the age of three or four, it turned out, could not distinguish between false beliefs and true ones, or so one kind of experiment showed.[35] Show a child in which of several boxes a piece of candy was hidden, lead her out of the room and in her absence shift the candy to another box, and now ask another child who has been present the whole time where the first child will look for the candy when she comes back into the room. He will predict that she will look where the candy was hidden in her absence. Children of this age seem not to be able, as it were, to grasp the idea of a false belief. This famous experiment produced a tidal wave of "yes, but" research, most of it brilliantly and fairly summarized in Janet Astington's masterful book,[36] and analyzed with great acumen for its theoretical presuppositions in a review article by Carol Feldman devoted to three of the four major books to appear on this work.[37]

But hold on. Could it be the case, really, that human three-year-olds are that backward when even young Old World monkeys intentionally deceive each other in their efforts to gain social advantage or food? Doesn't deliberately tricking another animal really indicate a distinction in the monkey's mind between true and false beliefs? (This is a question that assorted primatologists have directed their work to in a recent authoritative collection of papers brought together by Andrew Whiten.)[38] Surely it is counterintuitive that human three-year-olds at play can't do as well as young monkeys. Indeed, Chandler has demonstrated that young children who fail the False Belief Test *do* try to trick each other in spontaneous play.[39] Perhaps the best explanation of Chandler's finding is that Broca's area in the brain is only activated when the child has an intention and not when the child is only receptive, answering questions posed by others. And there is plenty of reason to believe that it is precisely Broca's area that is involved in dealing with "hypotheticals." Where indeed will another child look for candy when she returns to the room? Remember Sir Henry Head's famous aphasia patient, poised on the threshold of the doctor's office.[40] He becomes mute with indecision when asked: "Would you like to come in or stay there?" Yet asked about either alternative separately, he states his wish definitely and instantly. Well, the methodology I proposed at the outset suggests you should not only look at the False Belief Test but carry out a PET scan on the three-year-old's brain to see what conditions activate Broca's area. We also happen to know that the Machiavellian deceitfulness of monkeys and apes could not depend on Broca's area—they don't have one. So we are off and running on a new line.

4. *Enculturated chimpanzees.* We come now to the Rumbaughs' Kanzi. Consider his enculturation at the hands of a devoted band of caregivers working at the Georgia State Language Research Laboratory under the direction of Duane Rumbaugh and Sue Savage-Rumbaugh.[41] The roughest possible summary of their work is this: The more a chimpanzee is exposed to human treatment, treated *as if* he were human, the more likely he is to act in a human-like way. The Georgia group taught a young pygmy chimpanzee *(Pan paniscus),*

Kanzi, not only to communicate by using a board of visual symbols to make known what he had in mind or to answer questions, but also to get a firmer grip on the general notion that his human handlers were *intending to refer to something* by using the symbols on the board—a notion of intentionality, that a spoken word or arbitrary visual sign "stands for" something both for you and your interlocutor. Without distinctively human rearing, pygmy chimpanzees never exhibit such capacities—either in the wild or in the laboratory.

A recent study by Tomasello, Savage-Rumbaugh, and Kruger sheds light on this same topic, showing that "enculturation" depends upon being treated as if you were human.[42] Tomasello and his colleagues worked with imitation as their special tracer element—a phenomenon that is very human despite its being called "aping" in a standard thesaurus. They compared chimp-mother-reared young pygmy chimpanzees, human-reared ones, and young children (18 and 30 months of age). All subjects were shown novel actions performed on objects by familiar human caretakers and/or experimenters. The young human subjects were told "Do what I do" when shown the action, as were all the chimps, just to be scrupulous about experimental control. Would subjects, chimp and human, perform the modeled act immediately or later, and would they do so by imitating the model action or by producing the same outcomes by other means (emulation rather than imitation)?

It turned out that chimp-reared chimpanzees were much poorer on immediate imitation than human-reared ones or than human children of either age. On delayed imitation and emulation, the human-reared chimpanzees outperformed all the others, human and ape alike—even without the assistance of the gifted Kanzi, who was not in this experiment. Delayed imitation, of course, requires some sort of representation because the model is no longer present, and emulation demands some sense of the detachability of means and ends, that is, holding an end in mind while varying the means that might attain it.

How does one account for the remarkable increase in the "human" quality of the human-reared chimpanzees as revealed on these imitation tasks? I will quote from a letter that Tomasello wrote me in answer to this query:

> Kanzi and some other "enculturated" apes are different. Why? For precisely the reasons you articulate for children: from an early age Kanzi has spent his ontogeny building up a shared world with humans—much of the time through active negotiation. An essential element in this process is undoubtedly the behavior of other beings—i.e., human beings—who, on a daily basis, encourage Kanzi to share attention to objects with them, to perform certain behaviors they have just performed, to take their emotional attitudes toward objects, and so on and so forth. *Apes in the wild have no one who engages them in this way—no one who intends things about their intentional states.*[43]

So what about "active negotiation"? How crucial is it in intersubjectivity? I want to contrast negotiation in chimpanzees (this time *Pan troglodytes*) and in humans. The observations on the former come from an old study by Meredith Crawford on cooperative behavior in chimpanzees.[44] The task posed to a pair of animals was to pull in a sliding tray baited with food, but one that was too heavy for either to manage by himself. The animals (from the former Yale-Yerkes colony at Orange Park, Florida, and therefore well used to human beings and their experiments, though chimp-mother-reared) were not very good at the task. They seemed unable to indicate to each other what they wanted help about. One of them finally hit on a somewhat successful maneuver: getting the task all set up, starting to pull hard on the rope connected to the heavy sliding tray, and then poking the other one to draw attention to her strenuous pulling. It sometimes worked; the other animal would grasp the loose end of the rope and join in, as if mimetically or by empathy, or even in imitation. As we have already seen, higher primates show "knowledge" of intent in the acts of conspecifics, as in their Machiavellian deceit. But in the Crawford experiment, whatever operated seemed to do so in a rather hit-or-miss fashion. Contrast the impoverished negotiation of the chimpanzee pairs with what typically happens in human mother-child negotiation.

Consider an example of mother-child "book reading," where the mother was engaged in teaching her son, Jonathan, the names of things pictured on the pages of a book.[45] He and his mother were endlessly negotiating in a fashion that was as conventional as it was affable. At a superficial level, the negotiation was about what a thing should be called (signaled by the mother's typically inflected "What's that?"). More deeply, negotiation was about how things named should be situated, in what context they were to be construed. As soon as Jonathan could give a passably correct label in reply to his mother's standard "What's that?" question, she would begin a next "And what's the X doing?" routine. She was elaborating the name given to the object at the focus of their joint attention into a wider system of symbols—call it predication if you like. Indeed, Jonathan's mother even used a distinctive intonation pattern to indicate that she had extended the topic, reverting to the rising intonation she used whenever entering new intersubjective territory.

But there was one other thing operating, a more subtle matter, something that Sperber and Wilson call "the principle of relevance,"[46] although it might better be called the "presumption of relevance." In every exchange with Jonathan, his mother tried conspicuously to make sense of everything Jonathan said or did—as in one notable episode when he vetoed her proposal that the lady on the back of an English penny be labeled "the Queen," insisting on his own label, "Granny." Typically, she replied "All right, but it's sort of the same thing." Intersubjectivity, in a word, seems to be about "background knowledge"[47] as well as about a "target."

It is this close-textured pattern of reciprocity about the intentional states of one's partners that constitutes social-cognitive negotiation at the human, cultural level—human "attunement," to use Stern's term.[48] It does not exist "in the wild" even in such extraordinarily intelligent and socially sensitive primates as pygmy chimpanzees and orangutans. So when we speak of the "humanizing" effect of human culture, we must bear in mind the network of mutual expectations that it creates. Obviously, such a network is vastly empowered by the use of human language in our species, but mutual expectations work a small miracle for Kanzi, and even have an effect on the young human-nurtured chimpanzees in the microcosm explored by Tomasello and his colleagues. Even *Pan paniscus* seems to have a "zone of potential development"[49] that can benefit from human enculturation. And that is no small point in considering the course of primate evolution moving toward hominization.

All of which suggests strongly that the humanoid mind/brain complex does not simply "grow up" biologically according to a genetically predestined timetable but, rather, that it is opportunistic to nurturing in a human-like environment. To take a leaf from Gerald Edelman's book on "neural Darwinism,"[50] it seems reasonable to suppose that such neural equipment as the chimpanzee may have for supporting his "zone of potential development" may simply die when not activated by opportunities for developing culture-like mutual expectations. To revert to Geary's theory of biologically primary and secondary cognitive dispositions,[51] it may well be that the intrinsically non-rewarding secondaries require the support of just such networks of expectation.

III

I've said too little thus far about human speech and language. Merlin Donald[52] suggests that the passage from ape to man may have involved two revolutionary steps, the first endowing hominids with mimetic intelligence that enables them to model an action on another's acts or on his own previous actions, all of which prepared the ground for activities as varied as rehearsal-practice, group ritual, constructing to a model, and even practices of sympathetic magic. The second step, about a million years later, made possible more powerful forms of representing the world and provided the basis for lexico-grammatical speech. Linguistic nativists like Chomsky and Fodor are fond of referring to a "language organ" that developed independently of other human capacities and that makes it possible for human beings to develop various local languages as surface-structure realizations of some deeper linguistic principles.[53] We cannot know whether, in principle, such an assumption is logically necessary, as sometimes claimed, and we will never have the evidence available to make an empirical case for such a claim. In any event, this is not the place to argue the matter out. Let us simply agree that something in our genome makes us astonishingly adept at picking up the lexico-syntactic structure of any natural language.

But beyond that, what language permits is the construction and elaboration of that "network of mutual expectations" that is the matrix on which culture is constructed. It is this network that becomes shaped into the conventional patterning of Gricean maxims and implicatures,[54] into the felicity conditions on speech acts, and into the myriad of things that allow us to operate in the light of a presumption of relevance in our interactions. And above all, it is what enables meaning making to be such a powerful technique of adaptation in human culture. I am neither a nativist nor an anti-nativist, as must be evident by now, and I am prepared to leave wide open whether, say, the Wilson-Sperber relevance principle has some genetic base. I would be surprised if it didn't, just as surprised as if it were not institutionalized in a culture's systematic methods for exchanging respect and deference.

And with that I shall close. Let me put my conclusion in a few words. If psychology is to get ahead in understanding human nature and the human condition, it must learn to understand the subtle interplay of biology and culture. Culture is probably biology's last great evolutionary trick. It frees *Homo sapiens* to construct a symbolic world flexible enough to meet local needs and to adapt to a myriad of ecological circumstances. I have tried to show how crucial is man's capacity for intersubjectivity in this cultural adaptation. In doing so, I hope I have made it clear that, although the world of culture has achieved an autonomy of its own, it is constrained by biological limits and biologically determined predispositions. So the dilemma in the study of man is to grasp not only the causal principles of his biology and his evolution, but to understand these in the light of the interpretive processes involved in meaning making. To brush aside the biological constraints on human functioning is to commit hubris. To sneer at the power of culture to shape man's mind and to abandon our efforts to bring this power under human control is to commit moral suicide. A well-wrought psychology can help us avoid both these disasters.

NOTES

▼

1. CULTURE, MIND, AND EDUCATION

1. Though I use the expression "the computational view," there are in fact two such models, one based upon the idea of the mind as a set of computational devices that operate in parallel and without benefit of a central processing system, the other on the idea of a central processing unit that controls the sequential order of computational operations that must be performed to achieve solutions to particular problems. Though the differences between these two models are profound in many ways—particularly in their conceptions of the role of "rationality" and "experience"—that difference need not concern us. Compare, for example, David E. Rumelhart and James L. McClelland, eds., *Parallel Distributed Processing: Explorations in the Microstructure of Cognition,* vols. 1 and 2 (Cambridge, Mass.: MIT Press, 1986), with Philip N. Johnson-Laird, *The Computer and the Mind: An Introduction to Cognitive Science* (Cambridge, Mass.: Harvard University Press, 1988).

2. Judith W. Segal, Susan F. Chipman, and Robert Glaser, eds., *Thinking and Learning Skills* (Hillsdale, N.J.: Erlbaum, 1985); John T. Bruer, *Schools for Thought: A Science of Learning in the Classroom* (Cambridge, Mass.: MIT Press, 1993); Michelene T. H. Chi, Robert Glaser, and M. J. Farr, eds., *The Nature of Expertise* (Hillsdale, N.J.: Erlbaum, 1988).

3. Walter J. Ong, *Orality and Literacy: The Technologizing of the Word* (London: Routledge, 1991); David A. Olson, *The World on Paper: The Conceptual and Cognitive Implications of Writing and Reading* (Cambridge: Cambridge University Press, 1994).

4. Olson, *The World on Paper.*

5. Alfred L. Kroeber, "The Superorganic," *American Anthropologist,* 19(2) (1917): 163–213.

6. Some representative works in this cultural-psychological tradition are: Jerome Bruner, *Acts of Meaning* (Cambridge, Mass.: Harvard University Press, 1990); Michael Cole, *The Cultural Context of Learning and Thinking: An Exploration in Experimental Anthropology* (New York: Basic Books, 1971); Barbara

Rogoff, *Apprenticeship in Thinking: Cognitive Development in Social Context* (New York: Oxford University Press, 1990); Richard A. Shweder, *Thinking through Cultures: Expeditions in Cultural Psychology* (Cambridge, Mass.: Harvard University Press, 1991); James V. Wertsch, *Voices of the Mind: A Sociocultural Approach to Mediated Action* (Cambridge, Mass.: Harvard University Press, 1991). Its ancestry traces back to writers like Vygotsky, Durkheim, Schutz, and Max Weber: Lev S. Vygotsky, *Thought and Language* (Cambridge, Mass.: MIT Press, 1962); Emile Durkheim, *Elementary Forms of the Religious Life: A Study in Religious Sociology* (Glencoe, Ill.: Free Press, 1968); Alfred Schutz, *On Phenomenology and Social Relations: Selected Writings* (Chicago: University of Chicago Press, 1970); Max Weber, *Theory of Social and Economic Organization* (Glencoe, Ill.: Free Press, 1947).

7. Crane Brinton, *The Anatomy of Revolution* (New York: Vintage Books, 1965).

8. J. L. McClelland, "The Programmable Blackboard Model of Reading," in Rumelhart and McClelland, *Parallel Distributed Processing,* vol. 2, pp. 122–169; Roger C. Schank, *Tell Me a Story* (New York: Scribner's, 1990).

9. Melanie Mitchell, "What Can Complex Systems Approaches Offer the Cognitive Sciences?" Paper presented at the Annual Meeting of the Society for Philosophy and Psychology, State University of New York at Stony Brook, New York (June 10, 1995).

10. Dan Sperber and Deirdre Wilson, *Relevance: Communication and Cognition* (Cambridge, Mass.: Harvard University Press, 1986); H. Paul Grice, *Studies in the Way of Words* (Cambridge, Mass.: Harvard University Press, 1989).

11. Georg Henrik von Wright, *Explanation and Understanding* (Ithaca, N.Y.: Cornell University Press, 1971); Jerome Bruner, "Narrative and Paradigmatic Modes of Thought," in Elliot Eisner, ed., *Learning and Teaching the Ways of Knowing: Eighty-fourth Yearbook of the National Society for the Study of Education* (Chicago: University of Chicago Press, 1985), pp. 97–115.

12. von Wright, *Explanation and Understanding.*

13. Rumelhart and McClelland, eds., *Parallel Distributed Processing.*

14. Bruer, *Schools for Thought.*

15. Annette Karmiloff-Smith, *A Functional Approach to Child Language: A Study of Determiners and Reference* (Cambridge: Cambridge University Press, 1979); Karmiloff-Smith, *Beyond Modularity: A Developmental Perspective on Cognitive Science* (Cambridge, Mass.: MIT Press, 1992).

16. Melanie Mitchell, "What Can Complex Systems Approaches Offer the Cognitive Sciences?" Paper presented at the Annual Meeting of the Society for Philosophy and Psychology, State University of New York at Stony Brook, New York (June 10, 1995); James P. Crutchfield and Melanie Mitchell, *The*

Evolution of Emergent Computation, Santa Fe Institute Technical Report 94-03-012 (Santa Fe, N.J.: Santa Fe Institute, 1994).

17. Ann Brown and Joseph Campione have, for example, put the "rule of description" to work in their Oakland project. They make it a virtually obligatory step for their pupils. They even use a computer whose program requires a more general redescription of any specific "conclusion."

18. Allen Newell and Herbert A. Simon, *Human Problem Solving* (Englewood Cliffs, N.J.: Prentice-Hall).

19. Susan Chipman and Alan L. Meyrowitz, *Foundations of Knowledge Acquisition,* vols. 1 and 2 (Boston: Kluwer Academic Publishers, 1993).

20. Nelson Goodman, *Ways of Worldmaking* (Indianapolis: Hackett, 1978).

21. See, for example, Keith Oatley, *Best Laid Schemes: The Psychology of Emotions* (Cambridge: Cambridge University Press, 1992), or the pages of the journal *Cognition and Emotion* (Hove, East Sussex: Lawrence Erlbaum Associates).

22. Robert B. Zajonc, "Feeling and Thinking: Preferences Need No Inferences," *American Psychologist,* 35(2) (1980): 151–175; Richard S. Lazarus, "A Cognitivist's Reply to Zajonc on Emotion and Cognition," *American Psychologist,* 36 (1981): 222–223; Lazarus, "Thoughts on the Relations between Emotion and Cognition," *American Psychologist,* 37(9) (1982): 1019–1024; Zajonc, "On the Primacy of Affect," *American Psychologist,* 39(2) (1984): 117–123; Lazarus, "On the Primacy of Cognition," *American Psychologist,* 39(2) (1984): 124–129.

23. Bruner, *Acts of Meaning;* Carol Fleisher Feldman and David A. Kalmar, "Some Educational Implications of Genre-Based Mental Models," in David Olson and Nancy Torrance, eds., *Handbook of Education and Human Development* (Oxford: Blackwell, 1996), pp. 434–460.

24. For a fuller discussion of this point, see Goodman, *Ways of Worldmaking;* Richard Rorty, *Philosophy and the Mirror of Nature* (Princeton, N.J.: Princeton University Press, 1979).

25. David A. J. Richards, *Toleration and the Constitution* (New York: Oxford University Press, 1986); Richards, *Foundations of American Constitutionalism* (New York: Oxford University Press, 1989).

26. Burrhus Frederic Skinner, *Beyond Freedom and Dignity* (New York: Knopf, 1971); Stephen P. Stich, *From Folk Psychology to Cognitive Science: The Case Against Belief* (Cambridge, Mass.: MIT Press, 1983); Daniel C. Dennett, *Consciousness Explained* (Boston: Little, Brown, 1991).

27. Herbert L. A. Hart, *The Morality of the Criminal Law: Two Lectures* (Jerusalem: Magnes Press, Hebrew University, 1964); Hart, *Punishment and Responsibility: Essays in the Philosophy of Law* (New York: Oxford, 1968).

28. Stephen C. Levinson and Penelope Brown, "Immanuel Kant Against the Tenejapans: Anthropology as Empirical Philosophy," *Ethos,* 22(1) (1994): 3–41.

29. Vygotsky, *Thought and Language.*

30. Benjamin L. Whorf, *Language, Thought, and Reality: Selected Writings* (Cambridge, Mass.: Technology Press of MIT, 1956).

31. See Steven Pinker, *The Language Instinct* (New York: W. Morrow, 1994). For a well-reasoned refutation of this narrow conception, see Michael Tomasello, "Language Is Not an Instinct," *Cognitive Development,* 10 (1995): 131–156.

32. See, for example, Wolfgang Iser, *Laurence Sterne: Tristram Shandy* (Cambridge: Cambridge University Press, 1988); Julian Barnes, *Flaubert's Parrot* (New York: Knopf, 1985); Wayne C. Booth, *The Rhetoric of Fiction,* 2nd ed.(Chicago: University of Chicago Press, 1983).

33. For a good summary of these debates, see Bradd Shore, *Culture in Mind* (New York: Oxford University Press, 1996).

34. Alison F. Garton and Chris Pratt, *Learning to Be Literate: The Development of Spoken and Written Language* (Oxford: Basil Blackwell, 1989).

35. Roman Jakobson, "Poetry of Grammar and Grammar of Poetry," in Jakobson, *Selected Writings, III: Poetry of Grammar and Grammar of Poetry* (The Hague: Mouton, 1981), pp. 87–97.

36. Olson, *The World on Paper.*

37. Goodman, *Ways of Worldmaking.*

38. E. Sue Savage-Rumbaugh, Jeannine Murphy, Rose A. Sevcik, Karen E. Brakke, Shelly L. Williams, and Duane M. Rumbaugh, "Language Comprehension in Ape and Child," *Monographs of the Society for Research in Child Development,* 58 (3–4, Serial No. 233) (1993); Michael Tomasello, Ann Cale Kruger, and Hilary Horn Ratner, "Cultural Learning," *Behavioral and Brain Sciences,* 16 (1993): 495–552.

39. Colwyn B. Trevarthen, "Form, Significance, and Psychological Potential of Hand Gestures of Infants," in Jean-Luc Nespoulous, Paul Perron, and Andre Roch Lecours, eds., *The Biological Foundations of Gestures: Motor and Semiotic Aspects* (Hillsdale, N.J.: Erlbaum, 1986), pp. 149–202; Alison Gopnik, "How We Know Our Minds: The Illusion of First-Person Knowledge of Intentionality," *Behavioral and Brain Sciences* 16 (1993): 1–14; Alison Gopnik and Andrew N. Meltzoff, "Minds, Bodies, and Persons: Young Children's Understanding of the Self and Others as Reflected in Imitation and Theory of Mind Research," in Sue Taylor Parker, Robert W. Mitchell, and Maria L. Boccia, eds., *Self-Awareness in Animals and Humans: Developmental Perspectives* (Cambridge: Cambridge University Press, 1994), pp. 166–186.

40. Ignace Meyerson, *Les Fonctions Psychologiques et les Oeuvres* (Paris: J. Vrin, 1948); Meyerson, *Écrits, 1920–1983: Pour une Psychologie Historique* (Paris: Presses

Universitaires de France, 1987). An appreciation of Meyerson's work is contained in Françoise Parot, ed., *Les Oeuvres d'Ignace Meyerson: Un Hommage* (Paris: Presses Universitaires de France, in press), in which is included Jerome Bruner's "Meyerson aujourd'hui: Quelques Reflexions sur la Psychologie Culturelle."

41. This is a verbatim remark made to me by a ten-year-old in one of the Oakland classrooms, commenting on the plan his class was devising to deal with disasters like the oil spill from the *Exxon Valdez* two years earlier—a class project in ecology.

42. Lucien Febvre and H.-J. Martin, *L'Apparition du Livre*, L'Evolution de l'Humanité, 49 (Paris: Albin Michel, 1958); Lucien P. V. Febvre, *The Problem of Unbelief in the Sixteenth Century: The Religion of Rabelais* (Cambridge, Mass.: Harvard University Press, 1982); Febvre, *A Geographical Introduction to History* (Westport, Conn.: Greenwood Press, 1974); Marc L. B. Bloch, *Feudal Society* (Chicago: University of Chicago Press, 1961); Bloch, *French Rural History: An Essay on Its Basic Characteristics* (Berkeley: University of California Press, 1966); Bloch, *Land and Work in Mediaeval Europe: Selected Papers* (London: Routledge and Kegan Paul, 1967); François Furet, *In the Workshop of History* (Chicago: University of Chicago Press, 1984); François Dosse, *New History in France: The Triumph of the Annales* (Urbana: University of Illinois Press, 1994).

43. These sketches are exhibited at the Picasso Museum in Barcelona.

44. For a more general discussion of this process, see Eric Hobsbawm and Terence Ranger, eds., *The Invention of Tradition* (Cambridge: Cambridge University Press, 1983).

45. Sara Lawrence Lightfoot, *The Good High School: Portraits of Character and Culture* (New York: Basic Books, 1983).

46. Michael Cole and A. V. Belayeva, "Computer-Mediated Joint Activity and the Problem of Mental Development," *Soviet Journal of Psychology*, 12(2) (1991): 133–141.

47. Richard J. Herrnstein and Charles Murray, *The Bell Curve: Intelligence and Class Structure in American Life* (New York: Free Press, 1994); see also Steven Fraser, ed., *The Bell Curve Wars: Race, Intelligence, and the Future of America* (New York: Basic Books, 1995).

48. Howard Gardner, *Frames of Mind: The Theory of Multiple Intelligences* (New York: Basic Books, 1983).

49. *Faulkner v. Jones*, 51 F.3d 440 (1993).

50. See Thomas Ross, "The Richmond Narratives," 68 *Texas Law Review* 381 (1989): 1–28.

51. I am grateful to Daniel Rose for this example from an experimental public middle school in Harlem, Mott Hall Middle School, where a tutoring program has been sponsored for the past several years by the Rose Foundation.

The decision to sponsor and provide coaching for the school's chess club was taken by the school and the Foundation with full consciousness of the symbolism of chess as a "brainy" game.

52. Claude Lévi-Strauss, *Structural Anthropology* (New York: Basic Books, 1963).

53. Walter Lippmann, *Public Opinion* (New York: Harcourt, Brace, 1927); John Dewey, *The Public and Its Problems* (Chicago: Swallow Press, 1954).

54. Pierre Bourdieu, *Language and Symbolic Power* (Cambridge, Mass.: Harvard University Press, 1991).

55. Henri Tajfel, ed., *Differentiation between Social Groups: Studies in the Social Psychology of Intergroup Relations* (London: Academic Press, 1978); Tajfel, *Human Groups and Social Categories: Studies in Social Psychology* (Cambridge: Cambridge University Press, 1981).

56. Harry Judge, Michel Lemosse, Lynn Paine, and Michael Sedlek, *The University and the Teachers: France, the United States, England* (Wallingford: Triangle, 1994).

57. I had the privilege of participating in one such meeting of the province of Piedmont, held at Turin in July of 1993. The liveliness of the exchanges, as well as their coverage in such major newspapers as *La Stampa,* was striking.

58. There have of course been notable exceptions. One need only cite the work of Lawrence A. Cremin, *Popular Education and Its Discontents* (New York: Harper & Row, 1990); Theodore W. Schultz, *The Economic Value of Education* (New York: Columbia University Press, 1963); Neil Postman, *Conscientious Objections: Stirring Up Trouble about Language, Technology, and Education* (New York: Knopf, 1988); Pierre Bourdieu, *Language and Symbolic Power* (Cambridge, Mass.: Harvard University Press, 1991); Shirley Brice Heath, *Ways with Words: Language, Life, and Work in Communities and Classrooms* (Cambridge: Cambridge University Press, 1983); and most recently, Harry Judge, *The University and the Teachers: France, the United States, England* (Wallingford: Triangle, 1994). There has also been a recent and lively growth of studies in what has come to be called the "ethnography of the classroom," such as Hugh Mehan's *Learning Lessons: Social Organization in the Classroom* (Cambridge, Mass.: Harvard University Press, 1979), which, though limited to self-contained school communities, have shed much light on how broader authority and affiliative patterns within the culture mirror themselves in classroom practices.

59. Robert B. Reich, *The Work of Nations: Preparing Ourselves for Twenty-first-Century Capitalism* (New York: Knopf, 1991); Daniel Bell, *The Coming of Post-Industrial Society: A Venture in Social Forecasting* (New York: Basic Books, 1976).

60. James Clifford, *The Predicament of Culture: Twentieth-Century Ethnography, Literature, and Art* (Cambridge, Mass.: Harvard University Press, 1988).

61. See Peter B. Dow, *Schoolhouse Politics: Lessons from the Sputnik Era* (Cambridge, Mass.: Harvard University Press, 1991); Dorothy Nelkin, *Science Textbook Controversies and the Politics of Equal Time* (Cambridge, Mass.: MIT Press, 1977); Comptroller General of the United States, *Report to the House Committee on Science and Technology: Administration of the Science Education Project—Man: A Course of Study*, October 14, 1975.

62. George H. Mead, *Mind, Self, and Society from the Standpoint of a Social Behaviorist* (Chicago: University of Chicago Press, 1962); Paul Ricoeur, *Oneself as Another* (Chicago: University of Chicago Press, 1992); Nicholas Humphrey, *Consciousness Regained: Chapters in the Development of Mind* (Oxford: Oxford University Press, 1983); Robert Jay Lifton, *The Life of the Self: Toward a New Psychology* (New York: Basic Books, 1983).

63. Hazel Rose Markus and Shinobu Kitayama, "Culture and the Self: Implications for Cognition, Emotion, and Motivation," *Psychological Review*, 98(2) (1991): 224–253.

64. Jean Pierre Vernant, *Myth and Society in Ancient Greece* (Sussex: Harvester Press, 1980); Vernant, *The Origins of Greek Thought* (Ithaca, N.Y.: Cornell University Press, 1982); Vernant, *Myth and Thought among the Greeks* (London: Routledge, 1983); Vernant, *Myth and Tragedy in Ancient Greece* (Cambridge, Mass.: MIT Press, 1988).

65. John Campbell, *Past, Space, and Self* (Cambridge, Mass.: MIT Press, 1994).

66. Erich von Holst, *The Behavioural Physiology of Animals and Man: The Collected Papers of Erich von Holst* (Coral Gables, Fla.: University of Miami Press, 1973).

67. David Rubin, ed., *Remembering Our Past* (Cambridge: Cambridge University Press, 1996).

68. Markus and Kitayama, "Culture and the Self"; Kurt Lewin, Tamara Dembo, Leon Festinger, and Pauline Snedden Sears, "Level of Aspiration," in J. McV. Hunt, ed., *Personality and the Behavioral Disorders: A Handbook Based on Experimental and Clinical Research* (New York: Ronald Press, 1944), pp. 333–378; J. W. Atkinson, "Motivational Determinants of Risk-Taking Behavior," *Psychological Review*, 64 (1957): 359–372; J. W. Atkinson and N. T. Feather, eds., *A Theory of Achievement Motivation* (New York: Wiley, 1966).

69. Muzafer Sherif and Hadley Cantril, *The Psychology of Ego-Involvements, Social Attitudes, and Identification* (New York: John Wiley, 1947).

70. Bruner, *Acts of Meaning*; Vladimir Propp, *Morphology of the Folktale*, 2nd ed., rev. (Austin: University of Texas Press, 1968); William Labov and Joshua

Waletzky, "Narrative Analysis: Oral Versions of Personal Experience," in June Helm, ed., *Essays on the Verbal and Visual Arts: Proceedings of the 1966 Annual Spring Meeting of the American Ethnological Society* (Seattle: American Ethnological Society), pp. 12–44). We'll return to this topic in a later section.

71. For a pioneering discussion of competence, see R. W. White's classic "Motivation Reconsidered: The Concept of Competence," *Psychological Review*, 66 (1959): 297–323.

72. See Ruth F. Benedict, *Patterns of Culture* (Boston: Houghton Mifflin, 1959).

73. Pauline S. Sears and Vivian S. Sherman, *In Pursuit of Self-Esteem: Case Studies of Eight Elementary School Children* (Belmont, Calif.: Wadsworth, 1964).

74. Saul Rosenzweig, *Aggressive Behavior and the Rosenzweig Picture-Frustration Study* (New York: Praeger, 1978).

75. See Norman Garmezy and Michael Rutter, eds., *Stress, Coping, and Development in Children* (New York: McGraw-Hill, 1983); Jon Rolf, ed., *Risk and Protective Factors in the Development of Psychopathology* (Cambridge: Cambridge University Press, 1990); Marc Zimmerman and Revathy Arunkumar, "Resiliency Research: Implications for Schools and Policy," *Social Policy Report*, 8(4) (1994): 1–17.

76. Paulo Freire, *Pedagogy of the Oppressed*, new rev. 20th-anniversary ed. (New York: Continuum, 1994).

77. Pierre Bourdieu, *Distinction: A Social Critique of the Judgment of Taste* (Cambridge, Mass.: Harvard University Press, 1984); Roland Barthes, "Toys," in his *Mythologies* (New York: Hill and Wang, 1982), pp. 53–55.

78. Jerome S. Bruner, *The Process of Education* (Cambridge, Mass.: Harvard University Press, 1960); Bruner, *Toward a Theory of Instruction* (Cambridge, Mass.: Harvard University Press, 1966); Bruner, *The Relevance of Education* (New York: Norton, 1971).

79. See Jerome Bruner, "Narrative and Paradigmatic Modes of Thought," in Elliot Eisner, ed., *Learning and Teaching the Ways of Knowing: Eighty-fourth Yearbook of the National Society for the Study of Education* (Chicago: University of Chicago Press, 1985), pp. 97–115.

80. Jerome Bruner, "Life as Narrative," *Social Research*, 54(1) (1987): 11–32.

81. Donald P. Spence, *Narrative Truth and Historical Truth: Meaning and Interpretation in Psychoanalysis* (New York: W. W. Norton, 1982); Roy Schafer, *Retelling a Life: Narration and Dialogue in Psychoanalysis* (New York: Basic Books, 1992).

82. Ronald M. Dworkin, *Law's Empire* (Cambridge, Mass.: Harvard University Press, 1986); James Boyd White, *Heracles' Bow: Essays on the Rhetoric and Poetics of the Law* (Madison: University of Wisconsin Press, 1985).

83. Carol F. Feldman, Jerome Bruner, David Kalmar, and Bobbi Renderer, "Plot, Plight, and Dramatism: Interpretation at Three Ages," *Human Development,* 36(6) (1993): 327–342.

84. Jerome Bruner and Carol Feldman, "Theories of Mind and the Problem of Autism," in Simon Baron-Cohen, Helen Tager-Flusberg, and Donald J. Cohen, eds., *Understanding Other Minds: Perspectives from Autism* (Oxford: Oxford University Press, 1993), pp. 267–291; Oliver Sacks, "A Neurologist's Notebook: An Anthropologist on Mars," *The New Yorker,* 69(44) (1993): 106–125.

85. Bruno Bettelheim, *The Uses of Enchantment: The Meaning and Importance of Fairy Tales* (New York: Random House, 1989); Donald E. Polkinghorne, *Narrative Knowing and the Human Sciences* (Albany: State University of New York Press, 1988).

86. Shirley Brice Heath, *Ways with Words: Language, Life, and Work in Communities and Classrooms* (Cambridge: Cambridge University Press, 1983).

87. Simon Schama, *Dead Certainties: Unwarranted Speculations* (New York: Knopf, 1991).

88. See Bruner, "Narrative and Paradigmatic Modes of Thought"; Shelby Anne Wolf and Shirley Brice Heath, *The Braid of Literature: Children's Worlds of Reading* (Cambridge, Mass.: Harvard University Press, 1992); Carole Peterson and Allyssa McCabe, *Developmental Psycholinguistics: Three Ways of Looking at a Child's Narrative* (New York: Plenum, 1983); Allyssa McCabe and Carole Peterson, eds., *Developing Narrative Structure* (Hillsdale, N.J.: Erlbaum, 1991); *Journal of Narrative and Life History* (Hillsdale, N.J.: Erlbaum); Theodore R. Sarbin, ed., *Narrative Psychology: The Storied Nature of Human Conduct* (New York: Praeger, 1986); Richard J. Gerrig, *Experiencing Narrative Worlds: On the Psychological Activities of Reading* (New Haven, Conn.: Yale University Press, 1993).

89. Both the National Council of Teachers of Mathematics and the National Science Teachers Association are actively involved in such efforts. See, for example, *Curriculum and Evaluation Standards for School Mathematics* (Reston, Va.: National Council of Teachers of Mathematics, 1989), and *Professional Standards for School Mathematics* (Reston, Va.: National Council of Teachers of Mathematics, 1991). A report on the progress of these efforts is contained in Mary M. Lindquist, John A. Dossey, and Ina V. S. Mullis, *Reaching Standards: A Progress Report on Mathematics* (Princeton, N.J.: Policy Information Center, Educational Testing Service, undated [appeared 1995]).

90. A good example of the kind of material that might make the quest of science come more alive is Robert B. Silvers, ed., *Hidden Histories of Science* (New York: New York Review of Books, 1995), with accounts of the coun-

terintuitive dramas of discovery in the natural sciences as told by such master storyteller scientists as Stephen Jay Gould and Oliver Sacks.

2. FOLK PEDAGOGY

1. A. C. Kruger and M. Tomasello, "Cultural Learning and Learning Culture," in *Handbook of Education and Human Development* (Oxford: Blackwell, 1996).

2. M. Tomasello, A. C. Kruger, and H. Ratner, "Cultural Learning," *Behavioral and Brain Sciences,* 16(3) (1993): 495–511.

3. E. S. Savage-Rumbaugh, J. Murphy, R. A. Sevcik, K. E. Brakke, S. L. Williams, and D. L. Rumbaugh, "Language Comprehension in Ape and Child," *Monographs of the Society for Research in Child Development,* 58 (3–4, Serial No. 233) (1993).

4. R. S. Fouts, D. H. Fouts, and D. Schoenfeld, "Sign Language Conversational Interaction between Chimpanzees," *Sign Language Studies,* 42 (1984): 1–12; J. Goodall, *The Chimpanzees of Gombe: Patterns of Behavior* (Cambridge, Mass.: Harvard University Press, 1986).

5. Tomasello, Kruger, and Ratner, "Cultural Learning."

6. D. L. Cheney and R. M. Seyfarth, *How Monkeys See the World* (Chicago: University of Chicago Press, 1990).

7. E. Visalberghi and D. M. Fragaszy, "Do Monkeys Ape?" in S. Parker and K. Gibson, eds., *"Language" and Intelligence in Monkeys and Apes: Comparative Developmental Perspectives* (Cambridge: Cambridge University Press, 1991).

8. B. Rogoff, J. Mistry, A. Goncu, and C. Mosier, "Guided Participation in Cultural Activity by Toddlers and Caregivers," *Monographs of the Society for Research in Child Development,* 58 (8, Serial No. 236) (1993).

9. J. Bruner, *Acts of Meaning* (Cambridge, Mass.: Harvard University Press, 1990).

10. J. Astington, P. Harris, and D. Olson, eds., *Developing Theories of Mind* (Cambridge: Cambridge University Press, 1988).

11. C. Bereiter and M. Scardamaglia, *Surpassing Ourselves: An Inquiry into the Nature and Implications of Expertise* (Chicago: Open Court, 1993).

12. A. L. Brown and J. C. Campione, "Communities of Learning and Thinking, Or a Context by Any Other Name," in Deanna Kuhn, ed., *Developmental Perspectives on Teaching and Learning Thinking Skills, Contributions in Human Development,* 21 (Basel: Krager, 1990), pp. 108–126.

13. H. Gardner, *The Unschooled Mind* (New York: Basic Books, 1991), p. 253.

14. Tomasello, Kruger, and Ratner, "Cultural Learning."

15. K. Egan, *Primary Understanding* (New York: Routledge, 1988), p. 45.

16. V. Turner, *From Ritual to Theater: The Human Seriousness of Play* (New York: Performing Arts Journal Publications, 1982).

17. Brown and Campione, "Communities of Learning and Thinking."

18. See J. S. Bruner, J. J. Goodnow, and G. A. Austin, *A Study of Thinking* (New York: Wiley, 1956).

19. See also J. S. Bruner and D. R. Olson, "Learning through Experience and Learning through Media," in G. Gerbner, L. P. Gross, and W. Melody, eds., *Communications Technology and Social Policy: Understanding the New "Cultural Revolution"* (New York: Wiley, 1973).

20. Tomasello, Kruger, and Ratner, "Cultural Learning."

21. B. Latour and S. Woolgar, *Laboratory Life: The Social Construction of Scientific Facts* (Princeton, N.J.: Princeton University Press, 1986).

22. See T. Gladwin, *East Is a Big Bird* (Cambridge, Mass.: Harvard University Press, 1970).

23. C. F. Feldman, "Oral Metalanguage," in D. R. Olson and N. Torrance, eds., *Literacy and Orality* (Cambridge: Cambridge University Press, 1991), pp. 47–65.

24. B. Stock, *The Implications of Literacy* (Princeton, N.J.: Princeton University Press, 1983).

25. See J. Bruner, "From Joint Attention to the Meeting of Minds," in C. Moore and F. Dunham, eds., *Joint Attention* (New York: Academic Press, in press).

26. See J. Astington, *The Child's Discovery of the Mind* (Cambridge, Mass.: Harvard University Press, 1993) for a summary of this work.

27. A. Brown, "The Development of Memory: Knowing, Knowing about Knowing, and Knowing How to Know," in H. W. Reese, ed., *Advances in Child Development and Behavior,* vol. 10 (New York: Academic Press, 1975).

28. C. Bereiter and M. Scardamaglia, *Surpassing Ourselves: An Inquiry into the Nature and Implications of Expertise* (Chicago: Open Court, 1993); M. Scardamaglia, C. Bereiter, C. Brett, P. J. Burtis, C. Calhoun, and N. Smith Lea, "Educational Applications of a Networked Communal Database," *Interactive Learning Environments,* 2(1) (1992): 45–71; Ann L. Brown and Joseph C. Campione, "Communities of Learning and Thinking, Or a Context by any Other Name," in Deanna Kuhn, ed., *Developmental Perspectives on Teaching and Learning Thinking Skills,* Contributions in Human Development, 21 (Basel: Krager, 1990), pp. 108–126; Roy D. Pea, "Seeing What We Build Together: Distributed Multimedia Learning Environments for Transformative Communications," *The Journal of the Learning Sciences,* 3(3) (1994): 219–225.

29. See, for example, Ingrid Pramling, *Learning to Learn: A Study of Swedish Preschool Children* (New York: Springer-Verlag, 1990).

30. I. Hacking, *The Emergence of Probability: A Philosophical Study of Early Ideas about Probability, Induction, and Statistical Inference* (Cambridge: Cambridge University Press, 1975).

31. K. Popper, *Objective Knowledge: An Evolutionary Approach* (Oxford: Oxford U. Press, 1972).

32. T. Nagel, *The View from Nowhere* (New York: Oxford U. Press, 1986).

33. T. Kuhn, *The Structure of Scientific Revolutions* (Chicago: University of Chicago Press, 1962).

34. Personal communication.

35. M. Donaldson, *Human Minds: An Exploration* (London: Allen Lane, Penguin Press, 1992).

36. For a particularly thoughtful account of the Western orientation of anthropological writing, see Clifford Geertz, *Works and Lives: The Anthropologist as Author* (Stanford, Calif.: Stanford University Press, 1988).

3. THE COMPLEXITY OF EDUCATIONAL AIMS

1. R. J. Herrnstein and C. Murray, *The Bell Curve: Intelligence and Class Structure in American Life* (New York: Free Press, 1994).

2. C. Geertz, *After the Fact* (Cambridge, Mass.: Harvard U. Press, 1995); Geertz, *Local Knowledge* (New York: Basic Books, 1983).

3. J. Derrida, *Writing and Difference* (Chicago: U. of Chicago Press, 1978).

4. J. McV. Hunt, *Intelligence and Experience* (New York: Ronald Press, 1961).

5. For an overview of this work, see W. H. Calvin, *The Throwing Madonna: From Nervous Cells to Hominid Brains* (New York: McGraw-Hill, 1983).

6. M. R. Rosenzweig, "Environmental Complexity, Cerebral Change, and Behavior," *American Psychologist,* 21 (1996): 321–332.

7. M. A. Ribble, "Infantile Experience in Relation to Personality Development," in J. McV. Hunt, ed., *Personality and the Behavior Disorders* (New York: Ronald Press, 1944).

8. See B. S. Bloom, *Stability and Change in Human Characteristics* (New York: Wiley, 1964); see also Bloom, *Human Characteristics and School Learning* (Chicago: University of Chicago Press, 1976).

9. William Kessen, *The Rise and Fall of Development* (Worcester, Mass.: Clark U. Press, 1990).

10. See I. Kalins and J. Bruner, "The Coordination of Visual Observation and Instrumental Behavior in Early Infancy," *Perception,* 2 (1973): 307–314; H. Papousek, "From Adaptive Responses to Social Cognition: The Learning View of Development," in M. H. Bornstein and W. Kessen, eds., *Psychological Development from Infancy: Image to Intention* (Hillsdale, N.J.: Erlbaum, 1979).

11. P. Salapatek, "Pattern Perception in Early Infancy," in L. B. Cohen and P. Salapatek, eds., *Infant Perception: From Sensation to Cognition,* vol. 1 (New York: Academic Press, 1975).

12. N. H. Mackworth and J. S. Bruner, "How Adults and Children Search and Recognize Pictures," *Human Development*, 13(3) (1970): 149–177.

13. M. Scaife and J. S. Bruner, "The Capacity for Joint Visual Attention in the Infant," *Nature*, 253 (1975): 265–266; G. Stechler and E. Latz, "Some Observations on Attention and Arousal in the Human Infant," *Journal of the American Academy of Child Psychiatry*, 5 (1966): 517–525.

14. B. Koslowski and J. S. Bruner, "Learning to Use a Lever," *Child Development*, 43 (1972): 790–799.

15. M. Harrington, *The Other America: Poverty in the United States* (New York: Macmillan, 1962; rev. ed.: Penguin, 1981); Harrington, *The New American Poverty* (New York: Holt, Rinehart, and Winston, 1984).

16. S. W. Gray, R. A. Klaus, J. O. Miller, and B. J. Forrester, *Before First Grade: The Early Training Project for Culturally Disadvantaged Children* (New York: Teachers College Press, 1966); R. A. Klaus and S. W. Gray, *The Early Training Project for Disadvantaged Children: A Report after Five Years* (Chicago: University of Chicago Press, 1968); S. W. Gray, B. K. Ramsey, and R. A. Klaus, *From 3 to 20: The Early Training Project* (Baltimore: University Park Press, 1982); N. Hobbs, *The Troubled and Troubling Child: Reeducation in Mental Health, Education, and Human Services Programs for Children and Youth* (San Francisco: Jossey-Bass, 1982); N. Hobbs, P. R. Dokecki, K. V. Hoover-Dempsey, R. M. Moroney, M. W. Shayne, and K. H. Weeks, *Strengthening Families* (San Francisco: Jossey-Bass, 1984).

17. M. Cole and J. S. Bruner, "Cultural Differences and Inferences about Psychological Processes," *American Psychologist*, 26 (10) (1971): 867–876.

18. 347 U.S. 483 (1954).

19. R. J. Herrnstein, "IQ Testing and the Media," *The Atlantic Monthly* (August 1982): 68–74; A. R. Jensen, "How Much Can We Boost IQ and Scholastic Achievement?" *Harvard Educational Review*, 39(1) (1969): 1–123.

20. E. Zigler and J. Valentine, eds., *Project Head Start: A Legacy of the War on Poverty* (New York: Free Press, 1979); L. J. Schweinhart and D. P. Weikart, "Young Children Grow Up: The Effects of the Perry Preschool Program on Youths through Age 15," *Monographs of the High/Scope Educational Research Foundation*, No. 7 (1980); A. Clarke-Stewart, *Day Care: National Day Care Study Final Reports*, vols. 1–5 (Washington, D.C.: Day Care Division, Administration for Children, Youth, and Families [DHHS], 1982); W. S. Barnett, "Benefit-Cost Analysis of Preschool Education: Findings from a 25-Year Follow-up," *American Journal of Orthopsychiatry*, 63(4) (1993): 500–508. Most of the results reported have been drawn, to be sure, from "better" Head Starts (like the Perry Preschool Program). Though full results are not in, there is no reason to believe this program was different in kind from the others.

21. A. L. Brown, "The Advancement of Learning," *Educational Researcher,* 23(8) (1994): 4–12.

22. Ellen Langer, *Mindfulness* (Reading: Addison-Wesley, 1989).

23. I am grateful to Hanne Haavind and Vibeke Groever Auskrust of the University of Oslo for their accounts of this interesting project.

24. V. G. Paley, *You Can't Say You Can't Play* (Cambridge, Mass.: Harvard University Press, 1992).

25. P. Bourdieu, *Language and Symbolic Power* (Cambridge, Mass.: Harvard University Press, 1991).

26. For the benefit of those not acquainted with the American television culture of a generation ago, "Ozzie and Harriet" (Nelson) were a very well known married pair who starred in a long-running television serial best characterized as midway between a sitcom and a soap opera. For many viewers, they were the idealized American middle-class couple: moderately well off (though not conspicuously so), suburban, youngish with youngish kids, healthy, and conspicuously "trad" in the pattern of husband-at-work/mother-at-home.

27. The figures cited are drawn from D. J. Hernandez, *America's Children: Resources from Family, Government, and the Economy* (New York: Russell Sage Foundation, 1993).

28. H. Judge, *The University and the Teachers: France, the United States, England* (Wallingford: Triangle, 1994).

29. *A Nation at Risk: The Imperative for Educational Reform* (Washington, D.C.: U.S. Government Printing Office, 1983).

30. Ernest Boyer, Annual Report, Carnegie Endowment for the Advancement of Teaching, 1988.

4. Teaching the Present, Past, and Possible

1. One can only marvel at the contrast, say, between the interpretation of the legality of slavery offered by Justice Taney in *Dred Scott v. Sandford,* 60 U.S. 393 (1856), as opposed to the interpretation offered by Lord Mansfield in *Sommersett v. Stuart,* King's Bench: 12 George III A.D. (1771–72), Lofft, 20 Howell's State Trials 1. The difference lies entirely in how the concept of "Natural Law" is construed—Taney presuming it did not preclude slavery, Mansfield that it did. Both these distinguished jurists firmly believed that they were operating within the tradition of Anglo-Saxon common law.

2. Carol Fleisher Feldman, "Monologue as Problem-Solving Narrative," in Katherine Nelson, ed., *Narratives from the Crib* (Cambridge, Mass.: Harvard University Press, 1989), pp. 98–119.

3. Vladimir Propp, *Morphology of the Folktale,* 2nd ed. (Austin: University of Texas Press, 1968).

4. Northrop Frye, *Anatomy of Criticism* (Princeton: Princeton University Press, 1957).

5. Robin George Collingwood, *The Idea of History* (New York: Oxford University Press, 1956); Collingwood, *Essays in the Philosophy of History* (New York: McGraw-Hill, 1965); Clifford Geertz, *The Interpretation of Cultures* (New York: Basic Books, 1973); Geertz, *Local Knowledge;* Clifford Geertz, *After the Fact: Two Countries, Four Decades, One Anthropologist* (Cambridge, Mass.: Harvard University Press, 1995); James Clifford, *The Predicament of Culture: Twentieth Century Ethnography, Literature, and Art* (Cambridge, Mass.: Harvard University Press, 1988).

6. Cynthia Fuchs Epstein, *Deceptive Distinctions: Sex, Gender, and the Social Order* (New Haven: Yale University Press, 1988); James Deese, "Human Abilities versus Intelligence," *Intelligence,* 17 (1993): 107–116.

5. UNDERSTANDING AND EXPLAINING OTHER MINDS

1. R. Adolphs, D. Tranel, H. Damasio, and A. Damasio, "Impaired Recognition of Emotion in Facial Expressions following Bilateral Damage to the Human Amygdala," *Nature,* 372 (1994): 669–672.

2. C. Geertz, *After the Fact: Two Countries, Four Decades, One Anthropologist* (Cambridge, Mass.: Harvard University Press, 1995).

3. C. Geertz, *The Interpretation of Cultures* (New York: Basic Books, 1973).

4. S. J. Tambiah, *Magic, Science, Religion, and the Scope of Rationality* (Cambridge: Cambridge University Press, 1990).

5. F. Furet, *In the Workshop of History* (Chicago: University of Chicago Press, 1985).

6. P. Ariès, *Centuries of Childhood: A Social History of Family Life* (New York: Knopf, 1962).

7. G. A. de Laguna, *Speech, Its Function and Development* (New Haven: Yale University Press, 1927).

8. J. Astington, "Children's Understanding of the Speech Act of Promising," *Journal of Child Language,* 15 (1988): 157–173.

9. J. L. Austin, *How to Do Things with Words* (Oxford: Oxford University Press, 1962).

10. J. Dunn, *The Beginnings of Social Understanding* (Cambridge, Mass.: Harvard University Press, 1988).

11. M. Chandler, A. Fritz, and S. Hala, "Small Scale Deceit: Deception as a Marker of Two-, Three-, and Four-year-olds' Theories of Mind," *Child Development,* 60 (1989): 1263ff.

12. F. G. E. Happé, "The Autobiographical Writings of Three Asperger Syndrome Adults: Problems of Interpretation and Implications for Theory," in

U. Frith, ed., *Autism and Asperger Syndrome* (Cambridge: Cambridge University Press, 1991); J. Bruner and C. Feldman, "Theories of Mind and the Problem of Autism," in S. Baron-Cohen, H. Tager-Flusberg, and D. Cohen, eds., *Understanding Other Minds: The Perspective from Autism* (Cambridge: Cambridge University Press, 1993); O. Sacks, *An Anthropologist on Mars: Seven Paradoxical Tales* (New York: Knopf, 1995).

13. Anat Ninio and Jerome S. Bruner, "The Achievement and Antecedents of Labelling," *Journal of Child Language,* 5 (1978): 1–15.

14. M. Scaife and J. S. Bruner, "The Capacity for Joint Visual Attention in the Infant," *Nature,* 253(5489) (1975): 265–266.

15. Simon Baron-Cohen, "Predisposing Conditions for Joint Attention," in C. Moore and P. Dunham, eds., *Joint Attention* (Hillsdale, N.J.: Erlbaum, in press).

16. M. Tomasello, A. C. Kruger, and H. Ratner, "Cultural Learning," *Behavioral and Brain Sciences,* 16(3) (1993): 495–511. See also commentary on this article in the same issue by Jerome Bruner.

17. E. S. Savage-Rumbaugh, J. Murphy, R. A. Sevcik, K. E. Brakke, S. L. Williams, and D. L. Rumbaugh, "Language Comprehension in Ape and Child," *Monographs of the Society for Research in Child Development,* 58 (3–4, Serial No. 233) (1993); Tomasello, Kruger, and Ratner, "Cultural Learning."

18. E. Muybridge, *Horses and Other Animals in Motion: Forty-five Classic Sequences* (New York: Dover, 1985).

19. J. H. Flavell, F. L. Green, and E. R. Flavell, "Young Children's Knowledge about Thinking," *Monographs of the Society for Research in Child Development,* 60 (1, Serial No. 243) (1995).

20. Paul Harris, "The Rise of Introspection," *Monographs of the Society for Research in Child Development,* 60 (1, Serial No. 243) (1995): 97–103.

21. Umberto Eco, *The Aesthetics of Chaosmos: The Middle Ages of James Joyce* (Cambridge, Mass.: Harvard University Press, 1989).

22. D. C. Dennett, *Consciousness Explained* (Boston: Little, Brown, 1991).

23. J. Fodor, *Modularity of Mind: Faculty Psychology* (Cambridge, Mass.: MIT Press, 1983).

24. For example, N. Ach, *Ueber die Willenstätigkeit und das Denken* (1905). Referenced in E. G. Boring, *A History of Experimental Psychology,* 2nd ed. (New York: Appleton, 1950).

25. Johann F. Herbart, *Collected Works,* ed. K. Kehrbach and O. Fluegel (Leipzig, 1887–1912; reprinted 1963).

26. There are many things in this category, important matters that we do not understand but about which we are nonetheless obliged to converse. I include among them *love, reverence, envy, justice.* In the course of conversing we constitute recognizable entities by specifying practices and behaviors deemed

appropriate to them. This does not in any sense amount to a charge of non-rationality. Concepts and ideas that are constituted by such conventionalizing transactions make up most of what a culture is about.

27. Janet Wilde Astington and David R. Olson, "The Cognitive Revolution in Children's Understanding of Mind," *Human Development,* 38 (1995): 179–189.

28. Janet W. Astington, "Talking It Over with My Brain," *Monographs of the SRCD,* 60 (1, Serial No. 243) (1995), p. 109.

29. P. Harris, *Children and Emotion* (Oxford: Blackwell, 1989), cited by Astington, "Talking It Over with My Brain," p. 109.

30. Astington, "Talking It Over with My Brain," p. 109.

31. Roman Jakobson, *Selected Writings,* vol. 2: *Word and Language* (Amsterdam: Mouton, 1971).

32. E. Ochs, *Culture and Language Development* (Cambridge: Cambridge University Press, 1988).

33. H. Markus and S. Kitayama, "Culture and the Self: Implications for Cognition, Emotion, and Motivation," *Psychological Review,* 98 (1991): 224–253.

34. C. Goodwin and A. Duranti, "Rethinking Context: An Introduction," in A. Duranti and C. Goodwin, eds., *Reading, Thinking, Context: Language as an Interactive Phenomenon* (Cambridge: Cambridge University Press, 1992), pp. 1–42.

35. J. M. Bachnik and C. J. Quinn, eds., *Situated Meaning: Inside and Outside in Japanese Self, Society, and Language* (Princeton, N.J.: Princeton University Press, 1994).

36. A. Wierzbicka, *Semantics, Culture, and Cognition: Human Concepts in Culture-specific Configurations* (New York and Oxford: Oxford University Press, 1992).

37. Alfred L. Kroeber, "The Superorganic," *American Anthropologist,* 19(2) (1917): 163–213.

38. Ibid., p. 169.

39. Ibid., p. 195.

40. J. N. Spuhler, ed., *The Evolution of Man's Capacity for Culture* (Detroit: Wayne State University Press, 1959).

41. T. Nagel, "Reason and Relativism." The Trilling Lecture, delivered at Columbia University, spring 1995.

42. Astington and Olson, "The Cognitive Revolution in Children's Understanding of Mind," p. 187.

43. Geoffrey E. R. Lloyd, "Modes of Thought in Early Greek and Chinese Science." The Stubbs Lecture, delivered at the University of Toronto, 1993. To appear in David Olson and Nancy Torrance, eds., *Modes of Thought* (Cambridge: Cambridge University Press, in press).

44. Carol Feldman, Jerome Bruner, and David Kalmar, "Reply," *Human Development,* 36 (1993): 346–349.

45. J. Bruner, *Acts of Meaning* (Cambridge, Mass.: Harvard U. Press, 1990).

46. Bruner, "From Joint Attention to the Meeting of Minds."

47. B. Schieffelin and E. Ochs, "Language Socialization," *Annual Review of Anthropology,* 15 (1986): 163–246.

48. H. Clark, *Arenas of Language Use* (Chicago: U. of Chicago Press, 1992).

49. P. Bourdieu, *Language and Symbolic Power* (Cambridge, Mass.: Harvard University Press, 1991).

50. Tomasello, Kruger, and Ratner, "Cultural Learning."

51. S. Shanker, "Locating Bruner," *Language and Communication,* 13 (1993): 239–264; D. Sperber, "The Mind as a Whole" (review of Bruner, *Actual Minds, Possible Worlds*), *Times Literary Supplement,* Nov. 21 (1986): 1308–9.

52. Hilary Putnam, *Renewing Philosophy* (Cambridge, Mass.: Harvard University Press, 1992).

53. Alfred Kazin, *The Portable Blake* (N.Y.: Penguin, 1976), pp. 209–210.

6. NARRATIVES OF SCIENCE

1. Margaret C. Donaldson, *Children's Minds* (New York: Norton, 1978).

2. D. Wood, J. S. Bruner, and G. Ross, "The Role of Tutoring in Problem Solving," *Journal of Child Psychology and Psychiatry,* 17 (1976): 89–100.

3. Personal communication.

4. James Bryant Conant, *Harvard Case Histories in Experimental Science,* 2 vols. (Cambridge: Harvard University Press, 1957).

7. THE NARRATIVE CONSTRUAL OF REALITY

1. Donald P. Spence, *Narrative Truth and Historical Truth* (New York: W. W. Norton, 1982); Donald E. Polkinghorne, *Narrative Knowing and the Human Sciences* (Albany, N.Y.: SUNY Press, 1988).

2. M. H. Erdelyi, "A New Look at the New Look: Perceptual Defense and Vigilance," *Psychological Review,* 80 (1974): 1–25; J. Bruner, "Another Look at New Look 1," *American Psychologist,* 47 (1992): 780–783; Bruner, "The View from the Heart's Eye: A Commentary," in P. M. Niedenthal and S. Kitayama, eds., *The Heart's Eye* (San Diego: Academic Press, 1994), pp. 269–286.

3. A striking example of this new emphasis is provided in a study by Carol Fleisher Feldman, *The Development of Adaptive Intelligence* (San Francisco: Jossey-Bass, 1974).

4. J. Seeley Brown, A. Collins, and P. Duguid, "Situated Cognition and the Culture of Learning," *Educational Researcher,* 18 (1988): 32–42.

5. Harriet Zuckerman, *Scientific Elite: Nobel Laureates in the United States* (New York: Free Press, 1977).

6. T. Gladwin, *East Is a Big Bird;* R. Rosaldo, *Culture and Truth: The Remaking of Social Analysis* (Boston: Beacon Press, 1989); C. Geertz, *Local Knowledge* (New York: Basic Books, 1983); J. Bruner, *Acts of Meaning* (Cambridge, Mass.: Harvard University Press, 1990).

7. Susan Carey, *Conceptual Change in Childhood* (Cambridge, Mass.: MIT Press, 1985).

8. James D. Watson, *The Double Helix: A Personal Account of the Discovery of the Structure of DNA* (New York: Atheneum, 1968); Richard Feynman, *"Surely you're joking, Mr. Feynman": Adventures of a Curious Character* (New York: W. W. Norton, 1985); Abraham Pais, *Subtle Is the Lord: The Science and Life of Albert Einstein* (Oxford: Oxford University Press, 1982); Pais, *Einstein Lived Here: Essays for the Layman* (Oxford: Oxford University Press, 1994).

9. Ann L. Brown and Joseph C. Campione, "Communities of Learning and Thinking, Or a Context by Any Other Name," in Deanna Kuhn, ed., *Developmental Perspectives on Teaching and Learning Thinking Skills,* Contributions in Human Development, 21 (Basel: Karger, 1990), pp. 108–126.

10. Many of the points that will concern us in this chapter were first broached in scholarly discussion in 1981 in a collection of essays entitled *On Narrative* (W. J. T. Mitchell, ed. [Chicago: University of Chicago Press, 1981]). Some of the arguments in this chapter are, in effect, reflections on that collection.

11. Paul Ricoeur, *Time and Narrative,* vol. 1 (Chicago: University of Chicago Press, 1984).

12. W. Labov and J. Waletzky, "Narrative Analysis," in *Essays on the Verbal and Visual Arts* (Seattle: University of Washington Press, 1967); Labov, "Speech Actions and Reactions in Personal Narrative," *Georgetown University Round Table on Languages and Linguistics,* 1981, pp. 219–247.

13. Nelson Goodman, "Twisted Tales: or Story, Study, or Symphony," in Mitchell, ed., *On Narrative.*

14. *Kinds of Literature* (Cambridge, Mass.: Harvard University Press, 1982), p. 37.

15. Northrop Frye, *Anatomy of Criticism: Four Essays* (Princeton, N.J.: Princeton University Press, 1957).

16. In a study by Carol Feldman and David Kalmar, for example, a semi-autobiographical story by Primo Levi about an episode at a riverboat stop in rural Russia was read to some subjects as "autobiography," to another group as an adventure story. The former group, to take only one finding, found the characters in the story rather "thin"; the others found them "rich" and "suggestive." Such is the influence of genre even on the details of a textually identical account! See Carol Fleisher Feldman and David A. Kalmar, "Autobiography and

Fiction as Modes of Thought," in David Olson and Nancy Torrance, eds., *Modes of Thought: Explorations in Culture and Cognition* (Cambridge: Cambridge University Press, in press).

17. The information regarding these events is drawn from an article by Nuala O'Faolain in *The Irish Times* on September 9, 1994, reporting the packed audiences of middle-class women to whom Ms. O'Brien had been giving readings of her novels in the preceding week.

18. Clifford Geertz, "Blurred Genres: The Refiguration of Social Thought," in Geertz, *Local Knowledge: Further Essays in Interpretive Anthropology* (New York: Basic Books, 1983), pp. 19–35.

19. See Carol Fleisher Feldman, "Genres as Mental Models," in Massimo Ammaniti and Daniel N. Stern, eds., *Psychoanalysis and Development: Representations and Narratives* (New York: New York University Press, 1994), pp. 111–121.

20. Michel Leiris, *Manhood: A Journey from Childhood into the Fierce Order of Virility,* trans. Richard Howard (New York: Grossman, 1963).

21. "Interpretation and the Sciences of Man," in Paul Rabinow and William M. Sullivan, *Interpretive Social Science: A Reader* (Berkeley: University of California Press, 1979), p. 28.

22. We know very little about how human beings go about the hermeneutics of narrative. Its neglect by students of mind can probably be traced to its remoteness from both the rationalist and the empiricist traditions. There is much new interest in the nature and use of narrative, as in psychoanalysis—Donald P. Spence, *Narrative Truth and Historical Truth: Meaning and Interpretation in Psychoanalysis* (New York: W. W. Norton, 1982); Roy Schafer, *Retelling a Life: Narrative and Dialogue in Psychoanalysis* (New York: Basic Books, 1992); in life history writing—William Lowell Randall, *The Stories We Are: An Essay on Self-Creation* (Toronto: University of Toronto Press, 1995); and in clinical practice—Donald E. Polkinghorne, *Narrative Knowing and the Human Sciences* (Albany, N.Y.: SUNY Press, 1988). But this work is only lightly engaged with the study of the psychological processes that constitute hermeneutic activity.

23. Charles Taylor, "Interpretation and the Sciences of Man," in *Philosophy and the Human Sciences* (Cambridge: Cambridge University Press, 1985), p. 15.

24. Hadley Cantril, *The Invasion from Mars* (Princeton, N.J.: Princeton University Press, 1940).

25. Roland Barthes, *The Responsibility of Forms: Critical Essays on Music, Art, and Representation* (New York: Hill and Wang, 1985).

26. Roy Harris, "How Does Writing Restructure Thought?" *Language and Communication,* 9 (1989): 99–106.

27. See Hilary Putnam, *Mind, Language, and Reality* (Cambridge: Cambridge University Press, 1975), p. 278.

28. Hayden White, "The Value of Narrativity in the Representation of Reality," in Mitchell, ed., *On Narrative*.

29. Patricia Meyer Spacks, *Boredom: The Literary History of a State of Mind* (Chicago: University of Chicago Press, 1995).

30. For a good statement of Roman Jakobson's view, see his "Linguistics and Poetics," in T. Sebeok, ed., *Style in Language* (Cambridge, Mass.: MIT Press, 1960). See also his *Language in Literature* (Cambridge: Harvard University Press, 1987).

31. Gottlob Frege, "Über Sinn und Bedeutung," *Zeitschrift fur Philosophie und Philosophische Kritik,* 100 (1892): 25–50. Translated by Herbert Feigl as "On Sense and Nominatum," in Herbert Feigl and W. S. Sellars, eds, *Readings in Philosophical Analysis* (New York: Appleton-Century-Crofts, 1949).

32. See Henry A. Murray, "In Nomine Diaboli," *New England Quarterly,* 24 (1951): 435–452.

33. Judy Dunn, *The Beginnings of Social Understanding* (Cambridge, Mass.: Harvard University Press, 1988).

34. Ronald Dworkin, *Law's Empire* (Cambridge, Mass.: Harvard University Press, 1986).

35. Hayden White, "The Value of Narrativity in the Representation of Reality," in W. J. T. Mitchell, ed., *On Narrative* (Chicago: University of Chicago Press, 1981), pp. 1–23.

36. Carl G. Hempel, "Aspects of Scientific Explanation," in Hempel, *Aspects of Scientific Explanation and Other Essays in the Philosophy of Science* (New York: Free Press, 1965); Arthur C. Danto, *Narration and Knowledge* (New York: Columbia University Press, 1985).

37. Lawrence Stone, *The Causes of the English Revolution, 1529–1642* (London: Routledge and K. Paul, 1972); Louis Mink, "Narrative Form as a Cognitive Instrument," in Robert H. Canary and Henry Kozicki, eds., *The Writing of History: Literary Form and Historical Understanding* (Madison: University of Wisconsin Press, 1978); Dale H. Porter, *The Emergence of the Past: A Theory of Historical Explanation* (Chicago: University of Chicago Press, 1981).

38. See entry for W. T. Stace in *Encyclopedia of Philosophy* (New York: Macmillan and Free Press, 1967).

39. Jean Piaget, *The Grasp of Consciousness: Action and Concept in the Young Child,* trans. Susan Wedgwood (Cambridge, Mass.: Harvard University Press, 1976); Edouard Claparede, *Experimental Pedagogy and the Psychology of the Child* (New York: E. Arnold, 1911); Henri Louis Bergson, *Mind-Energy: Lectures and Essays* (New York: H. Holt, 1920).

40. Michael Riffaterre, *Fictional Truth* (Baltimore: Johns Hopkins University Press, 1990).

41. Roman Jakobson, "Closing Statement: Linguistics and Poetics," in Thomas A. Sebeok, ed., *Style in Language* (Cambridge, Mass.: Technology Press

of MIT, 1960), pp. 350–377; see also his "Poetry of Grammar and Grammar of Poetry," in Jakobson, *Selected Writings, III: Poetry of Grammar and Grammar of Poetry* (The Hague: Mouton, 1981), pp. 87–97.

42. Jerome Bruner, "Narrative and Paradigmatic Modes of Thought," in Elliot Eisner, ed., *Learning and Teaching the Ways of Knowing: Eighty-fourth Yearbook of the National Society for the Study of Education* (Chicago: University of Chicago Press, 1985), pp. 97–115.

43. I take the term from Stephen Toulmin's *Cosmopolis* (New York: Free Press, 1990), a work that provides a particularly sensitive discussion of the anti-illusionist role of science after the seventeenth century.

8. KNOWING AS DOING

1. Lev S. Vygotsky, *Thought and Language* (Cambridge, Mass.: MIT Press, 1962).

2. Harold Garfinkel, *Studies in Ethnomethodology* (Englewood Cliffs, N.J.: Prentice-Hall, 1967); Pierre Bourdieu, *Outline of a Theory of Practice* (Cambridge: Cambridge University Press, 1977); Erving Goffman, *The Presentation of Self in Everyday Life* (Garden City, N.Y.: Doubleday, 1959); Goffman, *Frame Analysis: An Essay on the Organization of Experience* (New York: Harper & Row, 1974).

3. John Seeley Brown, Allan Collins, and Paul Duguid, "Situated Cognition and the Culture of Learning," *Educational Researcher,* 18(1) (1988): 32–42.

4. Jerome S. Bruner, Rose R. Olver, Patricia M. Greenfield, et al., *Studies in Cognitive Growth: A Collaboration at the Center for Cognitive Studies* (New York: John Wiley & Sons, 1966).

5. Frederic Bartlett, *Thinking: An Experimental and Social Study* (New York: Basic Books, 1958).

6. Eleanor Rosch and Barbara B. Lloyd, eds., *Cognition and Categorization* (Hillsdale, N.J.: Erlbaum, 1978).

7. Robert Cover, *Narrative, Violence, and the Law* (Ann Arbor: University of Michigan Press, 1992); Cover, "Nomos and Narrative," *Harvard Law Review,* 97 (4) (1983): 4–68.

8. Claude Lévi-Strauss, *The Raw and the Cooked* (Chicago: University of Chicago Press, 1983).

9. PSYCHOLOGY'S NEXT CHAPTER

1. Rom Harré and Grant Gillett, *The Discursive Mind* (Thousand Oaks: Sage Publications, 1994); Kenneth J. Gergen, *Realities and Relationships: Soundings in Social Construction* (Cambridge, Mass.: Harvard University Press, 1994).

2. *Acts of Meaning* (Cambridge, Mass.: Harvard University Press, 1990).

3. Noam Chomsky, "Knowledge of Language," excerpted from the first John Locke Lecture, Oxford, April 29, 1969, in *Times Literary Supplement* (London), May 15, 1969.

4. R. D. Adolphs, D. Tranel, H. Damasio, and A. Damasio, "Impaired Recognition of Emotion in Facial Expressions Following Bilateral Damage to the Human Amygdala," *Nature,* 372 (1994): 669–672.

5. E. S. Savage-Rumbaugh, J. Murphy, R. A. Sevcik, K. E. Brakke, S. L. Williams, and D. M. Rumbaugh, "Language Comprehension in Ape and Child," *Monographs of the SRCD,* 58 (3–4, serial no. 233) (1993).

6. M. R. A. Chance and Clifford J. Jolly, eds., *Social Groups of Monkeys, Apes, and Men* (New York: Dutton, 1970).

7. A. L. Kroeber, "The Superorganic," *American Anthropologist,* 19 (1917): 163–213.

8. Clifford Geertz, *Local Knowledge* (New York: Basic Books, 1983).

9. David A. Olson, *The World on Paper: The Conceptual and Cognitive Implications of Writing and Reading* (Cambridge: Cambridge U. Press, 1994).

10. Ann L. Brown, "Knowing When, Where, and How to Remember: A Problem of Metacognition," in R. Glaser, ed., *Advances in Instructional Psychology,* 1 (Hillsdale, N.J.: Erlbaum, 1978), pp. 77–165.

11. S. B. Heath, *Ways with Words: Language, Life, and Work in Communities and Classrooms* (Cambridge: Cambridge University Press, 1983).

12. M. C. Potter, "Short-term Conceptual Memory for Pictures," *Journal of Experimental Psychology: Human Learning and Memory,* 2(5) (1976): 509–522; M. C. Potter and E. I. Levy, "Recognition Memory for a Rapid Sequence of Pictures," *Journal of Experimental Psychology,* 81(1) (1969): 10–15.

13. R. A. Shweder, *Thinking Through Cultures: Expeditions in Cultural Psychology* (Cambridge, Mass.: Harvard University Press, 1991).

14. Bradd Shore, *Culture in Mind: Meaning Construction and Cultural Cognition* (Oxford: Oxford University Press, 1996).

15. D. C. Geary, "Reflections of Evolution and Culture in Children's Cognition: Implications for Mathematical Development and Instruction," *American Psychologist,* 50(1) (1995): 24–37.

16. Rochel Gelman and C. R. Gallistel, *The Child's Understanding of Number* (Cambridge, Mass.: Harvard University Press, 1978).

17. Geertz, *Local Knowledge.*

18. See, for example, C. Trevarthen, "Form, Significance and Psychological Potential of Hand Gestures of Infants," in J.-L. Nespoulous, P. Perron, and A. R. Lecours, eds., *The Biological Foundations of Gestures: Motor and Semiotic Aspects* (Hillsdale, N.J.: Erlbaum, 1986), pp. 149–202; C. Trevarthen and H. Marwick, "Signs of Motivation for Speech in Infants, and the Nature of a Mother's Support for Development of Language," in B. Lindblom and R. Zetterstrom,

eds., *Precursors of Early Speech,* Proceedings of an International Symposium held at the Wenner-Gren Center, Stockholm, September 19–22, 1984 (New York: Stockton Press, 1986), pp. 279–308.

19. K. S. Lashley, "The Problem of Serial Order in Behavior," in F. Beach, D. O. Hebb, and H. Nissen, eds., *The Neuropsychology of Lashley* (New York: McGraw-Hill, 1960).

20. J. MacMurray, *Persons in Relation* (London: Faber, 1961).

21. D. Stern, *The First Relationship: Infant and Mother* (Cambridge, Mass.: Harvard University Press, 1977).

22. For example, J. Bowlby, *Attachment and Loss,* vol. 1: *Attachment* (New York: Basic Books, 1969).

23. Margaret S. Mahler, *The Selected Papers of Margaret S. Mahler, M.D.* (New York: J. Aronson, 1979); Fred Pine, *Developmental Theory and Clinical Process* (New Haven: Yale University Press, 1985).

24. Charles R. Darwin, *The Expression of the Emotions in Man and Animals* (New York: AMS Press, 1972; originally published 1899).

25. M. Scaife and Jerome Bruner, "The Capacity for Joint Visual Attention in the Infant," *Nature,* 253 (1975): 265–266.

26. Chris Moore and Phil Dunham, eds., *Joint Attention: Its Origins and Role in Development* (Hillsdale, N.J.: Erlbaum, in press).

27. E. Menzel, "A Group of Young Chimpanzees in a One-Acre Field," in M. Schrier and F. Stolnitz, eds., *Behavior of Non-Human Primates,* vol. 5 (New York: Academic Press, 1974).

28. R. W. Byrne and A. Whiten, "Computation and Mindreading in Primate Tactical Deception," in A. Whiten, ed., *Natural Theories of Mind: Evolution, Development and Simulation of Everyday Mindreading* (Oxford: Basil Blackwell, 1991), pp. 127–141.

29. Michael Argyle and Mark Cook, *Gaze and Mutual Gaze* (Cambridge: Cambridge University Press, 1976).

30. L. Kanner, *Childhood Psychosis* (New York: Wiley, 1973).

31. B. Hermelin and N. O'Connor, *Psychological Experiments with Autistic Children* (Oxford: Pergamon, 1970); S. Baron-Cohen, A. Leslie, and U. Frith, "Does the Autistic Child Have a Theory of Mind?" *Cognition,* 21 (1985): 37–46.

32. A. Leslie and D. Roth, "What Autism Teaches Us about Metarepresentation," in S. Baron-Cohen, H. Tager-Flusberg, and D. J. Cohen, eds., *Understanding Other Minds: Perspectives from Autism* (Oxford: Oxford University Press, 1993), pp. 83–111.

33. Jerome Bruner and Carol Feldman, "Theories of Mind and the Problem of Autism," in Baron-Cohen, Tager-Flusberg, and Cohen, eds., *Understanding Other Minds,* pp. 267–291; Francesca Happé, *Autism: An Introduction to Psychological Theory* (Cambridge, Mass.: Harvard University Press, 1994).

34. F. G. E. Happé, "The Autobiographical Writings of Three Asperger Syndrome Adults: Problems of Interpretation and Implications for Theory," in U. Frith, ed., *Autism and Asperger Syndrome* (Cambridge: Cambridge University Press, 1991); Oliver Sacks, *An Anthropologist on Mars: Seven Paradoxical Tales* (New York: Knopf, 1995).

35. H. Wimmer and J. Perner, "Beliefs about Beliefs: Representation and Constraining Function of Wrong Beliefs in Young Children's Understanding of Deception," *Cognition,* 13 (1983): 103–128.

36. Janet W. Astington, *The Child's Discovery of the Mind* (Cambridge, Mass.: Harvard University Press, 1993).

37. Carol Feldman, "The New Theory of Theory of Mind," *Human Development,* 35 (1992): 107–117.

38. A. Whiten, ed., *Natural Theories of Mind: Evolution, Development and Simulation of Everyday Mindreading* (Oxford: Basil Blackwell, 1991).

39. Michael J. Chandler, A. S. Fritz, and S. M. Hala, "Small Scale Deceit: Deception as a Marker of 2-, 3-, and 4-year-olds' Early Theories of Mind," *Child Development,* 60 (1989): 1263–1277.

40. Sir Henry Head, *Aphasia and Kindred Disorders of Speech* (Cambridge: Cambridge University Press, 1926).

41. E. S. Savage-Rumbaugh, J. Murphy, R. A. Sevcik, K. E. Brakke, S. L. Williams, and D. M. Rumbaugh, "Language Comprehension in Ape and Child," *Monographs of the Society for Research in Child Development,* 58 (3–4, Serial No. 233) (1993).

42. M. Tomasello, E. S. Savage-Rumbaugh, and A. C. Kruger, "Imitative Learning of Actions on Objects by Children, Chimpanzees, and Enculturated Chimpanzees," *Child Development,* 64 (1993): 1688–1705.

43. M. Tomasello, personal communication, 1994.

44. M. P. Crawford, "The Cooperative Solving of Problems by Young Chimpanzees," *Comparative Psychology Monographs,* 14 (2, Serial No. 68) (1937): 1–88.

45. See A. Ninio and J. Bruner, "The Achievement and Antecedents of Labelling," *Journal of Child Language,* 5 (1978): 1–15.

46. D. Sperber and D. Wilson, *Relevance: Communication and Cognition* (Oxford: Blackwell, 1986).

47. J. R. Searle, *The Rediscovery of the Mind* (Cambridge, Mass.: MIT Press, 1992).

48. Stern, *The First Relationship.*

49. See L. S. Vygotsky, *Mind in Society: The Development of Higher Psychological Processes* (Cambridge, Mass.: Harvard University Press, 1978).

50. G. M. Edelman, *Neural Darwinism: The Theory of Neuronal Group Selection* (New York: Basic Books, 1987).

51. Geary, "Reflections of Evolution and Culture in Children's Cognition."

52. Merlin Donald, *Origins of the Modern Mind: Three Stages in the Evolution of Culture and Cognition* (Cambridge, Mass.: Harvard University Press, 1991).

53. Chomsky, "Knowledge of Language"; J. A. Fodor, *The Modularity of Mind* (Cambridge, Mass.: MIT Press, 1983).

54. H. Paul Grice, "Logic and Conversation," Part I in *Studies in the Way of Words* (Cambridge, Mass.: Harvard University Press, 1989), pp. 3–143.

CREDITS

▼

Chapter 2 Adapted from an essay written with David R. Olson. An earlier version of this essay appears in *Handbook of Education and Human Development: New Models of Learning, Teaching, and Schooling,* ed. David R. Olson and Nancy Torrance (Oxford: Blackwell, 1996).

Chapter 3 Earlier versions were presented at the Hebrew Union College Conference on "The Future of Education" held in Cincinnati, Ohio, in November 1994, and at the Fifth Congress of the European Early Childhood Research Association held in Paris in September 1995, on the topic "Quels objectifs pédagogiques pour l'éducation préscholaire."

Chapter 4 Originally presented as a keynote address at the American Educational Research Association, New Orleans, April 7, 1994.

Chapter 5 Based on a commentary written in reply to an article by Janet Wilde Astington and David R. Olson, "The Cognitive Revolution in Children's Understanding of Mind," *Human Development* 38 (1995): 203–213.

Chapter 6 Presented as the Karplus Lecture to the National Council of Teachers of Science, Atlanta, April 7, 1990, and originally published in *Journal of Science Education and Technology* 1(1) (1992): 5–12.

Chapter 7 An earlier version was published in *Critical Inquiry* 18 (1991): 1–21.

Chapter 9 Originally presented as two lectures on "The Future of Psychology" at Georgetown University, 1995.

INDEX

▼

Bowlby, J., 176, 210n22
Boyer, Ernest, 85, 200n30
Boyle, Robert, 105
Bradbury, Malcolm, 139
Brakke, Karen E., 190n38, 196n3, 202n17, 209n5, 211n41
Brett, C., 197n28
Brinton, Crane, 188n7
Brown, Ann L., 58, 76, 86, 87, 93, 99, 169, 189n17, 196n12, 197nn17,27,28, 200n21, 205n9, 209n10
Brown, John Seeley, 154, 204n4, 208n3
Brown, Penelope, 190n28
Brown v. Board of Education, 73, 89, 95
Bruer, John T., 10, 187n1, 188n14
Bruner, Jerome S., 49, 88, 176, 177, 187n6, 188n11, 189n23, 191n40, 193n70, 194nn78,79,80, 195nn83,84,88, 196n9, 197nn18,25, 198n10, 199nn12,13,14,17, 202nn12,13,14,16, 204nn2,45,46, 205nn6,16, 208nn4,42, 210nn25,33, 211n45
Bullock, Lord, 71, 128
Burke, Edmund, 142
Burtis, P. J., 197n28
Byrne, R. W., 210n28

Calhoun, C., 197n28
Calvin, W. H., 198n5
Calvino, Italo, 96, 139, 142
Campbell, John, 193n65
Campione, Joseph C., 86, 189n17, 196n12, 197nn17,28, 205n9
Canary, Robert H., 207n37
Canonicity in narrative, 139–140, 141, 146, 147
Cantril, Hadley, 193n69, 206n24
Carey, Susan, 205n7
Center for Cognitive Studies, Harvard University, 155
Chance, M. R. A., 209n6
Chandler, Michael J., 104, 179, 201n11, 211n39
Cheney, D. L., 196n6
Chi, Michelene T. H., 187n1

Children, 24, 36–38, 49, 50–52, 56–57, 112–113; knowledge of culture, 20, 52; in poverty, 26–27, 71, 77, 79; creation of reality by, 39–42, 46; teachers and, 46–47, 49; theory of mind about, 49, 50, 93; learning and acquisition of knowledge, 51–52, 58, 60–63, 64; theory of mind of, 52, 57, 58, 101, 102, 103, 104, 107, 108–109, 111, 112, 114, 175, 178–179; as thinkers, 56–60, 64, 106; folk psychology of, 58–59; child rearing, 73, 76, 80–81; use of language, 109. *See also* Infant(s)
Child's Discovery of the Mind, The (Astington), 104
Chimpanzees and monkeys: teaching strategies of, 47–48, 53; theory of mind and, 48, 50, 176; eye-to-eye contact, 163, 176; deceit among, 179, 181; enculturated, 179–181, 182–183
Chipman, Susan F., 187n1, 189n19
Chomsky, Noam, 103, 161, 183, 209n3, 212n53
Claparède, Edouard, 207n39
Clark, H. H., 204n48
Clarke-Stewart, A., 199n20
Clifford, James, 33, 193n60, 201n5
Clinton, Bill, 33
Cognition, 12–13, 24, 50, 58, 71–72
Cohen, Donald J., 195n84, 202n12, 210nn32,33
Cohen, L. B., 198n11
Cole, Michael, 24, 187n6, 191n46, 199n17
Coleridge, Samuel Taylor, 143
Collaboration, 58, 68, 84, 87, 92–97
Collingwood, Robin George, 201n5
Collins, Allan, 204n4, 208n3
Common sense, 14, 16
Complementarity, 124–125
Computationalism, 1–12, 187n2
Computers, 2, 5, 7, 20, 24, 25, 45, 98
Conant, James Bryant, 126–127, 204n4
Conflict resolution, 30
Confrontation in narrative, 147, 148
Constructivism, 19–20. *See also* Reality: construction of